KD

Law of the United Kingdom and Ireland

Library of Congress Classification
2008

Prepared by the Cataloging Policy and Support Office
Library Services

LIBRARY OF CONGRESS
Cataloging Distribution Service
Washington, D.C.

This edition cumulates all additions and changes to subclass KD through Weekly List 2008/07, dated February 13, 2008. Additions and changes made subsequent to that date are published in weekly lists posted on the World Wide Web at

<http://www.loc.gov/aba/cataloging/classification/weeklylists/>

and are also available in *Classification Web*, the online Web-based edition of the Library of Congress Classification.

Library of Congress Cataloging-in-Publication Data

Library of Congress.
   Library of Congress classification. KD. Law of the United Kingdom and Ireland / prepared by the Cataloging Policy and Support Office, Library Services. — 2008 ed.
     p. cm.
   "This edition cumulates all additions and changes to subclass KD through Weekly list 2008/07, dated February 13, 2008. Additions and changes made subsequent to that date are published in weekly lists posted on the World Wide Web at <http://www.loc.gov/aba/ cataloging/classification/weeklylists/> and are also available in *Classification Web*, the online Web-based edition of the Library of Congress classification." — T.p. verso.
   Includes index.
   ISBN-13: 978-0-8444-1203-0
   ISBN-10: 0-8444-1203-1
   1. Classification, Library of Congress. 2. Classification—Books—Law. 3. Classification—Books—Great Britain. 4. Classification—Books—Ireland. 5. Law—Great Britain—Classification. 6. Law—Ireland—Classification. I. Library of Congress. Cataloging Policy and Support Office. II. Title. III. Title: Law of the United Kingdom and Ireland.
   Z696.U5K3 2008   025.4'634941—dc22   2008008431

For sale by the Library of Congress Cataloging Distribution Service,
101 Independence Avenue, S.E., Washington, DC 20541-4912.
Product catalog available on the Web at **www.loc.gov/cds**.

PREFACE

The first edition of subclass KD, *Law of the United Kingdom and Ireland*, developed by John Fischer, was published in 1973. A 1998 edition cumulated all changes that had been made to the schedule during the period 1973-1998. This 2008 edition cumulates changes made since the 1998 edition was published. It includes significant changes and simplifications that were made to Form Division Tables KD1, KD2, and KD3 in 2008.

Classification numbers or spans of numbers that appear in parentheses are formerly valid numbers that are now obsolete. Numbers or spans that appear in angle brackets are optional numbers that have never been used at the Library of Congress but are provided for other libraries that wish to use them. In most cases, a parenthesized or angle-bracketed number is accompanied by a "see" reference directing the user to the actual number that the Library of Congress currently uses, or a note explaining Library of Congress practice.

Access to the online version of the full Library of Congress Classification is available on the World Wide Web by subscription to *Classification Web*. Details about ordering and pricing may be obtained from the Cataloging Distribution Service at:

<http://www.loc.gov/cds/>

New or revised numbers and captions are added to the L.C. Classification schedules as a result of development proposals made by the cataloging staff of the Library of Congress and cooperating institutions. Upon approval of these proposals by the weekly editorial meeting of the Cataloging Policy and Support Office, new classification records are created or existing records are revised in the master classification database. Weekly lists of newly approved or revised classification numbers and captions are posted on the World Wide Web at:

<http://www.loc.gov/aba/cataloging/classification/weeklylists/>

Paul Weiss, senior subject cataloging policy specialist in the Cataloging Policy and Support Office, is responsible for coordinating the overall intellectual and editorial content of subclass KD. Kent Griffiths, assistant editor of classification schedules, is responsible for creating new classification records, maintaining the master database, and creating index terms for the captions.

Barbara B. Tillett, Chief
Cataloging Policy and Support Office

February 2008

KD51-9500	Law of England and Wales
KD51-59	Bibliography
KD62	Official gazettes
KD124-180	Legislation
KD124-150	Statues
KD166-173	Subordinate (Delegated legislation)
KD175-180	Prerogative legislation
KD187-300	Law reports and related materials
KD310	Encyclopedias
KD313	Law dictionaries. Words and phrases
KD315	Legal maxims. Quotations
KD318	Form books
KD327-332	Judicial statistics
KD336-340	Directories
KD345	Society and bar association journals
KD347	Congresses
KD353-358	Collections
KD370-379.5	Trials
KD370-376	Criminal trials and judicial investigations
KD378-379.5	Civil trials
KD392-400	Legal research. Legal bibliography
KD404	Legal composition and draftsmanship
KD411	Law reporting. Law reporters
KD417-452	Legal education
KD456	Law societies
KD460-510	The legal profession
KD512-513	Community legal services. Legal aid
KD530-632	History
KD640	Jurisprudence and philosophy of English law
KD654	Criticism. Legal reform. General administration of justice
KD658-669	General and comprehensive works
KD671	Common law
KD674	Equity
KD680-685	Conflict of laws
KD687	Retroactive law. Intertemporal law
KD691-700	General principles and concepts
KD703	Concepts applying to several branches of law
KD720-721	Private (Civil) law
KD723-785	Persons
KD723-746	General. Status. Capacity
KD750-785	Domestic relations. Family law

Law of England and Wales - Continued
KD810-1465	Property
KD810-815	General. Ownership. Possession
KD821-1195	Real property. Land law
KD833-1020.6	Land tenure. Transfer of rights in land. Real estate management
KD1034-1195	Public property. Public restraints on private property
KD1035	Conservation of natural resources
KD1040-1048	Roads
KD1070-1072	Water resources. Rivers. Water courses
KD1090-1107	Public land law
KD1125-1162	Regional and city planning. Zoning. Building
KD1171-1184	Housing. Slum clearance. City redevelopment
KD1185-1189	Eminent domain. Compulsory acquisition
KD1195	Public works
KD1205-1465	Personal property
KD1214-1225	Ownership and possession
KD1238-1465	Special kinds of personal property
KD1238-1450	Intangible. Choses in action
KD1261-1450	Intellectual property
KD1281-1325	Copyright
KD1345	Design protection
KD1360-1413.3	Patent law
KD1431-1445	Trademarks
KD1450	Goodwill. Business names. Registration and transfer of business names
KD1465	Government personal property
KD1480-1495	Trusts and trustees
KD1497	Estate planning
KD1500-1534	Succession upon death
KD1554-1920	Contracts
KD1554	General and comprehensive works
KD1559-1605	General principles
KD1610-1616	Government contracts. Public contracts. Purchasing and procurement
KD1621-1920	Particular contracts
KD1621-1630	Comprehensive. Mercantile law. Commercial law
KD1634	Contract of service. Master and servant

Law of England and Wales
Contracts
Particular contracts - Continued
KD1638-1642   Contract for work and labor (Contract for services).
Independent contractors
KD1650-1675   Sale of goods
KD1679-1685   Contracts involving bailments
KD1695-1699   Negotiable instruments
KD1715-1737   Banking
KD1740-1742   Loan of money
KD1752   Suretyship. Guaranty
KD1755-1763   Secured transactions
KD1774-1787   Marketing of securities. Investments. Stock exchange
transactions
KD1800-1847   Carriers. Carriage of goods and passengers
KD1800   General. Liability
KD1802   Carriage by land
KD1804   Carriage by air
KD1811-1834   Carriage by sea. Maritime (Commercial) law.
Admiralty
KD1836-1842   Maritime labor law. Merchant mariners
KD1845-1847   Marine insurance
KD1851-1913   Insurance
KD1920   Aleatory contracts. Wagering contracts
KD1924   Restitution. Quasi contracts. Unjust enrichment
KD1941-2004 Torts (Extracontractual liability)
KD2007   Compensation to victims of crime. Reparation
KD2020-2024 Agency
KD2040-2127 Associations
KD2046-2054   Unincorporated associations
KD2049-2054   Business associations. Partnership
KD2057-2127   Corporations. Juristic persons
KD2061-2062   Nonprofit corporations
KD2071-2127   Business corporations. Companies
KD2139-2172 Insolvency and bankruptcy. Creditors' rights
KD2185-2190 Economic policy. Economic planning
KD2200-2990 Regulation of industry, trade, and commerce.
Occupational law
KD2200   General. Comprehensive
KD2201   Board of Trade
KD2204-2233 Trade regulation. Control of trade practices
KD2204   General. Unfair trade practices
KD2206   Advertising

OUTLINE

Law of England and Wales
  Regulation of industry, trade, and commerce.
    Occupational law
    Trade regulation. Control of trade practices - Continued

KD2208-2209	Labeling
KD2212	Restraint of trade
KD2215	Price regulations
KD2218-2220	Monopolies. Antitrust laws
KD2225-2226	Unfair competition
KD2228	Trade associations
KD2230-2231	Weights and measures. Containers
KD2233	Standard time
KD2241-2370	Primary production. Extractive industries. Conservation of natural resources
KD2241-2295	Agriculture. Forestry
KD2310-2315	Fishery
KD2331-2370	Mining. Quarrying
KD2375-2398	Manufacturing industries
KD2405-2430	Food processing industries. Agricultural products
KD2435	Construction and building industry. Contractors
KD2455-2530	Trade and commerce
KD2535-2560	Public utilities
KD2571-2915	Transportation and communication
KD2940-2990	The professions
KD3000-3340	Social legislation
KD3001-3177	Labor law
KD3191-3273	Social insurance
KD3291-3315	Public welfare. Public assistance. Poor laws
KD3351-3382	Public health. Sanitation. Environmental pollution
KD3395-3417	Medical legislation
KD3420-3422	Veterinary laws. Veterinary hygiene
KD3424-3429	Prevention of cruelty to animals
KD3450-3462	Food. Drugs. Cosmetics
KD3466-3480	Alcohol. Alcoholic beverages. Liquor laws
KD3490-3516	Public safety
KD3492	Weapons. Firearms. Munitions
KD3494-3507	Hazardous articles and processes
KD3510	Accident control
KD3515-3516	Fire prevention and control. Explosives
KD3521-3529	Control of social activities
KD3523	Amusements
KD3525	Sports. Prizefighting. Horseracing

Law of England and Wales
Control of social activities - Continued
KD3527   Lotteries. Games of chance. Betting
and gambling

KD3527	Lotteries. Games of chance. Betting and gambling
KD3529	Other
KD3600-3689	Education
KD3710-3758	Science and the arts. Research
KD3720-3731	Performing arts
KD3736	Museums and galleries
KD3746	Libraries
KD3753-3756	Archives. Historical documents
KD3758	Educational, scientific, and cultural exchanges
KD3930	Constitutional and administrative law
KD3931-4645	Constitutional law
KD3931-3966	History
KD3931-3932	Sources
KD3934	General works
KD3938-3966	By period
KD3981-3990	General works
KD3995-4018	Constitutional principles
KD3995	Rule of law
KD4000-4010	Separation of powers. Delegation of powers
KD4015-4018	Sources and relationships of law
KD4030	Foreign relations
KD4050-4139	Individual and state
KD4050-4058	Nationality and citizenship
KD4080-4119	Civil and political rights and liberties
KD4124-4145	Control of individuals
KD4130-4145	Aliens
KD4185-4645	Organs of the government
KD4190-4381	The Parliament
KD4190-4246	Both Houses
KD4260-4290	House of Lords
KD4310-4381	House of Commons
KD4430-4531	The Crown and the Central Government (Executive branch)
KD4435-4456	The Crown
KD4462	The Prime Minister and the Cabinet
KD4467-4531	Government departments. Civil service
KD4645	The Judiciary. Judicial power
KD4650	National emblem. Seals
KD4656-4657	Decorations of honor. Awards of honor. Dignities

OUTLINE

Law of England and Wales - Continued

KD4746-4840	Local government
KD4871-4902	Administrative organization and procedure
KD5020-5025	Commonwealth and Empire
KD5110-5133	Government measures in time of war, national emergency, or economic crisis. Emergency economic legislation
KD5280-5752	Public finance
KD5280	General. History
KD5282	The Exchequer
KD5284-5286	Money. Currency. Banknotes. Coinage
KD5288	Foreign exchange regulations
KD5292	Budget. Government expenditures
KD5295	Expenditure control. Public auditing and accounting
KD5300	Public debts. Loans. Bond issues
KD5320-5694	National revenue
KD5320-5341	History
KD5351-5694	Particular sources of revenue
KD5351-5605	Taxation
KD5641-5694	Tariff. Customs duties
KD5710-5752	Local finance
KD6000-6355	National defense. Military law
KD6000-6012	Comprehensive. General
KD6030-6335	The military establishment. Armed Forces
KD6086-6228	Particular branches of service
KD6240-6248	Auxiliary services during war or emergency
KD6250	Military discipline
KD6270-6332	Military criminal law and procedure
KD6335	Civil status of members of the Armed Forces and auxiliary services. Civil law relating to soldiers, sailors, airmen, etc .
KD6338	Other defense agencies
KD6340	Civil defense
KD6355	War veterans
KD6850-7640	Courts. Procedure
KD6850-6857	History
KD6870-6992	Administration of justice. Courts and procedure before the Judicature Act of 1873
KD7000-7312	Administration of justice. Courts and procedure since the Judicature Act of 1873
KD7111-7261	Court organization and procedure
KD7325-7640	Civil procedure
KD7645-7647	Arbitration and award. Commercial arbitration
KD7850-8090	Criminal law

Law of England and Wales - Continued
KD8220-8469   Criminal procedure
KD8600-8790   Ecclesiastical law. Csanon law of the Church of
                        England. Church and state
KD8850-9355   Local laws
KD8850-9312   England
KD8850   Counties and shires
KD8860-9150   Cities, boroughs, and towns, etc.
KD8860-9142   London
KD9150   Other cites, boroughs, and towns, etc.
KD9350   Manors
KD9320-9355   Wales
KD9320   Counties and shires
KD9325   Cities, boroughs, and towns, etc.
KD9350   Manors
KD9400-9500   Law of Wales
KDC51-990   Law of Scotland
KDE21-580   Law of Northern Ireland
KDG(21)-540   Law of Isle of Man. Channel Islands
KDK21-1950   Law of Ireland (Eire)

KD

Law of England and Wales
    Including the United Kingdom as a whole and the common-law
        system (Anglo-American law) in general
  Bibliography
    For bibliography of special topics, see the topic, e.g., KD417,
        Legal education
    For manuals on legal bibliography, legal research, and the
        use of law books see KD392+

51	General
53	Checklists of statutes
54	Checklists of law reports
	Including Year Books
56	Library catalogs. Central catalogs
57	Sales catalogs. Want lists. Lists of duplicates
59	Indexes to periodical literature, society publications, and collections
	Class indexes to particular publications with the publication
	Official gazettes
62	London Gazette
<68-94>	Parliamentary publications
	see J301
<68>	Both Houses
<70-76>	House of Lords
<70>	Sessional Papers (Papers and bills)
<72>	Minutes of the House of Lords
<74>	Journals
<76>	Debates (Hansard)
<86-94>	House of Commons
<86>	Sessional Papers
	Including Command Papers and bills
	Class Command Papers with the subject if not collected
<88>	Votes and proceedings
<90>	Journals
<92>	Debates (Hansard)
<94>	Standing committee debates
	Legislation
	Statutes
	Public acts
	Public general acts
124	Serials
125	Sessional volumes
	By initial date of session
	General compilations. Collections
	Early and discontinued compilations. Statutes at large
129	Serials

	Legislation
	Statutes
	Public acts
	Public general acts
	General compilations. Collections
	Early and discontinued compilations. Statutes at large -- Continued
130	Monographs
	Arrange chronologically by initial date of period covered
	Current and continuing compilations
	Official editions
132	The Statutes revised
	By date of revision
135.A-Z	Unofficial editions, A-Z
	e.g.
135.B8	Butterworth's Annotated Legislation Service, 1947-
135.C8	Current Law Statutes Annotated, 1948-
135.H3	Halsbury's Statutes of England
135.L3	Law Reports Statutes, 1866-
137	Local, personal, and private acts
	War and emergency legislation see KD5110+
140	Abridgments and digests of statutes
141	Citators to statutes
	Indexes and tables to statutes
(142)	Chronological Table and Index of the Statutes see KD142.3
142.3	Chronological Table and Index of the Statutes. Chronological Table of the Statutes
142.4	Index to Statutes in Force. Index to the Statutes
142.6.A-Z	Other, A-Z
146	Expiring law continuance legislation
150	Statute law revision acts and committees
	Subordinate (Delegated) legislation
	Statutory rules and orders. Statutory Instruments
	Official editions
166	Serials
168.A-Z	Monographic collections
168.A2	Statutory Rules and Orders Revised; Statutory Rules and Orders Other than Those of Local, Personal, or Temporary Character, Issued Prior to 1890
168.A3	Statutory Rules and Orders Revised. Being the Statutory Rules and Orders in force on Dec. 31, 1903
168.A4	Statutory Rules and Orders and Statutory Instruments Revised to Dec. 31, 1948

	Legislation
	Subordinate (Delegated) legislation
	Statutory rules and orders. Statutory Instruments
	Official editions -- Continued
170	Indexes
171	Tables. Statutory Instruments Effects
173.A-Z	Unofficial editions, A-Z
173.H3	Halsbury's Statutory Instruments
	Prerogative legislation
175	Royal proclamations and instructions
	By editor, title, etc.
176	Orders-in-Council. Statutory proclamations
	Class here general collections only
	For ministerial regulations, see subject
178	Letters patent
180	Other
	Law reports and related materials
	Law reports
	Including both authorized (regular) and collateral reports
	Class reports on particular subjects with the subject
	By courts
	For arrangement by courts, see Sweet and Maxwell's Guide to Law Reports and Statutes. Fourth ed., 1962, pp. 123-130
	Common law courts
	Reports of various courts see KD270+
	Particular courts
	House of Lords
187.A-Z	Reports
	By initial date of period covered and reporter or title, A-Z
187.7	Court records and briefs
	By initial date of period covered
	King's (Queen's) Bench
190	Before the Year Books (To ca. 1280). By initial date of period covered
	Class here civil plea rolls and rolls containing both civil and crown pleas, e.g. Curia Regis rolls (1196-); Bracton's Note Book (1217-1240)
	Cf. KD225 Rolls of manorial courts
	Cf. KD7864.8 Crown plea rolls
	The Year Books (ca. 1280-1535)
	Texts
193	Serials
	By publisher, editor, or title

	Law reports and related materials
	Law reports
	By courts
	Common law courts
	Particular courts
	King's (Queen's) Bench
	The Year Books (ca. 1280-1535)
	Texts -- Continued
194	Monographs
	Arrange chronologically by initial date of period covered
196.A-Z	Abridgments. By author, A-Z
	e.g.
196.B7	Brooke, R., Graunde Abridgment
196.F5	Fitzherbert, A., Graunde Abridgment
197.A-Z	Indexes. Tables. By author, A-Z
	e.g.
197.F5	Fleetwood, W., Annalium Tam regum ...
198	General works
	Including guidebooks, commentaries, etc.
200	Private (named) reports. By initial date of period covered and by reporter or title, A-Z
	Subarrange each by Table KD6
	Cf. KD370+ State trials
200.3	Abridgments and digests not connected with any named reports
	By date of publication
200.4	Indexes and tables not connected with any named reports
	By date of publication
200.5	Selected cases
	By compiler, editor, or title
200.7	Court records and briefs (Collected by court)
	By initial date of period covered
	Court of Common Pleas
203	Private (named) reports. By initial date of period covered and by reporter or title, A-Z
	Subarrange each by Table KD6
203.3	Abridgments and digests not connected with any named reports
	By date of publication
203.4	Indexes and tables not connected with any named reports
	By date of publication
203.5	Selected cases
	By compiler, editor, or title

Law reports and related materials
 Law reports
  By courts
   Common law courts
    Particular courts
     Court of Common Pleas -- Continued
203.7   Court records and briefs (Collected by court)
              By initial date of period covered
             Court of Exchequer (Law)
208   Private (named) reports. By initial date of period
              covered and by reporter or title, A-Z
               Subarrange each by Table KD6
208.3   Abridgments and digests not connected with any
              name reports
               By date of publication
208.4   Indexes and tables not connected with any named
              reports
               By date of publication
208.5   Selected cases
               By compiler, editor, or title
208.7   Court records and briefs (Collected by court)
               By initial date of period covered
             Nisi Prius (Circuit) courts
210   Private (named) reports. By initial date of period
              covered and by reporter or title, A-Z
               Subarrange each by Table KD6
210.3   Abridgments and digests not connected with any
              name reports
               By date of publication
210.4   Indexes and tables not connected with any named
              reports
               By date of publication
210.5   Selected cases
               By compiler, editor, or title
210.7   Court records and briefs (Collected by court)
               By initial date of period covered
225   Manorial courts
              By initial date of period covered and by reporter or title,
               A-Z
              For listing, see Frederick C. Hicks, Materials and
               Methods of Legal Research. 3d rev. ed., 1942, pp.
               448-449
             County courts
228   Private (named) reports. By initial date of period
              covered and by reporter or title, A-Z
               Subarrange each by Table KD6

	Law reports and related materials
	Law reports
	By courts
	Common law courts
	Particular courts
	County courts -- Continued
228.3	Abridgments and digests not connected with any name reports
	By date of publication
228.4	Indexes and tables not connected with any named reports
	By date of publication
228.5	Selected cases
	By compiler, editor, or title
228.7	Court records and briefs (Collected by court)
	By initial date of period covered
	Equity courts
	Reports of various courts see KD232+
	Particular courts
	Court of Chancery
	Including reports, etc. relating to decisions of both Court of Chancery and other equity courts
232	Private (named) reports. By initial date of period covered and by reporter or title, A-Z
	Subarrange each by Table KD6
232.3	Abridgments and digests not connected with any named reports
	By date of publication
232.4	Indexes and tables not connected with any named reports
	By date of publication
232.5	Selected cases
	By compiler, editor, or title
232.7	Court records and briefs (Collected by court)
	By initial date of period covered
	Vice-Chancellors' Courts
234	Private (named) reports. By initial date of period covered and by reporter or title, A-Z
	Subarrange each by Table KD6
234.3	Abridgments and digests not connected with any named reports
	By date of publication
234.4	Indexes and tables not connected with any named reports
	By date of publication
234.5	Selected cases
	By compiler, editor, or title

KD

Law reports and related materials
Law reports
By courts
Common law courts
Particular courts
Court of Chancery
Vice-Chancellors' Courts -- Continued

234.7	Court records and briefs (Collected by court) By initial date of period covered
	Court of Exchequer (Equity)
236	Private (named) reports. By initial date of period covered and by reporter or title, A-Z Subarrange each by Table KD6
236.3	Abridgments and digests not connected with any named reports By date of publication
236.4	Indexes and tables not connected with any named reports By date of publication
236.5	Selected cases By compiler, editor, or title
236.7	Court records and briefs (Collected by court) By initial date of period covered
	Master of Rolls Court
238	Private (named) reports. By initial date of period covered and by reporter or title, A-Z Subarrange each by Table KD6
238.3	Abridgments and digests not connected with any named reports By date of publication
238.4	Indexes and tables not connected with any named reports By date of publication
238.5	Selected cases By compiler, editor, or title
238.7	Court records and briefs (Collected by court) By initial date of period covered
	Court of Requests (Equity)
240	Private (named) reports. By initial date of period covered and by reporter or title, A-Z Subarrange each by Table KD6
240.3	Abridgments and digests not connected with any named reports By date of publication
240.4	Indexes and tables not connected with any named reports By date of publication

Law reports and related materials
Law reports
By courts
Common law courts
Particular courts
Court of Requests (Equity) -- Continued
240.5   Selected cases
By compiler, editor, or title
240.7   Court records and briefs (Collected by court)
By initial date of period covered
Admiralty and ecclesiastical precedents
245   Combined reports
Admiralty reports see KD1811+
Ecclesiastical cases see KD8638+
Privy Council Cases (Judicial Committee)
For Privy Council decisions relating to a particular
jurisdiction, see the jurisdiction, e.g. India, KNS17+
247   Private (named) reports. By initial date of period
covered and by reporter or title, A-Z
Subarrange each by Table KD6
247.3   Abridgments and digests not connected with any
named reports
By date of publication
247.4   Indexes and tables not connected with any named
reports
By date of publication
247.5   Selected cases
By compiler, editor, or title
247.7   Court records and briefs (Collected by court)
By initial date of period covered
Special courts or reports on particular subjects
see the subject
Bail Court see KD7605
Bankruptcy see KD2141+
Crown (Criminal) cases see KD7864.8+
Election (Contested elections) see KD4380+
Private bills. Locus standi reports see KD4372
Registration cases (Registration of electors) see
KD4340
Reports in all the courts
Before 1865
270   General reports
e.g. English Reports - Full Reprint (1220-1866); The
Revised Reports (1785-1865); Jurist (1837-1866)
Law Journal Reports (1822-1831) see KD288.A2
Law Times Report, Old Series (1843-1859) see
KD288.A3

KD

Law reports and related materials
  Law reports
    Reports in all the courts -- Continued
      Since 1865
        The Law Reports
          Appellate Series

275	English and Irish Appeals (1866-1875)
275.2	Scotch and Divorce Appeals (1866-1875)
275.3	Privy Council Appeals (1866-1875)
275.4	Appeal Cases (1876-1890, 1891-)
	Chancery and Equity Series
276	Chancery Appeals (1865-1875)
276.2	Equity Cases (1865-1875)
276.3	Chancery Division (1875-1890, 1891-)
	Common Law Series
277	Queen's Bench Cases (1865-1875)
277.2	Queen's Bench Division (1875-1890)
277.3	Common Pleas Cases (1865-1875)
277.4	Common Pleas Division (1875-1880)
277.5	Exchequer Cases (1865-1875)
277.6	Exchequer Division (1865-1880)
277.7	Queen's and King's Bench (1891-)
	Probate, Divorce, and Admiralty Series
279	Probate and Divorce Cases (1865-1875)
279.2	Admiralty and Ecclesiastical Cases (1866-1875)
279.3	Probate, Divorce, and Admiralty Division (1875-1971)
279.4	Family Division (1972-)
	For admiralty cases from 1972 see KD277.7
	Restrictive Practices Cases see KD2218
282	Weekly Law Reports (1953-). Weekly Notes (1866-1952)
284	Digests
285	Index. Annually supplemented (Red Index)
	Current years covered by Pink Index published several times a year
288.A-Z	Other
	Digests relating to particular reports may be arranged (when applicable) by using consecutive Cutter numbers like .A222 below
288.A2	Law Journal Reports (1822-1831)
288.A22	Law Journal Reports, New Series (1832-1949)
288.A222	Law Journal quinquennial digest (1921-1925)
288.A3	Law Times Reports, Old Series (1843-1859)
288.A34	Law Times Reports (1859-1947)
288.A4	Weekly Reporter (1852-1906)
288.A5	Times Law Reports (1884-1952)

	Law reports and related materials
	Law reports
	Reports in all the courts
	Since 1865
	Other -- Continued
288.A6	All England Law Reports Reprint (1843-1935)
288.A64	All England Law Reports (1936-)
	Weekly Law Reports see KD282
	Weekly Notes see KD282
291.A-Z	Selected reports. By editor or title, A-Z
	e.g.
291.B75	British Ruling Cases (1900-1931)
291.E45	English Ruling Cases (1307-1908)
291.J87	Justice of the Peace Reports (1903-1926)
	Comprehensive abridgments and digests
	Including works relating to both legislation and law reports
	Class abridgments and digests relating to particular reports with such reports
295.A-Z	Before 1865. By editor, A-Z
	Including both law and equity
	Cutter numbers listed below are provided as examples
	For abridgments of the Year Books (e.g. R. Brooke, A. Fitzherbert) see KD196.A+
295.B3	Bacon, M., New Abridgment of the Law
295.C6	Comyns, J., Digest of the Laws of England
296.A-Z	Since 1865. By editor or title, A-Z
	Including both law and equity
	Cutter numbers listed below are provided as examples
296.C45	Chitty, E., Chitty's Index to All Cases Relating to Equity ...
	4th ed. (1883-1889)
	Class here also earlier editions
	Current law
296.C8	Consolidation
296.C82	Yearbook
	Citator
296.C84	Case citator
296.C85	Statute citator
296.E5	English and Empire Digest. The Digest
296.M4	Mews, J., Digest of English Case Law
	16 v. (1898)
296.M43	Mews, J., Digest of English Case Law. 2nd ed.
	24 v. (1925-1928). Annual supplements, periodically cumulated
300	Indexes. Tables
	Class indexes and tables relating to particular reports or abridgments and digests with such works

	Administrative decisions
	see subject
310	Encyclopedias
	e.g. Halsbury's Laws of England
313	Law dictionaries. Words and phrases
	For dictionaries on a particular subject, see subject
	For bilingual and multilingual dictionaries see K50+
315	Legal maxims. Quotations
318	Form books
	Class here general works only
	Form books on a particular subject are classed with the subject
<322>	Periodicals
	For periodicals consisting primarily of informative materials (Newsletters, bulletins, etc.) relating to a particular subject, see subject and form division, "Periodicals"
	For law reports, official bulletins or circulars, and official gazettes intended chiefly for the publication of laws and regulations, see appropriate entries in the text or form division tables
	For periodicals consisting predominantly of legal articles, regardless of subject matter and jurisdiction see K1+
(325)	Yearbooks
	Class here only publications issued annually, containing information, statistics, etc. about the year just passed
	For other publications appearing yearly see K1+
	Judicial statistics
327	General
330	Criminal statistics
331	Juvenile crime
332.A-Z	Other. By subject, A-Z
	Directories
	General
336	National. Regional
338.A-Z	Local. By county or city, A-Z
340.A-Z	By specialization, A-Z
340.B34	Bankruptcy
340.C65	Commercial law
	Law schools see KD422
	Patent attorneys see KD1413.3
345	Society and bar association journals
	Class here only journals restricted to society or bar association activities
	For journals devoted to legal subjects, either wholly or in part see K1+
347	Congresses
	Collections
353	Monographic series
354	Several authors. Festschriften

	Collections	
	Several authors. Festschriften -- Continued	
355	Minor collections. Anthologies	
356	Digests (Summaries, condensations of essays, periodical articles, etc.)	
358.A-Z	Individual authors, A-Z	

Under each:

.x	By date
.xA-.xZ	By editor, A-Z

Including collected opinions

	Trials
	Criminal trials and judicial investigations
	Collections
370	General
371.A-Z	Particular offenses, A-Z
371.H47	Heresy
371.L5	Libel and slander
371.M8	Murder
371.P6	Political offenses
	Including treason, sedition, etc.
371.R5	Riots
371.S48	Sex crimes
371.W56	Witchcraft
	Particular trials
	Including commentaries and stories on a particular trial, and including records and briefs
372.A-Z	Early through 19th century. By defendant or best known name, A-Z
373.A-Z	20th century. By defendant or best known name, A-Z
	Trials of peers
376.A3A-.A3Z	Collections
376.A4-Z	Particular trials. By defendant, A-Z
	Civil trials
378	Collections
	Particular trials
	Including commentaries and stories on a particular trial, and including records and briefs
	Cf. KD3089.5.A+ Railway labor disputes
	Cf. KD4381.A+ Contested elections
379.A-Z	Early through 19th century. By plaintiff, A-Z
379.5.A-Z	20th century. By plaintiff, A-Z
380.A-Z	21st century. By plaintiff, A-Z
	Legal research. Legal bibliography
	Class here works on methods of bibliographical research and how to find the law
392	General
	Electronic data processing. Information retrieval

	Legal research. Legal bibliography
	Electronic data processing. Information retrieval --
	Continued
394	General
394.5.A-Z	By subject, A-Z
394.5.C67	Court administration
394.5.L3	Land titles
400	Systems of citation. Legal abbreviations
404	Legal composition and draftsmanship
	For legislative drafting see KD4238
<407>	Paleography. Court hand
	see Z115
411	Law reporting. Law reporters
	Casebooks
	General see KD658
	By subject
	see the subject
	Legal education
417	Bibliography
<418>	Periodicals
	see K1+
419	Society publications
420	Congresses. Conferences
421	Yearbooks. Annual and periodical surveys
422	Directories
428.A-Z	Law school catalogs and bulletins
	By school, A-Z
430.A-Z	Legal education associations, A-Z
	e.g.
430.L4	Legal Education Association
432	General works. Standards. Criticism (Table KD3)
	Continuing (post-admission) legal education
434	General (Table KD3)
435	Judicial education (Table KD3)
	Study and teaching
	General works see KD432
436.A-Z	Particular subjects, A-Z
	Teaching methods
438	General
	Moot courts
440.A2A-.A2Z	General
440.A3-Z	Particular. By school, A-Z
442	Students' guides and textbooks
	For introductions to legal literature (legal bibliography)
	see KD392+
	For introductory surveys of the law see KD660
444	Prelaw-school education. Admission to law school

	Legal education
	Study and teaching -- Continued
	Law students
446	General
448.A-Z	Student associations, fraternities, etc., A-Z
452.A-Z	Particular law schools, A-Z
456.A-Z	Law societies, A-Z
456.C7	Order of the Coif
456.I6	The Institute
456.J87	Justice (Society)
	Legal education associations see KD430.A+
456.L6	Lowtonian Society
456.S4	Selden Society
	Inns of Court and Inns of Chancery see KD502+
	Law Society see KD509
	The legal profession
460	General. Law as a career (Table KD3)
461	Particular aspects
	Barristers
463	General (Table KD3)
464	Serjeants-at-law
	Solicitors
466	General (Table KD3)
468	Articled clerks
470	Notaries
472.A-Z	Particular classes of lawyers and types of careers, A-Z
472.B35	Bankruptcy lawyers
472.G6	Government service
472.I5	Industry. Corporate practice
472.M55	Minority lawyers
	Patent attorneys see KD1413
472.P82	Public interest
472.S35	Scriveners
472.W65	Women lawyers
	Practice of law
474	General (Table KD3)
	Biography of lawyers (Collective biography of members of the Inns of Court and Inns of Chancery) see KD503.2+
	Biography of lawyers (General collective biography) see KD536+
	Biography of lawyers (1066-ca. 1830) see KD620+
	Biography of lawyers (1830-) see KD630+
476	Admission to practice
	Legal ethics and legal etiquette. Professional discipline
	Cf. KD7286.J8 Judicial ethics
479	General (Table KD3)
482.A-Z	Special topics, A-Z

	The legal profession
	Practice of law
	Legal ethics and legal etiquette. Professional discipline
	Special topics, A-Z -- Continued
482.A4	Advertising
482.A6	Ambulance chasing
	Attorney and client
485	General (Table KD3)
486.A-Z	Special topics, A-Z
	Liability see KD486.M35
486.M35	Malpractice. Liability
	Economics of law practice
488	General
489	Fees
490	Attorney's lien
491	Marketing of legal services (Table KD2)
	Law office management
492	General
493	Attorneys' and legal secretaries' handbooks, manuals, desk-books, etc.
	Form books see KD318
495.A-Z	Special topics, A-Z
495.A3	Accounting
	For works on accounting in general for the use of attorneys see HF5601+
495.A87	Automation
	Legal advertising see KD703.N6
	Attorneys in nonjudicial government service see KD472.G6
	Bar associations. Solicitors' associations
498	General
	Class monographs and publications on particular subjects with the subject
	For bar association serial publications see KD345
	Particular types of organizations
	National
	Barristers
500	Senate of the Inns of Court and the Bar
	Formerly General Council of the Bar of England and Wales, and Senate of the Four Inns of Court
	Inns of Court and Inns of Chancery
502	General

The legal profession
Bar associations. Solicitors' associations
Particular types of organizations
National
Barristers
Inns of Court and Inns of Chancery -- Continued
Particular inns
Including collective biography of members, memorials, etc.
For individual biography (1066-ca. 1830) see KD621.A+
For individual biography (1831-1900) see KD631.A+
For individual biography (1901-   ) see KD632.A+
Inns of Court
General see KD502

504.A-Z	Individual, A-Z
504.G7	Gray's Inn
504.I5	Inner Temple
504.L5	Lincoln's Inn
504.M5	Middle Temple
504.S4	Serjeants' Inn

Inns of Chancery
General see KD502

505.A-Z	Individual, A-Z
505.B37	Barnard's Inn
505.C5	Clement's Inn
505.C55	Clifford's Inn
505.S7	Staple Inn
507	Doctors' Commons

Solicitors

509	Law Society (United Kingdom)

Including predecessor associations, e.g., Incorporated Law Society

510.A-Z	Local associations, lawyers' clubs, etc. By place, A-Z

Subarrange by association, A-Z
Lawyers in literature
see subclasses PB-PZ
Legal anecdotes. Wit and humor see K183+
Community legal services. Legal aid. Legal assistance to the poor

512	General (Table KD2)

Legal aid societies see KD509+
Public defenders see KD8358

513.A-Z	Local agencies and organizations. By place, A-Z

Subarrange each by Table KD4

	History
	Including works on the history of modern law
	For works on the history of a particular subject, see the subject
530	Sources
532	General (Table KD3)
	Biography
	Collective
536	General
537.A-Z	Local, A-Z
	Individual (1066-ca. 1830) see KD621.A+
	Individual (1830-) see KD631+
	Particular aspects
540	Influence of foreign law
	e.g. Influence of Roman law
540.5.A-Z	Other, A-Z
540.5.R4	Influence of religion. The Bible in English law
	By period
	Anglo-Saxon period (to 1066)
	Sources
542	General and comprehensive collections
543	Statutes. Anglo-Saxon dooms
	e.g. Dooms of Alfred
544	Norman compilations. Custumals. Law books
	e.g. Liber Quadripartitus (1114); Consiliatio Cnuti. Laws of Canute (1110-1130); Leges Henrici (1114-1118); Leges Edwardi Confessoris (1130-1135)
546	Formularies
	Documents
548	Royal
549	Private
550	Land books
552	Contemporary treatises
	e.g. Rectitudines singularum personarum (also known as De dignitate hominum Anglosaxonum)
	Treatises. Monographs
554	General
555	Special aspects
	Norman period (1066 to ca. 1200)
	Sources
558	Exchequer rolls
560	Collections of judgments
562	Law books
	e.g. Statuta et consuetudines Normanniae (Établissement et coutumes de Normandie); Summa de legibus consuetudinum Normanniae (Summa de legibus in Curia Laicali; Grand coutumier de Normandie) (ca. 1270-1275)

	History
	By period
	Norman period (1066 to ca. 1200)
	Sources -- Continued
564	Diplomata (Cartularies)
566	Treatises. Monographs
	Anglo-Norman period. Common law (1066 to ca. 1830)
	Sources
570	General collections
571	Laws: Statutes, statute rolls, charters. By date
	For session laws see KD125
572	Private compulations. Custumals
	Judicial sources
574	Chancery records
	For calendars and inventories see DA25
	Reports see KD190+
576	Writs (Brevia)
	e.g. Old Natura Brevium; Registrum omnium brevium ... (1531)
578	Records. Records of litigation
	For civil plea rolls see KD190
	For crown plea rolls see KD7864.8
580	Precedents
	Public records
	For calendars and inventories see DA25
582	Domesday Book. Surveys
584	Pipe rolls (Rotuli Pipea)
586	Exchequer rolls (Rotuli scaccarii)
587	Rolls of letters patent and letters close
588	Fine rolls. Charter rolls
590	Diplomata (Charters of feoffment. Grants of franchises)
594	Manorial laws
	Class here general collections only
	For rolls of manorial and other local courts see KD225
	For laws of particular manors (England) see KD9310.A+
	For laws of particular manors (Wales) see KD9350.A+
597	Municipal and mercantile customs
600	Contemporary treatises. Law books
	e. g.
600.B73	Bracton, H.: De legibus et consuetudinibus Angliae libri quinque (1248-1258)
600.D5	Dialogus de Scaccario
600.F59	Fleta, seu Commentarius juris Anglicani (ca. 1290)
600.F6713	Fortescu, J., De laudibus legum Angliae (1468-1471)

	History
	By period
	Anglo-Norman period. Common law (1066 to ca. 1830)
	Sources
	Contemporary treatises. Law books -- Continued
600.G5513	Glanvill: Tractatus de legibus consuetudinibus et regni Angliae (1187-1189)
600.H3	Hale, M.: The History of the Common Law of England (1713)
600.H67	Horn, A.: the Mirrour of Justices (1285-1290)
600.S4413	Seldon, J., Ad Fletam dissertatio (1647)
	Treatises. Monographs
	General
606	Comprehensive
	By period
608	From the Norman conquest (1066) to the death of Edward I (1307)
610	From Edward II (1307) to Henry VIII (1547)
612	From Henry VIII (1547) to ca. 1775
614	From ca. 1775 to the law reform (ca. 1830)
	Biography
620	Collective
	For local biography see KD537.A+
621.A-Z	Individual, A-Z
	Subarrange each by Table KD7
	Including criticism
	Recent history, since ca. 1830
	Sources (Legislation) see KD124+
	Sources (Law reports) see KD186.2+
626	Treatises. Monographs
	Biography
630	Collective
	For local biography see KD537.A+
	Individual
631.A-Z	1831-1900
	Subarrange each by Table KD7
632.A-Z	1901-
	Subarrange each by Table KD7
	Jurisprudence and philosophy of English law
	Class here general doctrines of English legal institutions, including those of the common law system (Anglo-American law) in general.
	For works on the philosophy of particular branches of the law (e.g., Constitutional or criminal law), see those subjects
	For works by British authors on legal philosophy in general see K201+
640	General (Table KD3)

	Jurisprudence and philosophy of English law -- Continued
	Rule of law in the United Kingdom see KD3995
	Relationship of law to other disciplines, subjects, or phenomena see K486+
654	Criticism. Legal reform. General administration of justice (Table KD3)
	Cf. KD6850+ Judiciary
	Cf. KD7876 Criminal justice
	General and comprehensive works
	Collections see KD353+
658	Casebooks. Readings
660	Treatises
661	Compends. Courses of study
662	Minor and popular works
663	Examination aids
664	Miscellaneous individual addresses and essays
	For collected essays see KD354
665.A-Z	Works for particular groups of users, A-Z
665.A25	Accountants
	Administrators, Arts see KD665.A77
665.A43	Aged. Older people. Retired persons
665.A77	Arts administrators
665.B86	Businesspeople. Foreign investors
665.C6	Consumers
665.E5	Engineers
665.F3	Farmers
	Cf. KD1020.4 Rural estate management
	Foreign investors see KD665.B86
665.G95	Gypsies. Romanies
665.J6	Journalists
665.N87	Nurses
	Older people see KD665.A43
665.P6	Police
	Retired persons see KD665.A43
	Romanies see KD665.G95
665.S6	Social workers
665.T4	Technologists
	Urban realty owners and managers see KD1020.6
667.A-Z	Works on diverse legal aspects of a particular subject and falling within several branches of the law, A-Z
667.A5	Animals
667.C65	Computers
667.D6	Dogs
667.G37	Gardens
	Handbooks for legal services to the poor see KD667.P68
667.H6	Horses
	For sale of horses see KD1657.H6

	General and comprehensive works
	Works on diverse legal aspects of a particular subject and
	falling within several branches of the law, A-Z --
	Continued
667.H85	Human body
	Legal protection of the poor see KD667.P68
667.M4	Meetings
667.M63	Mobile homes
667.O28	Oath
667.P68	Poverty. Legal protection of the poor. Handbooks for legal
	services
667.P83	Public interest law
669.A-Z	Foreign language treatises. By language, A-Z
	Translations from English are classed with original
671	Common law (Table KD3)
674	Equity (Table KD3)
	Usage and customs see KD693
	Conflict of laws
	For conflict of laws between the United States and Great
	Britain see KF416.A+
680	General (Table KD3)
681.A-Z	Particular aspects, A-Z
	Incidental questions see KD681.P74
681.P74	Preliminary questions
681.R34	Remedies
681.R4	Renvoi
685.A-Z	Particular branches and subjects of the law, A-Z
	Bankruptcy see KD685.I5
685.C6	Contracts. Obligations. Debtor and creditor (Table KD4)
685.F65	Foreign exchange (Table KD4)
	Foreign judgments see KD7121
685.I5	Insolvency and bankruptcy (Table KD4)
685.I54	Intellectual property (Table KD4)
685.L3	Labor law (Table KD4)
685.L55	Limitation of actions (Table KD4)
685.M3	Marriage. Divorce. Marital property (Table KD4)
685.P47	Persons (Table KD4)
685.S9	Succession upon death (Table KD4)
685.T67	Torts (Table KD4)
685.T7	Transfer of property (Table KD4)
	Including chattels
687	Retroactive law. Intertemporal law
	General principles and concepts
	Comprehensive works see KD657+
	Particular aspects
691	Statutory construction and interpretation (Table KD3)
693	Usage and custom

	General principles and concepts
	Particular aspects -- Continued
695	Stare decisis
700	Codification (Table KD3)
	Classification of library collections of legal literature see Z697.L4
703.A-Z	Concepts applying to several branches of the law, A-Z
703.D3	Damages (Table KD4)
	Cf. KD1602 Breach of contract. Remedies
703.E7	Estoppel (Table KD4)
703.G6	Good faith (Table KD4)
703.L5	Limitation of actions (Table KD4)
	Cf. KD1697.L5 Negotiable instruments
	Cf. KD7455 Civil procedure
703.N6	Notice. Legal advertising (Table KD4)
703.N84	Nullity (Table KD4)
703.P9	Public policy (Table KD4)
703.R4	Recording and registration (Table KD4)
	Cf. KD746 Persons
	Cf. KD984 Real property
703.T5	Time (Computation of time) (Table KD4)
703.W34	Waiver (Table KD4)
	Private (Civil) law
720	General and comprehensive works
721	General principles and concepts
	Persons
723	General. Status. Capacity
	Natural persons
	Civil status
725	Domicile
	Cf. KD3311 Public welfare
727	Name (Table KD3)
	Nobility see KD4265+
728	Coats of arms. Court of Chivalry (Table KD3)
	Decorations of honor. Awards of honor. Dignities see KD4656+
729	Absence. Missing persons. Presumption of death
	Capacity and disability
732	General
734	Women (Table KD3)
	For married women see KD758
735	Minors. Children (Table KD3)
	Including liability
	Mentally ill. People with mental or physical disabilities
	For care of the mentally ill see KD3412
737	General (Table KD2)
738.A-Z	Particular diseases or impairments, A-Z

Persons
  General. Status. Capacity
    Natural persons
      Capacity and disability
        Mentally ill. People with mental or physical disabilities
        Particular diseases or impairments, A-Z -- Continued

738.D7	Drunkards
	Lunacy proceedings. Court of Protection
740	General (Table KD3)
741	Receivers for mentally disordered persons
744.A-Z	Other, A-Z
744.A5	Aliens
	Cf. KD4130+ Control of individuals
744.J4	Jews
	Cf. KD4102.J4 Civil and political rights and liberties
744.U53	Unborn children. Nasciturus
746	Recording and registration. Registers of births, marriages, and deaths. Birth and death certificates (Table KD3)
	Juristic persons, corporate persons, associations, etc. see KD2040+
	Domestic relations. Family law
750	General (Table KD2)
	Domestic relations courts and procedure
751	General (Table KD2)
752	Summary jurisdiction and procedure (Table KD2)
	Marriage. Husband and wife
	Cf. KD7973 Conjugal violence
753	General (Table KD2)
754	Betrothal. Breach of promise
755	Performance of marriage. Civil and religious celebrations (Table KD3)
756	Void and voidable marriage. Nullity (Table KD3)
	Rights and duties of husband and wife
758	Civil status of married women (Table KD3)
	Property relationships
760	General (Table KD3)
761.A-Z	Particular modes of matrimonial property relations, A-Z
761.S4	Separate property
762	Marriage settlements. Antenuptial contracts
	Divorce. Nullity. Separation
764	General (Table KD2)
769	Maintenance. Alimony
771	Unmarried couples (Table KD2)
	Parent and child
772	General (Table KD3)

	Persons
	Domestic relations. Family law
	Parent and child -- Continued
774	Legitimacy. Legitimation. Paternity (Table KD3)
775	Illegitimate children. Affiliation (Table KD3)
777	Adoption (Table KD3)
	Parental rights and duties. Property of minors. Custody
	Including works on access to children and on parental kidnapping
779	General (Table KD2)
780	Child support. Desertion and non-support (Table KD3)
785	Guardian and ward (Table KD2)
	Agency see KD2020+
	Property
810	General. Ownership. Possession (Table KD2)
811	Particular aspects and relationships
	For equitable conversion see KD858
	Particular kinds of property
813	Alien property. Enemy property
	Cf. KD1607 Trading with the enemy
	Matrimonial property see KD760+
815	Public property. Government property
	Including both real and personal property
	For public real property see KD1034+
	Real property. Land law
821-830	General (Table KD1)
831	Special aspects and relationships
	e.g. Public control. Public policy
	Land tenure
833	General
	Feudal tenure
834	General (Table KD2)
	Particular kinds
	Free tenure
835	General (Table KD2)
836.A-Z	Particular types, A-Z
836.B8	Burgage
836.G3	Gavelkind
836.K5	Knight's service
836.S4	Serjeanty
	Unfree tenure
837	General
838.A-Z	Particular types, A-Z
838.M3	Manors. Copyholds (Table KD4)
838.V5	Villeinage (Table KD4)
839	Inquisitiones post mortem
	Estates and interests

Property
  Real property. Land law
    Land tenure
      Estates and interests -- Continued
841   General
842   Special aspects
        Particular estates and interests (legal or equitable)
         Freehold estates
          Fee simple
845   General
           Particular kinds
            Allotments. Small holdings see KD907+
850   Flats. Horizontal property. Housing
             condominium
854   Fee tail. Entailed interests
           For words of limitation, Shelley's case see
            KD869
           For fines and recoveries see KD992
          Life interests. Possessory estates
857   General
           Fixtures. Improvements see KD917
           Rights of user. Waste. Dilapidations. Repairs
            see KD919
           Dower. Curtesy see KD1523.D6
         Estates less than freehold
          Leasehold interests. Landlord and tenant see
           KD891+
858   Equitable ownership. Equitable conversion
859   Uses and trusts. Statute of uses (Table KD3)
861   Settlements and trusts for sale. Settled land (Table
          KD3)
         Future estates and interests
          Including works on future interests in both real and
           personal property
863   General (Table KD3)
865   Power of appointment
866   Reversions. Reversionary interests
867   Remainders. Contingent remainders. Executory
           devices (Table KD3)
869   Words of limitation. Rule in Shelley's case
871   Rule against perpetuities (Table KD3)
873   Mortmain (Table KD3)
        Concurrent ownership. Co-ownership
         Including works on concurrent ownership in both real
          and personal property
878   General
880   Joint tenancy

Property
  Real property. Land law
    Land tenure
      Estates and interests
        Particular estates and interests (legal or equitable)
          Concurrent ownership. Co-ownership
            Joint tenancy -- Continued

883	Partition
	Estates and interests arising from marriage see KD1523.D6
	Tenancy. Leaseholds. Landlord and tenant
891-900	General (Table KD1)
902	Rent. Rent control (Table KD2)
	Particular kinds of leaseholds
905	Business and professional tenancies. Commercial leases (Table KD2)
	Farm tenancy. Agricultural holdings acts. Allotments. Small holdings
907	General (Table KD2)
908.A-Z	Special topics, A-Z
908.A3	Agricultural arbitration
908.V3	Valuation of tenant right
910	Distress (Table KD3)
911	Housing courts (Table KD2)
	Rights and interests incident to ownership and possession. Interests less than estates
915	General
917	Fixtures. Improvements (Table KD3)
919	Rights of user. Waste. Dilapidations. Repair (Table KD3)
	Cf. KD8733 Ecclesiastical dilapidations
921	Boundaries. Fences (Table KD2)
923	Riparian rights. Water rights of individuals (Table KD3)
925	Action to recover the possession of land. Ejectment (Table KD3)
	For trespass to land see KD1966
	Right to dispose of land
928	Restraint of alienation
	Rights to use and profits of another's land. Incorporeal hereditaments
935	General
	Easement and profits
936	General
	Easements
937	General (Table KD3)
	Particular kinds

Property
  Real property. Land law
    Land tenure
      Estates and interests
        Rights and interests incident to ownership and
            possession. Interests less than estates
          Rights to use and profits of another's land.
              Incorporeal hereditaments
            Easement and profits
              Easements
                Particular kinds -- Continued

938	Right of way (Table KD3)
940	Light and air. Ancient lights (Table KD3)
942	Party walls. Support of land (Table KD3)
950	Profits à prendre
952	Commons and inclosures (Table KD3)
954	Restrictive covenants (Table KD3)
956	Rent charges
	Annuities see KD1240
	Tithe rent charges see KD8747
960.A-Z	Particular topics, A-Z
960.P7	Prescription

      Transfer of rights in land
        Transfer inter vivos

966	General. Vendor and purchaser (Table KD2)
	Estate agents. Real estate agents see KD2517.E7
	Conveyances. Title investigation. Abstracts
971-980	General. Deeds (Table KD1)
982	Title investigation. Abstracts (Table KD3)
984	Registration (Table KD2)
986	Conveyancing costs (Table KD3)
988	Description of land. Surveying
	Other modes of transfer
989	Adverse possession
990	Auction sales
992	Fines and recoveries (Table KD3)
	Prescription see KD960.P7

        Transfer by will see KD1501+
        Intestate succession see KD1522+
        Unclaimed estates see KD1534
        Lands Tribunal see KD1187
      Mortgages. Liens. Land charges

1010	General
	Particular types
1013	Mortgages (Table KD3)
1016	Land charges (Table KD3)
	For local land charges see KD1128

	Property
	Real property. Land law -- Continued
	Real estate management
1020	General
1020.4	Rural estate management
1020.6	Urban estate management
	Public property. Public restraints on private property
1034	General
1035	Conservation of natural resources (Table KD2)
	Roads
1040	General. Highway law (Table KD3)
1043	Highway finance
	Road construction contracts and specifications see KD1641
1045	Roadside protection. Rights of way (Table KD3)
	Including restrictions on signboards, advertising, etc.
1048	Foot trails
	Water resources. Rivers. Water courses
1070	General (Table KD2)
	Riparian rights see KD923
1071	Flood control (Table KD2)
1072	River and harbor improvement (Table KD2)
	Water pollution see KD3367+
	Public land law
1090	General
	Reclamation. Land drainage
1095	General (Table KD3)
1098	Shore protection
	National preserves
1102	Crown lands (Table KD3)
	National parks and recreation grounds. Open spaces. "Access to the countryside." Wilderness preservation
1105	General (Table KD3)
1107.A-Z	Special topics, A-Z
	Caravan sites development see KD1107.T7
1107.T7	Trailer camps sites development
	Cf. KD2517.T7 Trailer camp regulations
	Architectural and historic monuments see KD3740
	Regional and city planning. Zoning. Building
1125	General. Land development (Table KD2)
1128	Land Commission. Local land changes (Table KD3)
	Betterment levy see KD5539
	Lands Tribunal see KD1187
	Particular land uses and zoning controls
1132	Sex-oriented businesses (Table KD2)
	Building laws

	Property
	Real property. Land law
	Public property. Public restraints on private property
	Regional and city planning. Zoning. Building
	Building laws -- Continued
1140	General (Table KD2)
1152	Model building bylaws
1154.A-Z	Particular types of buildings, A-Z
1154.S3	School buildings
1154.T4	Theaters
1160	Electric conduits and installations
1162	Plumbing. Sewers and drains. Pipe fitting (Table KD3)
	Housing. Slum clearance. City redevelopment
	Cf. KD1616 Public housing contracts
1171-1180	General (Table KD1)
1183	Housing finance (Table KD3)
1184	Discrimination in housing (Table KD2)
	Eminent domain. Compulsory acquisition
1185	General (Table KD2)
1187	Lands Tribunal
1189	Nationalization
	For the nationalization of a particular industry, see the industry
	Requisitioned land and war works see KD5126+
1195	Public works
	Personal property
1205	General. Personal actions (Table KD2)
	Ownership and possession
	Fixtures see KD917
	Acquisition of property
1214	General
	Original acquisition
1215	General
1217	Particular modes of acquisition, A-Z
	Treasure trove see KD5333.T7
	Transfer
1220	Choses in possession
	Bill of sale see KD1683
	Sale see KD1650+
	Auction sale see KD1660
	Transfer on death see KD1515.L4
1222	Bailment (Table KD3)
	For contracts involving bailments see KD1679+
	Transfers as security see KD1755+
1225	Actions to recover personal property. Replevin
	For trover and conversion see KD1970

Property
    Personal property -- Continued
        Special kinds of personal property
            Tangible. Choses in possession see KD1220
            Intangible. Choses in action
1238   General
                Particular kinds of choses in action
                    Debts see KD1740
1240   Annuities
                    Negotiable instruments see KD1695+
                    Shares, stocks, and debentures (Marketing) see
                        KD1774+
                    Shares, stocks, and debentures (Corporate finance.
                        Issuing of securities) see KD2096
                Intellectual property
1261-1270   General (Table KD1)
                        For antitrust aspects see KD1371
                    Copyright
1281-1290   General (Table KD1)
                        Formalities. Administration
1293   General
1295   Registration
                        Particular branches
                            Literary copyright
1300   General. Authorship (Table KD3)
                                Protected works
1301   General (Table KD2)
1303.A-Z   Particular types of works, A-Z
1303.C65   Computer programs. Computer software
                                            (Table KD4)
1305   Scope of protection
                                    General see KD1300
1305.2   Mechanical reproduction. Reprinting.
                                        Dissemination
1305.3   Performing rights
1305.5   Public lending rights (Table KD3)
1310   Musical copyright (Table KD3)
                                Works of art and photography
1320   General. Works of art (Table KD2)
1325   Designs and models (Table KD3)
1340   Author and publisher. The publishing contract
                                    (Table KD3)
1345   Design protection (Table KD3)
                                    Including protection by copyright or patent
                                    Cf. KD1325 Design copyright
                                    Cf. KD1398 Design patent
                            Patent law and trademarks

KD

Property
  Personal property
    Special kinds of personal property
      Intangible. Choses in action
        Particular kinds of choses in action
          Intellectual property
            Patent law and trademarks -- Continued

1360	General (Table KD2)
1361-1370	Patent law (Table KD1)
1371	Special aspects
	Including relationship to antitrust laws
1374	Procedures. The Patent Office
	Inventions
1384	General (Table KD2)
1387.A-Z	Particular products and processes, A-Z
1387.B55	Biotechnology
1387.C4	Chemicals
	Employees' inventions
1390	General
1391	Government employees
1394	Use of inventions by the Crown. Awards to inventors (Table KD3)
1398	Designs and models (Table KD2)
1400	Licenses. Compulsory licenses
1401	Assignments. Patent conveyancing
1411	Infringement. Patent litigation and procedure
1413	Patent attorneys. Patent practice
1413.3	Directories. By date
	Trademarks
1431-1440	General. Common-law trademarks (Table KD1)
1442	Procedure. Registration (Table KD3)
1443	Service marks (Table KD2)
	Marks of origin
1444	General
1445.A-Z	By product, A-Z
1450	Goodwill. Business names. Registration and transfer of business names (Table KD3)
1465	Government personal property
	Cf. KD3755 Public Record Office. Record management
	Unfair competition see KD2225+
	Trusts and trustees
1480	General (Table KD2)
	Particular kinds of trusts
1483	Private trusts. General trusts (Table KD2)
	Constructive trusts see KD1925
1485	Resulting trusts

	Trusts and trustees
	Particular kinds of trusts -- Continued
	Charitable trusts
	Cf. KD873 Mortmain
	Cf. KD8740 Church land
1487	General (Table KD3)
1488	Cy pres doctrine
	Tax reliefs see KD5500
	Trusts for sale see KD861
	Trustees
1491	Trust companies
	Public trustees see KD1530.S6
	Special topics
1493	Liability. Breach of trust
1495	Accounting
	Legal investments. Trust investments see KD1787+
1497	Estate planning
	Succession upon death
1500	General (Table KD2)
	Testate succession. Wills
1501-1510	General (Table KD1)
	Texts of wills see CS1+
1514.A-Z	Contested wills. By testator, A-Z
1515.A-Z	Special topics, A-Z
	Bequests see KD1515.L4
	Cy pres doctrine see KD1488
1515.E5	Election
1515.F3	Family provisions
1515.L4	Legacies. Bequests
	Power of appointment see KD865
	Probate law and practice
1518	General. Probate courts (Table KD2)
1519.A-Z	Special topics, A-Z
	Adoption see KD777
	Intestate succession
1522	General (Table KD2)
1523.A-Z	Special topics, A-Z
1523.D6	Dower and curtesy (Table KD4)
1523.P7	Primogeniture (Table KD4)
	Cf. KD836.G3 Gavelkind
	Cf. KD854 Fee tail. Entailed interests
	Administration of decedents' estates. Personal
	representatives
1528	General (Table KD2)
1530.A-Z	Special topics, A-Z
1530.A3	Accounting (Table KD4)

KD

Succession upon death
  Administration of decedents' estates. Personal
    representatives
    Special topics, A-Z -- Continued

1530.S6   Small estates administration. Public trustees (Table
                 KD4)
               Estate and death duties see KD5561
               Estate planning see KD1497
1534   Unclaimed estates. Heirless property. Bona vacantia
                 Cf. KD839 Inquisitiones post mortem
Contracts
1554   General and comprehensive works (Table KD2)
          General principles
            Formation of contract
1559   General (Table KD2)
1561   Consideration
1563   Conditions
1568   Formalities. Written contracts. Contracts under seal.
                Statute of frauds (Table KD3)
            Parties to contract
1571   Joint obligations. Correality and solidarity
1573   Contract for the benefit of third persons
1574   Assignment of contracts. Subrogation
            Void and voidable contracts
1576   General
              Unlawful contracts
1578   General
1580.A-Z   Special, A-Z
                  Restraint of trade see KD2212
                  Sunday legislation see KD2488
                  Trading with the enemy see KD1607
1580.U7   Usury
                  Cf. KD1740 Loan of money
                Wager see KD1920+
            Lack of genuine consent
1582   Duress. Undue influence
1583   Mistake. Fraud. Misrepresentation (Table KD3)
          Discharge of contract
1588   General
1590   Performance
1594   Accord and satisfaction
1596   Supervening impossibility
            Limitation of actions (General) see KD703.L5
            Limitation of actions (Procedure) see KD7455+
            Bankruptcy see KD2141+
          Breach of contract. Remedies
1600   General (Table KD2)

Contracts
  General principles
    Breach of contract. Remedies -- Continued
      Particular remedies
1602   Damages. Assumpsit
1603   Specific performance (Table KD3)
        Injunction see KD7578
1605   Rescission and restitution (Table KD3)
    Special aspects
1607   Effects of war on contracts. Trading with the enemy (Table KD3)
    Government contracts. Public contracts. Purchasing and procurement
1610   General
1611   Municipal contracts
1613   War contracts. Defense contracts. Military procurement (Table KD3)
    Construction and building contracts
1615   General (Table KD2)
1616   Public housing (Table KD2)
    Particular contracts
1621-1630   Comprehensive. Mercantile law. Commercial law (Table KD1)
      Agency see KD2020+
      Banking see KD1715+
      Bankruptcy see KD2141+
      Business associations see KD2049+
      Carriers. Carriage of goods and passengers
        For land and air, see KD1802+
        For maritime commercial law and admiralty, see KD1811+
      Commercial arbitration see KD7645+
      Commercial Court see KD7182
      Communication see KD2845+
      Companies. Business corporations see KD2071+
      Contracts involving bailments see KD1679+
      Cooperative societies see KD2120+
      Corporations see KD2057+
      Industry. Trade. Commerce. Occupational law see KD2200+
      Insurance see KD1851+
      Investments see KD1774+
      Loan of money see KD1740
      Marketing of securities. Stock exchange see KD1774+
      Negotiable instruments see KD1695+
      Partnership see KD2051+
      Sale of goods see KD1650+
      Secured transactions see KD1755+

KD

Contracts
  Particular contracts
    Comprehensive. Mercantile law. Commercial law --
      Continued
     Suretyship. Guaranty see KD1900+
     Trademarks see KD1431+
     Transportation see KD2571+
     Unfair competition see KD2225+
    Contract of service. Master and servant

1634   General (Table KD3)
     Apprentices see KD3165
     Merchant mariners see KD1836+
     Civil service see KD4510+
    Contract for work and labor (Contract for services).
      Independent contractors

1638   General
1640   Mechanics' liens. Workers' liens. Contractors' liens
     Particular types of contracts
1641   Building and construction. Engineering (Table KD3)
        Cf. KD1140+ Building laws
        Cf. KD1615+ Government contracts
        Cf. KD2435 Regulation of construction and building
1642.A-Z   Other, A-Z
1642.C65   Computer contracts (Table KD4)
1642.S55   Shipbuilding contracts (Table KD4)
1642.T73   Transportation contracts (Table KD4)
        Including travel contracts and package tours
  Sale of goods
1650   General (Table KD2)
   Formation of contract
1653   General
1654.A-Z   Special topics, A-Z
     C.I.F. and F.O.B. clauses see KD1673
1654.C6   Conditions and warranties. Implied warranties
1657.A-Z   Particular goods and chattels, A-Z
1657.B6   Boats
1657.H6   Horses
   Transfer of property and title
1660   Auction sales (Table KD3)
   Documents of title
1663   General
1664   Bills of lading
     Ocean bills of lading see KD1827
1667   Warehouse receipts
   Conditional transfer, conditional sale, installment sale,
    hire-purchase see KD1759
   Performance

	Contracts
	Particular contracts
	Sale of goods
	Performance -- Continued
1671	General
1673	Overseas sales. C.I.F. clause. F.O.B. clause
	Right of unpaid seller
	Liens see KD1762+
1675	Stoppage in transitu
	Contracts involving bailments
	Cf. KD1222 Bailment
1679	General (Table KD3)
	Particular contracts
1681	Deposit of goods. Warehouses (Table KD3)
	For warehouse receipts see KD1667
	For warehouse regulations see KD2525+
1681.5	Bailment of securities (Table KD3)
1683	Bill of sale (Table KD3)
1685	Innkeeper and guest
	For hotel and restaurant trade see KD2517.H6
	Carriers see KD1800+
	Partnership see KD2051+
	Negotiable instruments
1695	General (Table KD2)
	Bills of exchange
1696	General (Table KD3)
1697.A-Z	Special topics, A-Z
1697.L5	Limitation of actions
1697.P7	Protest
1699	Checks (Table KD3)
	Securities (Bailment) see KD1681.5
	Securities (Marketing) see KD1774+
	Securities (Issuing and sale) see KD2096
	Warehouse receipts see KD1667
	Banking
1715	General (Table KD2)
	Particular kinds of banks and other deposit taking and
	financing companies and institutions
1718	National banks. Central banks. Banks of issue
	Cf. KD5284+ Banknotes
1720	Savings banks (Table KD3)
1722	Cooperative societies
1723	Agricultural cooperative credit associations
1726	Building societies (Table KD3)
	Friendly societies see KD1913
	Trust companies see KD1491
1733	Deposits

	Contracts
	Particular contracts
	Banking -- Continued
1734	Collecting of accounts. Collection laws
	Collection agencies see KD2517.C6
1735	Letters of credit (Table KD3)
1737.A-Z	Other, A-Z
1737.E44	Electronic funds transfer (Table KD4)
1737.R43	Record keeping (Table KD4)
	Including bank secrets, money laundering
1740	Loan of money. Debtor and creditor. Interest. Usury (Table KD3)
	Cf. KD1580.U7 Unlawful contracts
1742	Pawnbroking (Table KD3)
1752	Suretyship. Guaranty (Table KD3)
	For suretyship insurance, bonding see KD1900+
	Secured transactions
1755	General. Consumer credit (Table KD2)
	Particular transactions
1757	Chattel mortgages
1759	Conditional sale. Installment sale. Hire-purchase (Table KD3)
	Liens
1762	General (Table KD3)
1763.A-Z	Particular kinds, A-Z
	Prefer secured obligation
	Attorneys' lien see KD490
	Contractors' lien see KD1640
	Maritime liens see KD1834.B6
	Mechanics' liens see KD1640
	Workers' liens see KD1640
	Suretyship and guaranty see KD1752
	Marketing of securities. Investments. Stock-exchange transactions
	For the issuing and sale of securities see KD2096
1774	General (Table KD3)
1777.A-Z	Particular transactions, A-Z
1777.D47	Derivative securities (Table KD4)
1777.I58	Insider trading in corporate securities (Table KD4)
1778.A-Z	Particular stock exchanges, A-Z
	e.g.
1778.L6	London Stock Exchange (Table KD4)
1782	Investment trusts. Investment companies (Table KD3)
	Particular securities

Contracts
  Particular contracts
    Marketing of securities. Investments. Stock-exchange
      transactions
      Particular securities -- Continued
1787   Legal investments. Trust investments (Table KD2)
                For mortgages see KD1013
                For stocks see KD2096
                For industrial bonds (debentures) see KD2108
                For government bonds see KD5300
    Carriers. Carriage of goods and passengers
1800   General. Liability (Table KD3)
1802   Carriage by land (Table KD3)
                For motor carriers see KD2591+
                For railways see KD2651+
                For Commercial Court see KD7182
1804   Carriage by air (Table KD3)
                Cf. KD2732 Regulation of commercial aviation
      Carriage by sea. Maritime (Commercial) law. Admiralty
1811-1820   General. Affreightment (Table KD1)
                Admiralty and Ecclesiastical Precedents see KD245+
        Liability
1825   General. Maritime torts. Collisions at sea (Table
                KD3)
1826   Average
1827   Ocean bills of lading (Table KD3)
        High Court of Admiralty
1832   General (Table KD3)
1833   Admiralty proceedings (Table KD2)
1834.A-Z   Special topics, A-Z
1834.B6   Bottomry and respondentia. Ship mortgages.
                  Maritime liens (Table KD4)
1834.C5   Charter parties (Table KD4)
1834.D4   Demurrage. Lay days (Table KD4)
1834.S4   Salvage. Wreck (Table KD4)
1834.T67   Towage (Table KD4)
      Maritime labor law. Merchant mariners
                For war services see KD6244+
1836   General (Table KD2)
1837   Qualification. Certification (Table KD3)
1839   Maritime labor unions. Collective labor agreements.
              Labor disputes and arbitration (Table KD3)
            Accommodation on shipboard see KD2762
1842   Protection of labor. Labor hygiene and safety (Table
              KD2)
      Marine insurance
1845   General (Table KD2)

                      Contracts
                        Particular contracts
                          Carriers. Carriage of goods and passengers
                            Marine insurance -- Continued
                              Particular risks

1847   War risks
                                  For reinsurance war risks see KD1907+
                          Insurance
                            Including regulation of insurance business
1851-1860   General (Table KD1)
1862   Insurance business. Agents. Insurance brokers
                          Insurance fraud see KD8001
                          Particular branches
                            Personal insurance
                              Life
1864   General (Table KD2)
1866   Life insurance companies. Finance
1868.A-Z   Particular plans and modes of payment, A-Z
1868.I6   Industrial insurance (Table KD4)
1871   Health. Medical care
                            For state medicine see KD3210+
                          Accident
1874   General (Table KD2)
1875.A-Z   Special topics, A-Z
1875.W3   War risks (Table KD4)
1877   Burial
1879   Business insurance (Table KD2)
                            Including particular types of businesses, e.g. construction
                              companies
                          Property insurance
                            For war damage compensation, see KD5120.6,
                              KD5124.6, KD5128.6
1881   General
1885   Fire (Table KD2)
                          Marine insurance see KD1845+
1886   Aviation (Table KD2)
1887.A-Z   Other hazards, A-Z
1887.B8   Business interruption (Table KD4)
                          Casualty insurance
1890   General liability
                          Particular risks
1892   Motor vehicle (Automobile) insurance (Table KD3)
1894   Unsatisfied judgment funds. Motor Insurers'
                                Bureau
1896.A-Z   Other, A-Z
1896.P64   Pollution liability insurance
1896.P7   Products liability insurance

	Contracts
	Particular contracts
	Insurance
	Particular branches -- Continued
	Suretyship. Guaranty
	For contract of suretyship see KD1752
1900	General
	Bonding
1902	Bail bonds
	Guaranty
1904	Credit insurance
	Reinsurance
1906	General
	War risks
1907	General
	Reinsurance agreements
1909	General
1911.A-Z	Particular agreements. By company, A-Z
1913	Fraternal insurance. Friendly societies (Table KD2)
	Social insurance see KD3191+
	Aleatory contracts. Wagering contracts
1920	Betting and gambling
	Lotteries (Regulation) see KD3527
	Lotteries (Criminal law) see KD8072
	Insurance see KD1851+
1924	Restitution. Quasi contracts. Unjust enrichment (Table KD3)
1925	Remedies. Constructive trust
	Torts (Extracontractual liability)
1941-1950	General. Liability. Damages (Table KD1)
1952	Respondeat superior
	Particular torts
	Torts in respect to persons
1954	Personal injuries. Death by wrongful act (Table KD3)
	Cf. KD1999+ Vicarious liability
	Cf. KD2004 Government liability
	Violation of privacy
1956	General (Table KD3)
1957.A-Z	Special aspects, A-Z
1957.C65	Computers and privacy (Table KD4)
	Privacy and computers see KD1957.C65
	Torts in respect to reputation
1960	General. Libel and slander (Table KD3)
	Disparagement (Unfair competition) see KD2226.D5
	Abuse of legal process
	Maintenance and champerty see KD8057
1962	Malicious prosecution
1963	Deceit. Fraud

	Torts (Extracontractual liability)
	Particular torts -- Continued
	Unfair competition see KD2225+
1966	Trespass to land. Squatting (Table KD3)
	For ejectment see KD925
1968	Nuisance (Table KD3)
	For abatement of public nuisance see KD3372+
1970	Torts affecting chattels. Trespass to goods. Conversion. Trover (Table KD2)
	Negligence
1975	General (Table KD3)
1976	Contributory negligence
1977	Liability for condition and use of land (Table KD3)
1978	Malpractice (Table KD2)
	For malpractice and tort liability of particular professions, see the profession
1980.A-Z	Particular types of accidents, A-Z
1980.A8	Automobile accidents (Table KD4)
	Cf. KD1894 Unsatisfied judgment funds
1980.B84	Building accidents (Table KD4)
	Marine accidents see KD1825
	Railroad accidents see KD2698
	Strict liability. Liability without fault
1983	General
1985	Damage caused by animals
	Products liability
	For products liability insurance see KD1896.P7
1987	General (Table KD2)
1988.A-Z	By product, A-Z
1988.D78	Drugs (Table KD4)
1988.M42	Medical instruments and apparatus (Table KD4)
	Environmental damages
1989	General (Table KD2)
1989.5	Oil pollution damages (Table KD2)
	Parties to actions in tort
	Corporations
1990	General
1990.5.A-Z	Particular kinds of corporations, A-Z
1990.5.B35	Banks. Lender liability
	Lender liability see KD1990.5.B35
	Minors. Children see KD735
1991	Municipal corporations
1994	Public officers and government employees
1996	Labor unions
	Liability for torts of others. Vicarious liability
1999	Master and servant
	For respondeat superior see KD1952

	Torts (Extracontractual liability)
	Liability for torts of others. Vicarious liability -- Continued
2002	Employers' liability. Fellow servant rule (Table KD3)
2004	Government torts. Crown proceedings (Table KD3)
2007	Compensation to victims of crimes. Reparation (Table KD3)
	Including injuries to both person and property and compensation by government
	Agency
2020	General (Table KD2)
	Special topics
2022	Power of attorney (Table KD2)
2024.A-Z	Particular types of agency, A-Z
	Auctioneers see KD2517.E7
2024.B7	Brokers. Commission merchants. Factors (Table KD4)
	For estate agents, real estate agents see KD2517.E7
	Cf. KD989+ Auction sales of real property
2024.S4	Ship brokers (Table KD4)
	Associations
2040	General (Table KD2)
	Including business enterprises in general, regardless of form of organization
2042	Accounting law. Auditing. Financial statements (Table KD2)
	For corporation accounting see KD2098
	For practice of accountancy see KD2974+
2043	Business records. Record keeping and retention (Table KD2)
	Unincorporated associations
2046	General
2047.A-Z	Particular types of associations, A-Z
	Building societies see KD1726
2047.C6	Clubs (Table KD4)
	Friendly societies see KD1913
	Labor unions see KD3050+
	Business associations. Partnership
2049	General
	Partnership
2051	General (Table KD3)
2052	Particular aspects
2054	Limited partnership
	Corporations. Juristic persons
2057	Corporations in general (Table KD3)
2058	Particular aspects
2059.A-Z	Special topics, A-Z
2059.U5	Ultra vires doctrine (Table KD4)
	Nonprofit corporations
2061	General

	Associations
	Corporations. Juristic persons
	Nonprofit corporations -- Continued
2062	Particular types
	Foundations. Endowments see KD1487+
	Business corporations. Companies
	Including joint-stock companies
2071-2080	General (Table KD1)
	Government regulation and control. Licensing
2083	General (Table KD2)
2084	Foreign corporations. Multinational enterprises (Table KD2)
2085	Incorporation. Corporate charters and bylaws. Promoters. Prospectus (Table KD3)
	Management
2088	General (Table KD3)
2089	Board of directors. Officers (Table KD3)
	Corporate finance. Capital. Dividends
2094	General (Table KD2)
2096	Issuing of securities (Table KD3)
	For security exchanges see KD1774+
2098	Accounting. Auditing. Financial statements (Table KD3)
	For practice of accountancy see KD2974+
	Shares and shareholders' rights. Stock transfers
2100	General
2101	Disclosure requirements (Table KD2)
2104	Stockholders' meetings (Table KD3)
2106	Stock transfers
2108	Debentures. Bonds. Preferred stocks
2109	Receivers for debenture holders
	Particular types of corporations or companies
2112	Subsidiary and parent companies. Holding companies
	Monopolies. Combines see KD2218+
2115	Private companies. Family companies. Close companies (Table KD3)
2117	Publicly chartered corporations. Chartered companies
	Public corporations see KD4481+
	Cooperative societies
2120	General
	Agricultural cooperative credit associations see KD1723
	Building societies see KD1726
2122	Industrial and provident societies (Table KD3)
2125	Dissolution. Liquidation (Table KD3)
2127	Consolidation and merger (Table KD3)
	Municipal corporations see KD4770+

	Insolvency and bankruptcy. Creditors' rights
2139	General
	Bankruptcy
2141-2150	General (Table KD1, modified)
2146.4	Collections of legal advertisements
	Bankruptcy court and procedure
2153	General (Table KD3)
2155.A-Z	Special topics,A-Z
2155.C5	Costs (Table KD4)
2155.R4	Receivers in bankruptcy. Trustees. Liquidators (Table KD4)
2160	Priority of claims
2162	Fraudulent conveyances (Table KD3)
2163.A-Z	Particular types of bankrupts, A-Z
2163.C65	Construction industry (Table KD4)
2164.A-Z	Other topics, A-Z
	Debtors' relief
2166	General (Table KD3)
2168	Wartime relief
	For debtors' relief in particular wars see KD5114+
2170	Composition. Receivership to avoid bankruptcy. Deeds of arrangement (Table KD3)
2172.A-Z	Other forms of debtors' relief
2172.A7	Assignments for benefit of creditors
	Economic policy. Economic planning
2185	General (Table KD2)
2190	Foreign investments (Table KD2)
	Regulation of industry, trade, and commerce. Occupational law
2200	General. Comprehensive (Table KD3)
2201	Board of Trade
	Trade regulations. Control of trade practices. Consumer protection
	For economic emergency legislation see KD5110+
	Cf. KD1261+ Design protection, patent law, trademarks, and goodwill
	Cf. KD2225+ Unfair competition
2204	General. Unfair trade practices (Table KD3)
	Advertising
2206	General (Table KD2)
	Legal advertising see KD703.N6
	Labeling
	Including misbranding
2208	General
2209.A-Z	By product, A-Z
	Drugs, pharmaceutical products, narcotics see KD3460+

Regulation of industry, trade, and commerce. Occupational
  law
  Trade regulations. Control of trade practices. Consumer
    protection
    Labeling
      By product, A-Z -- Continued
        Economic and industrial poisons see KD3503+

2209.F6	Food (Table KD4)
	Hazardous substances see KD3494+
	Poisons see KD3462
2212	Restraint of trade (Table KD2)
2215	Price regulations (Table KD2)
	For price control in time of war or national emergency see KD5114+
	Monopolies. Antitrust laws
	For works on antitrust aspects of a particular industry or trade, see the industry or profession
	Cf. KD2112 Holding companies
2218	General. Restrictive Practices Court (Table KD2)
2220.A-Z	Special topics, A-Z
	Labor unions see KD3050+
	Patents see KD1361+
	Unfair competition
	Cf. KD1431+ Trademarks
	Cf. KD2204 Unfair trade practices
2225	General (Table KD2)
2226.A-Z	Particular aspects and special topics, A-Z
	Commercial espionage see KD2226.T7
2226.D5	Disparagement in advertising
2226.D8	Dumping
	Industrial espionage see KD2226.T7
2226.P76	Product counterfeiting
2226.S4	Secret commissions and bribes
2226.T7	Trade secrets. Industrial espionage. Commercial espionage
2227	Small business (Table KD2)
2228	Trade associations
	Weights and measures. Containers
2230	General. Standards (Table KD2)
2231.A-Z	By product, A-Z
2231.B7	Bread (Table KD4)
2231.C6	Coal (Table KD4)
2231.F6	Food (Table KD4)
2231.G6	Gold. Silver (Table KD4)
	Including assaying and hallmarks

	Regulation of industry, trade, and commerce. Occupational law
	Trade regulations. Control of trade practices. Consumer protection -- Continued
2233	Standard time (Table KD3)
	Including regulation of calendar
	For computation of time see KD703.T5
	For Sunday legislation see KD2488+
	Primary production. Extractive industries. Conservation of natural resources
	Agriculture. Forestry
2241	General (Table KD3)
	Economic assistance
2245	General
	Agricultural cooperative credit associations see KD1723
	Price supports
2247	General
	By commodity
2248.A-Z	Field crops, A-Z
2248.G7	Grain
2248.W4	Wheat
2250	Marketing agreements. Marketing controls
2254	Farm producers' and marketing cooperatives (Table KD2)
	Standards and grading
	For containers, measurements see KD2230+
2256	General
	Particular commodities
2257.A-Z	Field crops, A-Z
2257.S4	Seeds
	Livestock and meat
2259	General
2260.A-Z	Particular kinds, A-Z
2260.C3	Cattle. Beef
	Dairy products see KD2423
2263.A-Z	Other, A-Z
	Livestock industry and trade. Cattle raising
	For the meat industry see KD2417+
	Cf. KD3420+ Veterinary laws. Veterinary hygiene
2267	General. Cattle industry (Table KD3)
2272	Poultry industry
	Dairy industry see KD2423
2280	Forestry. Timber laws (Table KD3)
2285	Beekeeping. Apiculture (Table KD3)
	Game, bird, and fish protection
	Cf. KD2310+ Fishery law
2290	General. Game laws. Protection of birds (Table KD2)

KD

	Regulation of industry, trade, and commerce. Occupational law
	Primary production. Extractive industries. Conservation of natural resources
	Agriculture. Forestry
	Game, bird, and fish protection -- Continued
2295.A-Z	Particular animals and birds, A-Z
2295.S9	Swans
	Fishery
2310	General (Table KD2)
2315.A-Z	Particular fish or marine fauna, A-Z
	Including conservation, control, and regulation of industry
2315.H4	Herring
2315.S3	Salmon
	Mining. Quarrying
	For mine safety see KD3172.M5+
2331-2340	General (Table KD1)
	Coal
2350	General (Table KD2)
2360	Nationalization of coal industry (Table KD2)
2365.A-Z	Particular metals, A-Z
2365.I7	Iron (Table KD4)
2365.T5	Tin (Table KD4)
	Cf. KD6990 Court of Stannaries
	Petroleum. Oil and gas
2366	General (Table KD2)
2368	Submerged land legislation. Offshore oil (Table KD2)
2370.A-Z	Other, A-Z
2370.S3	Sand and gravel industry
	Manufacturing industries
	Chemical industries
2375	General (Table KD3)
2376.A-Z	Particular products, A-Z
2376.C4	Celluloid
2376.D9	Dyes and dyestuffs
2376.F4	Fertilizers and feeding stuffs
	Textile industry
2380	General (Table KD3)
	Textile fabrics
2382	General
2383.A-Z	Particular products, A-Z
2383.C6	Cotton fabrics
	Clothing industry
2385	Fur trade
	Individual types of manufacture
2395.A-Z	Major and heavy industries, A-Z
2395.I7	Iron and steel

Regulation of industry, trade, and commerce. Occupational
law
Manufacturing industries
Individual types of manufacture
Major and heavy industries, A-Z -- Continued
2395.S5   Shipbuilding
Cf. KD2830+ Merchant marine
2398.A-Z   Consumer products. Light industries, A-Z
2398.B56   Biotechnology industries
2398.B6   Book industries and trade
2398.E6   Enameled ware
2398.H6   Hollow ware
Food processing industries
2405   General
For food adulteration and inspection see KD3455
Agricultural products
Cereal products
2408   Baking industry (Table KD3)
2411   Sugar refining (Table KD3)
2415.A-Z   Other, A-Z
2415.T6   Tobacco products
Meat industry
2417   General. Meat inspection (Table KD2)
2423   Dairy industry. Dairy products industry. Milk production
and distribution (Table KD3)
2430.A-Z   Beverages, A-Z
2430.C3   Carbonated beverages. Soft drinks
Liquor, alcoholic beverages see KD3466+
2435   Construction and building industry. Contractors (Table KD2)
For building laws see KD1140+
For building contracts see KD1641
Trade and commerce
For commercial law (General) see KD1621+
For trade regulations see KD2204+
2455   General (Table KD3)
International trade
2460   General. Export and import controls and regulations
(Table KD2)
For trade agreements see KD5655+
Export trade. Export controls and regulations
2463   General (Table KD3)
2466.A-Z   Particular commodities, A-Z
2466.G7   Grain (Table KD4)
2466.M3   Malt (Table KD4)
2466.W6   Wool (Table KD4)
Dumping see KD2226.D8

	Regulation of industry, trade, and commerce. Occupational law
	Trade and commerce
	International trade -- Continued
	Import trade. Import controls and regulations
	For tariff see KD5641+
2470	General (Table KD3)
2472.A-Z	Particular countries, A-Z
	e.g.
2472.F7	France (Table KD4)
2475.A-Z	Particular commodities, A-Z
2475.B4	Beef (Table KD4)
2475.G7	Grain (Table KD4)
2475.T6	Tobacco (Table KD4)
2480	Wholesale trade
	Retail trade
2485	General (Table KD3)
	Conditions of trading
2488	Sunday legislation (Table KD3)
2490	Franchises (Table KD3)
	Price maintenance. Competition
2492	General (Table KD3)
2494	Trading stamps
	Particular modes of trading
2500	Markets. Fairs (Table KD3)
2500.3	Direct selling (Table KD3)
2501	Mail-order business (Table KD3)
2503	Vending machines
2510.A-Z	Particular products, A-Z
2510.A8	Automobiles
2510.G76	Groceries
	Secondhand trade
2512	General
2513.A-Z	Particular types, A-Z
	Pawnbrokers see KD1742
2513.S3	Scrap metal industry (Table KD4)
	Service trades
2515	General. Licensing
2517.A-Z	Particular trades, A-Z
	Auctioneers see KD2517.E7
2517.B4	Beauty shops (Table KD4)
	Brokers, commission merchants, factors see KD2024.B7
	Caravan sites see KD2517.T7
2517.C6	Collection agencies (Table KD4)
	For collection laws see KD1734

	Regulation of industry, trade, and commerce. Occupational law
	Trade and commerce
	Service trades
	Particular trades, A-Z
2517.E7	Estate agents. Real estate agents. Auctioners (Table KD4)
	Cf. KD989+ Auction sale of real property
2517.G3	Garages (Table KD4)
2517.H6	Hotels. Restaurants (Table KD4)
	Cf. KD1685 Innkeeper and guest
	Insurance agents see KD1862
	Nursing homes see KD2517.O43
2517.O43	Old age homes. Nursing homes (Table KD4)
2517.P5	Photographers (Table KD4)
	Real estate agents see KD2517.E7
	Ship brokers see KD2024.S4
2517.T67	Tourism (Table KD4)
2517.T7	Trailer camps (Table KD4)
	For trailer camp development see KD2517.T7
2517.U5	Undertakers (Table KD4)
	Warehouses
	For warehouse contracts see KD1681+
2525	General. Storage
	Special-purpose warehouses
2530	Bonded warehouses
	Public utilities
	Including private and publicly owned utilities
	Regulated industries in general
2535	General. Comprehensive (Table KD2)
2538	Valuation
	Particular utilities
	Power supply
2540	General
	Electricity
2545	General (Table KD2)
2545.5	Ratemaking
2550	Gas (Table KD2)
2555	Water
	Including water supply
2560	Atomic power
	Cf. KD3497 Public safety
	Transportation and communication
	Including government-owned and municipal services
2571-2580	General. Comprehensive (Table KD1)
2582	Ministry of Transport
2584	Nationalization of transportation
	Road traffic. Automotive transportation

KD

	Regulation of industry, trade, and commerce. Occupational law
	Transportation and communication
	Road traffic. Automotive transportation -- Continued
2591-2600	Motor vehicles in general (Table KD1)
2603	Safety equipment. Weight restrictions (Table KD3)
2605	Registration. Title transfer
2607	Drivers' license (Table KD3)
	Unsatisfied judgment funds, Motor Insurers' Bureau see KD1894
2611.A-Z	Particular vehicles, A-Z
2611.B5	Bicycles
2611.T7	Traction engines
2611.T76	Trucks
	Traffic regulations and enforcement
2617	General (Table KD2)
2618	Criminal provisions. Traffic violations. Drunk driving (Table KD2)
2620	Highway safety. Traffic signs. Grade crossings. Railroad crossings (Table KD2)
2622	Parking rules (Table KD2)
	Carriage of passengers and goods
2625	General motor carrier regulations (Table KD3)
2627	Licensing (Table KD3)
2632	Passengers carriers. Bus lines
2634	Taxicabs
2636	Carriers of goods. Trucklines
	Railways
2651-2660	General. Corporate structure. Regulation of industry (Table KD1)
	For Commercial Court see KD7182
2665	Railways lands. Private sidings
2668	Finance
	Operation of railways
	Rates and ratemaking
2680	General (Table KD2)
2684	Transport Tribunal. Railway Rates Tribunal. Railway and Canal Commission. Railway Commission (Table KD2)
	Liability
2696	General. Damage to property
2698	Personal injury
	Cf. KD2002 Employers' liability
2710	Local transit. Light railways (Table KD3)
2714	Pipelines
	Aviation
	Aviation in general

	Regulation of industry, trade, and commerce. Occupational law
	Transportation and communication
	Aviation
	Aviation in general -- Continued
2720	General. Comprehensive (Table KD2)
2723	Air traffic rules. Air safety. Airworthiness (Table KD2)
2726	Licensing pilots
2732	Commercial aviation. Airlines (Table KD3)
	Water transportation. Navigation and shipping
2750	General. Comprehensive (Table KD2)
	Merchant mariners see KD1836+
	War legislation see KD6240+
	Ships
2755	General (Table KD2)
2757	Ships' papers. Registry (Table KD2)
	Safety regulations
2760	General. Inspection (Table KD2)
2762	Accommodation of mariners on shipboard
2764	Lifesaving apparatus
2768.A-Z	Particular types of vessels, A-Z
2768.P5	Pleasure craft. Yachts. Small boats
2768.T8	Tugboats
2770.A-Z	Particular types of cargo, A-Z
2770.E9	Explosives. Munitions (Table KD4)
2770.G7	Grain (Table KD4)
2770.P4	Petroleum (Table KD4)
2772.A-Z	Special topics, A-Z
2772.N64	Noise control (Table KD4)
	Navigation and pilotage
2780	General. Coastwise navigation (Table KD3)
	For international rules of the road at sea see K4184
	Particular waterways
	Canals
2784	General
2785.A-Z	Particular canals, A-Z
2785.W6	Worcester & Birmingham Canal
2787	Rates, tolls, charges (Table KD3)
	Rivers
2789	General
2790.A-Z	Particular rivers, A-Z
2790.T4	Thames
	Harbors and ports
2792	General (Table KD2)
2794	Port charges. Mercantile Marine Fund
2796.A-Z	Particular ports, A-Z

KD

	Regulation of industry, trade, and commerce. Occupational law
	Transportation and communication
	Water transportation. Navigation and shipping
	Harbors and ports
	Particular ports, A-Z
2796.B7	Bristol
2796.H3	Hartlepool
2796.L5	Liverpool
2796.L6	London
	For Port of London Authority see KD9120
2798	Artificial islands
	Shipping laws. The merchant marine
2810	General (Table KD2)
	For war and emergency measures see KD6240+
	Regulation of shipping industry
2815	General (Table KD2)
2818	Passenger accommodations. Steerage passengers (Table KD3)
	Merchant marine
2830	History. Navigation acts (Table KD3)
2833	General. Comprehensive
	Finance
2836	General
2838	Shipping subsidies. Cargo preference (Table KD3)
	Cf. KD2830 Navigation acts
2840	Ground effect machines. Hovercraft (Table KD3)
	Postal service
2845	General (Table KD2)
	Organization and administration
2847	General
2849	Officers and personnel
	Including salaries, wages, and pensions
	Classification of mails. Rates
2852	General
2854.A-Z	Special classes, A-Z
2854.P3	Parcel post
2858.A-Z	Other services, A-Z
2858.P6	Postal notes
2860	Rates. Postage. Modes of collecting (Table KD2)
	Mass media
	Cf. KD4112 Freedom of press and information
	Cf. KD4114 Press censorship
2870	General (Table KD2)
2875	Press law (Table KD2)
	Radio and telecommunication
2880	General. Comprehensive (Table KD2)
2885	Telegraph (Table KD2)

	Regulation of industry, trade, and commerce. Occupational law
	Transportation and communication
	Mass media
	Radio and telecommunication -- Continued
2890	Telephone (Table KD3)
	Radio communication
2900	General (Table KD3)
	Including radio and television combined
2905	Radio stations. Licensing (Table KD3)
2915	Television (Table KD2)
	The professions
2940	General (Table KD3)
2941	Professional corporations (Table KD2)
	Particular professions
	The health professions
	For medical legislation see KD3395+
2945	General. Physicians (Table KD3)
	Medical associations
2950	General
2952.A-Z	Particular associations, A-Z
2952.R5	The Royal College of Physicians of London
2960.A-Z	Special topics, A-Z
2960.E4	Medical education (Table KD4)
2960.F4	Fees. Medical economics (Table KD4)
2960.M55	Malpractice (Table KD4)
2960.P3	Medical partnership. Group medical practice (Table KD4)
2965.A-Z	Particular branches of medicine, A-Z
2965.D4	Dentists and dental specialists (Table KD4)
2965.G95	Gynecologists. Obstetricians (Table KD4)
	Obstetricians see KD2965.G95
2965.P75	Psychiatrists. Psychotherapists. Psychologists (Table KD4)
	Psychologists see KD2965.P75
	Psychotherapists see KD2965.P75
2965.R33	Radiologists (Table KD4)
2965.S66	Sports medicine (Table KD4)
2968.A-Z	Auxiliary professions, A-Z
2968.M5	Midwives (Table KD4)
2968.N8	Nurses (Table KD4)
	Occupational therapists see KD2968.T47
2968.P4	Pharmacists (Table KD4)
	Physical therapists see KD2968.T47
2968.T47	Therapists, Physical. Occupational therapists (Table KD4)

KD

	Regulation of industry, trade, and commerce. Occupational law
	The professions
	Particular professions -- Continued
	Economic and financial advisors
	Including malpractice
2974	Accountants. Auditors (Table KD3)
	For accounting law see KD2042
	For corporation accounting see KD2098
	For tax accounting see KD5387
	Tax consultants see KD5395
	Lawyers see KD460
	Engineering and construction
2978	Architects
2980	Engineers
2990.A-Z	Other professions, A-Z, A-Z
2990.C4	Chemists
2990.L37	Landscape architects
	Social workers see KD3302
	Teachers see KD3636+
2990.V4	Veterinarians
	Social legislation
3000	General (Table KD3)
	Labor law
3001-3010	General (Table KD1)
3015	Administration. Ministry of Labor
	Management-labor relations
3040	General (Table KD3)
	Fair and unfair labor practices see KD3095
3045	Employee participation in management (Table KD3)
	Including works councils
	Labor unions
3050	General (Table KD3)
	Union security. Union shop
3051	General (Table KD3)
3053	Open and closed shop. Right-to-work laws (Table KD3)
	Collective bargaining. Collective labor agreements
3062	General (Table KD3)
3064.A-Z	Particular industries and occupations, A-Z
3064.E4	Electric industries
	Collective labor disputes
3070	General (Table KD3)
3071	Arbitration. Conciliation (Table KD2)
3073	Industrial courts and tribunals
	Particular industries see KD3089+
	Strikes. Boycotts

Social legislation
  Labor law
    Management-labor relations
      Labor unions
        Collective labor disputes
          Strikes. Boycotts -- Continued
3076   General (Table KD3)
                  For particular industries see KD3089+
3077   Picketing
                Wartime labor disputes. Munitions of war acts.
                  Munitions tribunals
                    For wartime regulation of wages and hours of
                      labor see KD3120+
3086   1914-1918
3087   1939-1945
                By industry
3089   Railways
3089.5.A-Z   Particular cases. By company, A-Z
3091.A-Z   Other, A-Z
3091.A9-.A91   Automobile industry (Table KD8)
3091.B9-.B91   Building and construction industries (Table KD8)
3091.C6-.C61   Coal mining industry (Table KD8)
                  Construction industry see KD3091.B9+
3091.F5-.F51   Firearms industry (Table KD8)
3091.F53-.F531   Fishing industry (Table KD8)
3091.P7-.P71   Printing industry (Table KD8)
3091.S8-.S81   Street railroads. Motorbus lines (Table KD8)
3091.W6-.W61   Wool industry (Table KD8)
            Labor standards
3095   General. Labor conditions (Table KD2)
              Employment and dismissal
3096   General (Table KD3)
                  For individual labor contracts see KD1634+
3097   Personnel records (Table KD2)
                Preferential employment
3098   Veterans
                    Cf. KD4520 Veterans' preference in civil service
3101   Covenants not to compete (Table KD2)
                Discrimination in employment and its prevention
3102   General. Racial discrimination (Table KD2)
3103.A-Z   Particular groups, A-Z
3103.O43   Older people (Table KD4)
3103.W6   Women (Table KD4)
                Dismissal. Resignation. Job security
3110   General (Table KD2)
3111   Dismissal pay (Table KD2)

KD

	Social legislation
	Labor law
	Labor standards -- Continued
	Wages. Minimum wage
	Including Wage and Hour laws
3118	General (Table KD2)
	War and emergency legislation. By period
	Cf. KD3126.A+ Particular industries
3120	1914-1918 (Table KD2)
3121	1939-1945 (Table KD2)
	Wage discrimination. Equal pay for equal work see KD3102+
3124.A-Z	Types of wages. Modes of remuneration, A-Z
	Bonus system see KD3124.P7
3124.C45	Checkweighting
	Incentive wages see KD3124.P7
3124.P3	Payment in kind. Truck system
3124.P7	Profit sharing. Incentive wages. Bonus system (Table KD4)
	Truck system see KD3124.P3
3126.A-Z	Particular industries and groups of employees, A-Z
3126.A4	Agriculture
3126.B3	Baking industry
3126.B65	Boot and shoe workers
	Box industry see KD3126.P3
3126.B7	Broom and brush industry
3126.B8	Button industry
3126.C3	Carbonated beverage industry
	Chainmaking industry see KD3126.I7
3126.C5	Clothing industry
3126.C64	Coffin and casket industry
	Confectionary industry see KD3126.B3
3126.C65	Container industry
3126.C67	Corset industry
3126.C68	Cotton-waste industry
3126.C8	Cutlery industry
3126.D3	Dairy industry
3126.D7	Dressmakers
3126.F4	Feather industry. Artificial flower industry
3126.F5	Flax and hemp industry
3126.F87	Fur industry
3126.F875	Furniture industry
3126.H3	Hat industry
3126.I7	Iron and steel industry
3126.J8	Jute industry
3126.K4	Keg and drum industry
3126.L3	Lace and lacemaking

Social legislation
  Labor law
    Labor standards
      Wages. Minimum wage
        Particular industries and groups of employees, A-Z -- Continued
3126.L38   Laundry workers
3126.L5   Linen industry
3126.M4   Men's furnishings industry
3126.M47   Metalworkers
3126.N4   Netmaking and repair industry
3126.P3   Paper bag and box industry
3126.R3   Ragpickers
3126.R6   Ropemakers
3126.R8   Rubber industry
3126.S3   Sack and bag industry
3126.S33   Sawmill workers
3126.S5   Shoe polish industry
          Tailoring see KD3126.C5
3126.T4   Textile workers
3126.T63   Tobacco manufacture
3126.T68   Toy industry
3126.T7   Transportation workers
3126.W3   Waste products industry
          Weavers see KD3126.T4
      Nonwage payments. Fringe benefits
3130   General (Table KD3)
        Pension and retirement plans
3131   General (Table KD3)
3132   Pension trusts (Table KD3)
      Hours of labor. Night work
3136   General (Table KD3)
        Children see KD3159
        Women see KD3161
3140.A-Z   Particular industries and groups of employees, A-Z
3140.B3   Baking industry (Table KD4)
3140.C6   Coal industry (Table KD4)
3140.R4   Retail and service establishments (Table KD4)
3142   Vacations. Holidays. Leaves of absence
3143   Sick leave (Table KD2)
3144   Parental leave (Table KD2)
        Including maternity leave
      Labor discipline. Work rules
3146   General (Table KD2)
3148   Shop committees. Shop stewards. Work councils. Whitley councils
3150   Grievances. Grievance procedure

Social legislation
Labor law -- Continued
Protection of labor. Labor hygiene and safety
3156   General (Table KD3)
3159   Child labor (Table KD3)
Including hours of child labor
3161   Woman labor (Table KD3)
Including hours of woman labor
3163   Home labor
3165   Apprentices. Learners (Table KD3)
Labor hygiene and safety. Hazardous occupations.
Safety regulations
3168   General (Table KD3)
3170   Factory inspection (Table KD2)
3172.A-Z   By industry or type of labor, A-Z
3172.A4   Agriculture (Table KD4)
3172.C6   Construction industry (Table KD4)
3172.D58   Diving operations (Table KD4)
3172.E38   Education (Table KD4)
3172.F6   Foundries (Table KD4)
3172.L3   Laundries (Table KD4)
3172.L4   Lead industry (Table KD4)
Mining
3172.M5   General (Table KD4)
3172.M53   Coal mining (Table KD4)
3172.O33   Offshore oil and gas (Table KD4)
3172.P55   Plastics industry (Table KD4)
3172.T3   Tanning (Table KD4)
3172.W62   Wood-using industries (Table KD4)
3177.A-Z   Labor law of particular industries or types of employment,
A-Z
3177.C65   Construction industry (Table KD4)
Cf. KD3172.C6 Safety regulations
3177.H5   Highway transport workers (Table KD4)
3177.J65   Journalists (Table KD4)
3177.L6   Longshoremen (Table KD4)
3177.M42   Medical personnel (Table KD4)
Merchant mariners see KD1836+
3177.O35   Offshore oil industry workers (Table KD4)
Social insurance
3191-3200   General (Table KD1)
Particular branches
Health insurance
Cf. KD1871 Private insurance
3205   General (Table KD2)
3207.A-Z   Particular industries and groups, A-Z
3207.A4   Agricultural laborers

Social legislation
  Social insurance
    Particular branches
      Health insurance -- Continued
        National Health Service. State medicine

3210   General (Table KD2)
3213.A-Z   Particular services and benefits, A-Z
3213.O6   Ophthalmic services
      Workers' compensation
3221-3230   General (Table KD1)
3235   Occupational diseases (Table KD3)
      Social security. Old age and disability pensions
3241-3250   General (Table KD1)
3252   Contributions. Social security taxes (Table KD2)
          Withholding of both income and social security taxes
            see KD5490+
      Unemployment insurance
3261-3270   General (Table KD1)
3273   Labor exchanges. Youth employment service
  Public welfare. Public assistance. Poor laws
3291-3300   General. Public institutions (Table KD1)
3302   Social work. Social workers. Social services (Table KD3)
    Particular groups
3304   Maternal and infant welfare
3305   Children and young persons. Child and youth welfare
        (Table KD3)
3306   Older people
      The poor
3310   General. Almshouses (Table KD2)
3311   Domicile requirements. Settlement and removal (Table
          KD3)
      People with disabilities. Vocational rehabilitation
3313   General
3315   Blind (Table KD3)
      Veterans see KD6355
      National Health Service. State medicine see KD3210+
3340   Birth control. Family planning. Population control (Table
        KD2)
       Cf. KD7969 Abortion (Criminal law)
  Public health. Sanitation. Environmental pollution
3351-3360   General (Table KD1)
       Including model ordinances and bylaws
3362.A-Z   Particular kinds of group hygiene, A-Z
       Labor hygiene see KD3168+
3365   Disposal of the dead. Burial and cemetery laws (Table KD3)
       For undertakers see KD2517.U5
    Contagious and infectious diseases

	Public health. Sanitation. Environmental pollution
	Contagious and infectious diseases -- Continued
3367	General. Reporting (Table KD3)
3368.A-Z	Particular diseases, A-Z
3368.A54	AIDS (Table KD4)
	Particular measures
3369	Immigration inspection. Quarantine
3370	Immunization. Vaccination
	Meat inspection see KD2417
	Environmental pollution
	Including abatement of public nuisances
3372	General (Table KD2)
3375	Water pollution. Drainage (Table KD2)
	Cf. KD1162 Plumbing. Sewers and drains
3378	Air pollution. Control of smoke, noxious gases, etc. (Table KD2)
3380	Noise control (Table KD2)
3382.A-Z	Other public health hazards and measures, A-Z
3382.E58	Environmental impact charges. Environmental taxes (Table KD4)
3382.R44	Refuse disposal (Table KD4)
	Medical legislation
	For physicians and related professions see KD2945+
3395	General (Table KD3)
	Hospitals and other medical institutions
3400	Hospitals (Table KD2)
3405.A-Z	Other health services, A-Z
	Ambulance service see KD3405.E45
3405.E45	Emergency medical services. Ambulance service
3405.S3	Schools. School health services
	Cf. KD1154.S3 School buildings
	Biomedical engineering. Medical technology
	Including human experimentation in medicine
3407	General (Table KD2)
3409	Transplantation of organs, tissues, etc. (Table KD2)
	Including xenografts and donation of organs, tissues, etc.
3410.A-Z	Special topics, A-Z
3410.E88	Euthanasia. Right to die. Living wills (Table KD4)
3410.G45	Medical genetics (Table KD4)
3410.I54	Informed consent (Table KD4)
	Living wills see KD3410.E88
3410.R43	Medical records (Table KD4)
	Right to die see KD3410.E88
	Pharmacies see KD2968.P4

Medical legislation -- Continued

3412	The mentally ill (Table KD3)
	For civil status of insane persons see KD737+
	For lunacy proceedings see KD740+
	For criminal liability see KD7897
3413.A-Z	Disorders of character, behavior, and intelligence, A-Z
3413.A4	Alcoholism (Table KD4)
	Drug addiction see KD3413.N3
3413.N3	Narcotic addiction. Drug addiction (Table KD4)
3415	Artificial insemination. In vitro fertilization (Table KD2)
3417	Eugenics. Sterilization (Table KD2)
	Veterinary medicine and hygiene. Veterinary public health
	For veterinarians, practice of veterinary medicine see
	KD2990.V4
3420	General. Reporting (Table KD3)
3422.A-Z	Particular measures, A-Z
	Animal protection. Animal welfare. Animal rights
	Including prevention of cruelty to animals
	For animal rights as a social issue see HV4701+
3424	General (Table KD3)
3426	Animal experimentation and research (Table KD3)
	Including vivisection and dissection
3427	Slaughtering of animals (Table KD3)
3429.A-Z	Special topics, A-Z
3429.K45	Kennels (Table KD4)
3429.P48	Pet shops (Table KD4)
	Food. Drugs. Cosmetics
3450	General. Comprehensive (Table KD3)
	For regulation of food processing industry see KD2405+
	Food law
3453	General (Table KD3)
3455	Adulteration. Inspection (Table KD3)
3456.A-Z	Food products, A-Z
3456.I54	Infant formulas (Table KD4)
3456.P7	Preservatives. Food additives (Table KD4)
	Drug laws
3460	General (Table KD3)
3462	Narcotics. Poisons (Table KD3)
	Cf. KD3503+ Economic and industrial poisons, Toxic
	substances
	Pharmacies see KD2968.P4
	Alcohol. Alcoholic beverages. Liquor laws
3466-3475	General (Table KD1)
3477.A-Z	Particular products, A-Z
3477.B4	Beer (Table KD4)
3480.A-Z	Special topics, A-Z
3480.L6	Local option

	Public safety
3490	General
3492	Weapons. Firearms. Munitions (Table KD3)
	Hazardous articles and processes
	Including transportation by land
	For transportation of explosives and munitions by sea
	see KD2770.E9
3494	General (Table KD3)
3495	Hazardous waste disposal (Table KD2)
	Particular products and processes
3497	Atomic power. Radiation (Table KD3)
3498	Explosives (Table KD3)
3500	Inflammable materials (Table KD3)
	Economic and industrial poisons. Toxic substances
3503	General
3505.A-Z	Particular substances, A-Z
	Herbicides see KD3505.P46
3505.P46	Pesticides. Herbicides (Table KD4)
3505.W4	White phosphorus matches (Table KD4)
3507.A-Z	Other, A-Z
	Accident control
3508	General (Table KD3)
3510	Steam boilers (Table KD3)
	Fire prevention and control
	Cf. KD3500 Inflammable materials
3515	General (Table KD3)
3516	Fire departments. Fire fighters (Table KD3)
	Control of social activities
3521	General (Table KD2)
3523	Amusements
3525	Sports. Prizefighting. Horse racing
3527	Lotteries. Games of chance. Gambling (Table KD3)
	Cf. KD8072 Criminal law
3529	Other
	Education
	Education in general. Public education
3600	General and comprehensive (Table KD3)
3605	Special aspects. Church and education. Denominational schools
	School government and finance
3607	General
3609	School districts
	Individual school districts are classed under the jurisdiction from which they derive their authority
3611	School boards. Boards of education
	Finance
3616	General (Table KD3)

	Education
	Education in general. Public education
	School government and finance
	Finance -- Continued
3617	Educational vouchers (Table KD3)
	Students. Compulsory education
3624	General
3628	School attendance and truancy
3632	Religious and patriotic observances. Bible reading.
	Religious instruction
	Teachers
3636	General (Table KD3)
3638	Education and training
3640	Salaries, pensions, etc. (Table KD3)
	Elementary and secondary education
3648	General (Table KD3)
3650	Secondary education
	Curricula. Courses of instruction
3652	General
	Vocational education
3660	General (Table KD2)
	For vocational rehabilitation see KD3313+
3662	Technical education. Manual training
	Particular types of students
3664	Students with physical disabilities
3666	Students with mental disabilities
3670	Private education. Private schools
	Higher education. Colleges and universities
3680	General
3685	Finance
3687	Student aid. Scholarships
3688	Students. Legal status of students. Student government.
	Student discipline
3689.A-Z	Particular colleges and universities, A-Z
	Science and arts. Research
3710	General
3715.A-Z	Particular branches and subjects, A-Z
3715.L3	Laboratories (Table KD4)
	The arts
	Performing arts
3720	General
	Theater and theaters
	Cf. KD1154.T4 Theater buildings
	Cf. KD3523 Amusements (Control of social activities)
3725	General (Table KD3)
3726	Censorship (Table KD3)
	Motion pictures

	Science and arts. Research
	The arts
	Performing arts
	Motion pictures -- Continued
3730	General (Table KD3)
3731	Censorship (Table KD3)
3736	Museums and galleries
3740	Historic buildings and monuments. Architectural landmarks (Table KD2)
3746	Libraries (Table KD3)
	Archives. Historical documents
3753	General
3755	Public Record Office. Record management
3756	Access to public records. Freedom of information (Table KD2)
	Including databases and data protection
3758	Educational, scientific, and cultural exchanges
	Constitutional and administrative law
3930	General works (Table KD3)
	Constitutional law
	History
	For history of a particular subject of constitutional and administrative law, see the subject
	General
	Sources
3931	Bibliography
3932	Collected documents. Sourcebooks
3934	General works (Table KD3)
	By period
	Early and medieval to 1485
3938	General (Table KD9)
3939	Anglo-Saxon to 1066 (Table KD9)
	Medieval, 1066-1485
3941	General (Table KD9)
3942	From Norman Conquest to Magna Carta, 1066-1215 (Table KD9)
	Magna Carta, 1215
3944.A-Z	Texts
3944.A3	Latin. By date of imprint
3944.A4	English. By date of imprint
3944.A5-Z	Other languages. By language, A-Z
3946	Treatises. Monographs (Table KD3)
	Including collected essays, symposia, etc.
3948	Magna Carta to 1485 (Table KD9)
	Modern England, 1485-
3951	Comprehensive, to the present (Table KD9)
3952	16th century, Tudor, 1485-1603 (Table KD9)

Constitutional law
  History
    By period
      Modern England, 1485- -- Continued
        17th century, Stuart and Revolution, 1603-1702

3954	General (Table KD9)
3956	Early Stuart (Table KD9)
3958	Commonwealth and Protectorate, 1649-1660 (Table KD9)
3959	Restoration, 1660-1689 (Table KD9)
3960	William and Mary, 1689-1702 (Table KD9)
3962	18th century, 1702-1832 (Table KD9)
3964	19th century, 1832-1899 (Table KD9)
3966	20th century (Table KD9)
3981-3990	General works (Table KD1)
	Constitutional principles
3995	Rule of law
	Act of State see KD4450
4000	Separation of powers. Delegation of powers
4005	Conflict of interests (General). Incompatibility of offices. Ethics in government (Table KD3)
4010	Executive privilege. Crown privilege
	Judicial review of administrative acts see KD4902
	Sources and relationships of law
4015	International and municipal law. Treaties and agreements
4018	Statutory law and delegated legislation (Table KD3)
	Cf. KD4885 Administrative law
4025	Structure of government. Jurisdiction (Table KD3)
	Foreign relations
4030	General
	Foreign service see KD4474+
	Individual and state
	Nationality and citizenship
4050	General (Table KD2)
	Acquisition and loss
4053	General
4056	Naturalization (Table KD3)
4058.A-Z	Particular groups, A-Z
4058.J48	Jews
4058.W6	Women
	Civil and political rights and liberties
4080	General (Table KD3)
	For rule of law see KD3995
	Particular groups
4095	Racial minorities. Discrimination in general (Table KD3)

	Constitutional law
	Individual and state
	Civil and political rights and liberties
	Particular groups -- Continued
	Religious minorities
	Cf. KD8600+ Church and state
4100	General (Table KD3)
	Including Corporation act, 1661. Test act, 1673
4102.A-Z	Particular, A-Z
	Cf. KD744.A+ Capacity and disability
4102.C3	Catholics (Table KD4)
4102.D5	Dissenters. Nonconformists (Table KD4)
4102.J4	Jews (Table KD4)
4102.M86	Muslims (Table KD4)
	Nonconformists see KD4102.D5
4102.Q3	Quakers (Society of Friends) (Table KD4)
4103	Sex discrimination (Table KD2)
	Particular constitutional guarantees
4106	Due process of law (Table KD3)
	Freedom of expression
4110	General
4112	Freedom of the press and of information
	For press law see KD2875
4114	Press censorship
	Motion picture censorship see KD3731
	Theater ownership see KD3726
4117	Freedom of assembly and association
4119	Freedom of petition
	Freedom of religion and conscience see KD4100+
	Habeas corpus see KD7612
	Right of privacy see KD1956+
	Self-incrimination see KD8386
	Control of individuals
4122	Identification. Registration (Table KD3)
4124	Passports (Table KD3)
	Aliens
	Cf. KD4130+ Capacity and disability
4130	General
	Immigration
4134	General (Table KD3)
4139.A-Z	Temporary admission of particular groups, A-Z
4139.S7	Student workers
	Particular controls and procedures
4140	Visas (Table KD3)
	Public health inspection, quarantine, see KD3369
4141	Other (Table KD3)
	Including controls on employment

Constitutional law
  Individual and state
    Control of individuals
      Aliens -- Continued
        Particular classes of immigrants
4142   Refugees. Asylum seekers (Table KD3)
        Particular ethnic groups
4145   Pakistanis (Table KD3)
4160   Internal security. Control of subversive activities
    Church and state see KD8600+
    Organs of the government
4185   General (Table KD3)
      Election law see KD4321+
      The Parliament
        History
4190   General (Table KD3)
          By period
4193   Medieval to 1485
           Modern, 1485
4195   General
4197   16th century, Tudor, 1485-1603
4198   17th century
4199   18th century to 1832
4200   19th century. Reform. 1832 to end of the century
4205   20th century
4210   General. Organization (Table KD2)
4215   Rules and procedure (Table KD2)
4220   Parliamentary reporting
        Parliamentary debates (Hansard) (House of Lords) see KD76
        Parliamentary debates (Hansard) (House of Commons) see KD92
        Royal prerogative to dissolve Parliament see KD4446
        The legislative process
4230   General
4235   Committees (Table KD3)
          Legislative investigations
           see the subject
4238   Bill drafting (Table KD3)
           For legal composition, language of the law see KD404
4242   Private bill procedure (Table KD3)
           Cf. KD4286 House of Lords
           Cf. KD4370+ House of Commons
4244   Bills of attainder (Table KD3)
           Including cases
        Legal status of legislators

Constitutional law
  Organs of the government
    The Parliament
      Legal status of legislators -- Continued
4246   Parliamentary immunity and privileges (Table KD3)
                Contested elections see KD4380+
      House of Lords
                For House of Lords as judicial court see KD7632
4260   General
              Membership
4263   Lords spiritual
                Lords temporal. Peers
4265   General (Table KD2)
4265.5   Peerage claims
                    Cf. KD275+ Cases and claims of peerage
4265.5.A2A-.A2Z   Collective
4265.5.A3-Z   Particular, A-Z
                  Trial of peers. Lord High Steward see KD8283
                  Trials of peers see KD376.A+
              Rules and procedure
4275.A3   Legislative documents. By date
4275.A4   Standing orders. By date
4275.A5-Z   Treatises. Monographs
              Committees
4280   General. Committees of the whole House
4281.A-Z   Particular committees, A-Z
4286   Private bill procedure (Table KD3)
4290   Powers and functions
                  For particular powers, see the subject
                  Judicial powers (Highest court of civil appeal) see
                    KD7632
                  Judicial powers (Original criminal jurisdiction) see
                    KD8283
                  Judicial powers (Highest court of criminal appeal) see
                    KD8429+
      House of Commons
4310   General
4314   Membership
              Election law
                  Including works on election law in general, not limited to
                    the House of Commons
4321-4330   General (Table KD1)
              Suffrage
4332   General (Table KD3)
                Particular groups of voters
4334   Service voters. Soldiers
4336   Women

Constitutional law
Organs of the government
The Parliament
House of Commons
Election law
Suffrage -- Continued

4340	Registration. Qualifications
4342	Absentee voting
	Service voters, soldiers see KD4334
4346	Election districts. Apportionment (Table KD3)
4347	Local elections (Table KD3)
4349	Corrupt practices (Table KD3)
	Organization. Legislative process
	Rules and practice
4354.A3	Legislative documents. By date of publication
4354.A4	Standing orders. By date of publication
	For standing orders on private bills see KD4370+
4354.A5	Parliamentary precedents (Decisions)
4354.A6-Z	Treatises. Monographs
	Committees
4358	General. Committees of the whole House
4361.A-Z	Particular committees, A-Z
4361.S8	Select Committee on Statutory Rules and Orders
	Private bill procedure
4370	General. Court of Referees (Table KD2)
4372	Locus standi reports. Private bill reports
4373	Impeachment power and procedure (Table KD3)
	Cf. KD7105.5 Impeachment of law officers of the Crown
	Legal status of members
4375	Salaries, pensions, etc. (Table KD3)
	Contested elections
4380	General
	Cases
4381.A3	Collections. By date
4381.A4-Z	Particular cases. By incumbent, A-Z
	The Crown and the Central Government (Executive branch)
4430	General
	The Crown
	Royal prerogative
4435	General (Table KD3)
	Prerogative in domestic affairs
	Ecclesiastical prerogative see KD8603
4440	War and emergency powers

	Constitutional law
	Organs of the government
	The Crown and the Central Government (Executive branch)
	The Crown
	Royal prerogative
	General
	Prerogative in domestic affairs
	War and emergency powers -- Continued
4442	Martial law. Civilians under military justice (Table KD3)
	Escheat see KD1534
	Prerogative to confer titles of nobility see KD4265+
	Prerogative to confer decorations of honor, awards of honor, and dignities see KD4656+
4446	Power to dissolve Parliament
	Executive privilege. Crown privilege see KD4010
	Treasure trove see KD5333.T7
	Wreck see KD1834.S4
	Prerogative in foreign affairs
4450	Act of State
4452	Treatymaking power
4456.A-Z	Other topics, A-Z
4456.C6	Coronation. Court of Claims (Table KD4)
4456.R4	Regency (Table KD4)
4456.R44	Religion of the monarch (Table KD4)
4456.S8	Succession to the throne (Table KD4)
4456.T5	Title of the monarch (Table KD4)
4460	The Privy Council (Table KD3)
	For Judicial Committee of the Privy Council (General) see KD7134+
	For Judicial Committee of the Privy Council (Appellate procedure) see KD7634
4462	The Prime Minister and the Cabinet
	Government departments. Civil service
4467	General (Table KD3)
	Particular departments. Boards
	Including proposed departments or boards
4472	Foreign Office
	The Foreign Service
4474	General
4477	Legal status of Foreign Service personnel
	Including salaries, allowances, pensions, etc.
	Advisory committees, Royal Commissions, etc.
4479	General

Constitutional law
  Organs of the government
    The Crown and the Central Government (Executive
      branch)
      Government departments. Civil service
      Particular departments. Boards
        Advisory committees, Royal Commissions, etc. --
          Continued
        Particular
          see the subject
      Public corporations

4481	General
	Particular
	see the subject
	Civil service. Government officials and employees
	Cf. KD4805+ Local civil service
4510	General. Qualifications for employment. Civil
	Service Commission (Table KD2)
4513	Civil service examinations (Table KD3)
	Conditions and restrictions of employment.
	Employment discipline
4515	General
4517	Political activities
	Types and modes of employment
4520	Veterans' preference
	Employment relations
4524	Labor unions. Arbitration. Conciliation (Table KD3)
	Tenure and remuneration
4527	General (Table KD3)
4528	Salaries (Table KD3)
4529	Retirement. Pensions (Table KD3)
4531	Leave regulations
	Particular departments
	see the department
4645	The Judiciary. Judicial power
	Constitutional status only
	Cf. KD6850+ Courts and procedure. Administration of
	justice. Organization of the judiciary
4650	National emblem. Seals
	Decorations of honor. Awards of honor. Dignities
4656	Civilian
4657	Military
	Local government
4746	History
4751-4760	General (Table KD1)
	Including wartime and emergency legislation
	Particular aspects

	Local government
	Particular aspects -- Continued
4765	Relation to central government
	Types of local authorities
	Municipal government. Municipal services
4770	General. Municipal corporations. Cities. Boroughs (Table KD2)
4772	Charters and ordinances. Local law
	Including borough customs, model ordinances, and drafting manuals
	Tort liability see KD1991
4776.A-Z	Special topics, A-Z
4776.A5	Annexation. Borough boundaries. Alteration of area
	Municipal officials. Organs of government
4778	General
4779.A-Z	Particular officers and organs, A-Z
4779.L6	Local councils
4781.A-Z	Special topics, A-Z
	Municipal civil service see KD4807+
	County government
4785	General. County council (Table KD3)
4787	Urban districts
4789	Rural districts
4791	Parishes (Table KD2)
4795	Special districts. Special authorities. Joint boards
	General
	For particular types of districts, etc., see the subject, e.g. KD3609 (School districts).
	For individual districts, etc., see jurisdiction from which they derive their authority
	Local elections see KD4347
	Local finance see KD5710+
	Local civil service
4805	General
	Municipal civil service
4807	General (Table KD3)
	Retirement. Pensions
4809	General (Table KD3)
4812.A-Z	Particular departments or positions, A-Z
	Fire fighters see KD3516
4812.P6	Police (Table KD4)
	Teachers see KD3640
	County civil service
4816	General
4818	Tenure and remuneration. Salaries. Pensions
4831-4840	Police and power of the police (Table KD1)
	Metropolitan Police see KD9140

	Local government
	Local civil service
	Police and power of the police -- Continued
	Police personnel (Salaries, tenure, etc.) see KD4812.P6
	Administrative organization and procedure
4871-4880	General. Administrative law (Table KD1)
	The administrative process. Regulatory agencies
4882	General (Table KD2)
4885	Legislative functions. Delegated legislation. Statutory rules and orders. Statutory instruments (Table KD2)
4890	Judicial functions. Procedure. Special (Administrative) tribunals (Table KD2)
	For particular administrative tribunals, see the subject
4895	Tribunals of inquiry. Governmental investigations (Table KD2)
4900	Abuse of administrative power. Ombudsman (Table KD2)
4902	Judicial review. Appeals (Table KD3)
	Tort liability of the government and public officers see KD2004
	Commonwealth and Empire
5020	General (Table KD2)
5025	Constitutional structure and relations
	Government measures in time of war, national emergency, or economic crisis. Emergency economic legislation
5110	General (Table KD2)
	By period
	In case of doubt, prefer classification with general subject
5114-5117	To 1914 (Table KD10)
5118-5121	1914-1918 (Table KD10)
5122-5125	1919-1939 (Table KD10)
5126-5129	1939-1945 (Table KD10)
5130-5133	1945- (Table KD10)
	Public finance
5280	General. History (Table KD2)
5282	The Exchequer
	Money. Currency. Banknotes. Coinage
5284	General (Table KD3)
5286	Coinage. Mint regulations
5288	Foreign exchange regulations (Table KD3)
5292	Budget. Government expenditures
5295	Expenditure control. Public auditing and accounting (Table KD3)
5300	Public debts. Loans. Bond issues (Table KD3)
	National revenue
	History
5320	General (Table KD3)
	Older forms of revenue

	Public finance
	National revenue
	History
	Older forms of revenue -- Continued
	Public domain
5323	General
5324.A-Z	Particular sources of revenue, A-Z
5324.P8	Purveyance
	Taxes
5326	General
5327.A-Z	Particular forms, A-Z
5327.H5	Hidage
5327.S5	Ship money
5329	Fees and fines
5330	Forfeitures
	Regalia. Royal prerogative
5332	General
5333.A-Z	Particular types, A-Z
5333.T7	Treasure troves
	Wartime finance
5336	General
	By period
5338	To the end of the 17th century (Table KD3)
5339	18th and 19th centuries (Table KD3)
5340	World War I (Table KD3)
5341	World War II (Table KD3)
5345	General (Table KD2)
	For the Exchequer see KD5282
	Particular sources of revenue
	Taxation
5351-5360	General (Table KD1)
5365	Tables
	Tax saving. Tax planning
	Class here works on tax planning in general and tax planning relating to income tax
	For tax planning relating to other taxes, see those taxes
5370	General (Table KD3)
5372	Tax havens (Table KD3)
	Tax administration and procedure
5375	General
5377	Board of Inland Revenue
	Double taxation
5380	General (Table KD3)
5382	Domicile (Table KD3)
	Tax collection
5385	General
5387	Tax accounting

Public finance
  National revenue
    Particular sources of revenue
      Taxation
        Tax administration and procedure -- Continued
          Procedure. Practice

5395	General
5398	Settlements (Table KD3)
5401	Remedies. Tax courts. Tax boards. Tax appeals (Table KD3)
	Tax treatment of special activities
5405	Bankruptcy (Table KD2)
5410	Criminal law. Tax evasion (Table KD2)
	Particular taxes
5415	Several. Collective (Table KD2)
	e.g. Income, estate, and gift taxes
	Income tax
5421-5430	General (Table KD1)
5431	Income tax tables
	Tax planning see KD5370+
	Allowances and deductions
5450	General
	Particular kinds
5452	Depreciation allowances. Capital allowances (Table KD3)
	Expenses
5460	General
5462.A-Z	Particular kinds, A-Z
5462.M3	Maintenance relief
5462.R4	Repairs
5462.R45	Retirement contributions
5467	Surtaxes
5467.5	Tables
	Undistributed profits see KD5521+
	Excess profit taxes see KD5511+
	Particular sources of income
5471	Income from ownership of land and buildings (Property tax). Tax on occupier of land (Schedules A and B) (Table KD3)
5473	Pensions and annuities
	Capital investment
5475	General. Securities
5477	Dividends. Interest
5479	Foreign investments
5481	Salaries and wages
5483.A-Z	Other, A-Z
5483.A4	Alimony and support

Public finance
 National revenue
  Particular sources of revenue
   Taxation
    Particular taxes
     Income tax
      Particular sources of income
       Other, A-Z -- Continued
5483.D35   Damages. Settlements
5483.G3   Gambling gains
5483.I53   Industrial property
                    Including copyright, patents, trademarks, etc.
5483.L4   Leases
5483.L5   Life insurance proceeds
                  Settlements see KD5483.D35
                  Support see KD5483.A4
                 Particular methods of assessment and collections
5490   Payroll deduction. Withholding tax (Table KD3)
                  Social security taxes see KD3252
5494.A-Z   Particular classes of taxpayers, A-Z
5494.A4   Aliens (Table KD4)
5494.F37   Farmers (Table KD4)
5494.N6   Nonresidents (Table KD4)
5494.T7   Trusts (Table KD4)
5500   Income of nonprofit associations, nonprofit
                    corporations, foundations, endowments,
                    pension funds (Table KD3)
                 Income of business organizations
                    Including works on profitmaking and nonprofit
                      organizations
5501   General (Table KD3)
5502   Partnerships and joint ventures (Table KD3)
                  Juristic persons. Corporations
                    For nonprofit corporations see KD5500
5504   General (Table KD3)
5506   Profit tax. National defense contribution
                    (Table KD3)
5507   Income tax (Table KD3)
5509   Corporation tax (Table KD3)
                  Excess profits tax
5511   General (Table KD3)
5512   Excess profits levy (Table KD3)
5514   Excess profits duty (Table KD3)
                  Surtaxes
5521   Undistributed profits
5523   Cooperatives
5524   Family corporations

Public finance
National revenue
Particular sources of revenue
Taxation
Particular taxes
Income tax
Income of business organizations
Juristic persons. Corporations -- Continued

5526.A-Z	Particular lines of corporate business, A-Z
5526.B6	Brewing industry
5526.F65	Forestry
5526.I56	Insurance companies
5526.M5	Mining. Petroleum industry
	Petroleum see KD5526.M5
5526.R3	Railroads (Table KD4)
5526.S5	Shipping
5528.A-Z	Special topics, A-Z
5528.C65	Corporate reorganization (Table KD4)
5528.M4	Mergers (Table KD4)
5528.S25	Sale of business enterprises. Stock transfer (Table KD4)
	Stock transfer see KD5528.S25

Property taxes. Taxation of capital

5532	General (Table KD3)
5533	Wealth tax (Table KD3)

Real property taxes

5534	General. Valuation of land and buildings (Table KD2)

Class here works dealing with several taxes affecting real property, including works on valuation of both real and personal property and valuation for both tax and other purposes, e.g. eminent domain, insurance

5535	Land tax (Table KD3)
5536	Land values duties. Mineral rights duties (Table KD3)
5538	Land value tax
5539	Betterment levy. Development gains tax (Table KD3)
5545	Real estate transactions

Other taxes on capital and income

5550	Capital gains tax (Table KD3)

Estate, inheritance, and gift taxes

5560	General (Table KD2)
5561	Death duties. Estate duty. Legacy duty. Succession duty (Table KD2)
5563	Gift taxes

	Public finance
	National revenue
	Particular sources of revenue
	Taxation
	Particular taxes -- Continued
	Indirect taxes. Sales or turnover taxes
5580	General
	Purchase tax
5584	General (Table KD3)
5585.A-Z	By commodity or industry, A-Z
5585.P7	Printing
5586	Value-added tax (Table KD3)
	Sales taxes. Excise duty
5588	General (Table KD2)
	Particular commodities, services, transactions
	Alcohol. Alcoholic beverages. Liquor taxes
5590	General (Table KD2)
5591.A-Z	Particular alcoholic beverages, A-Z
5591.B4	Beer (Table KD4)
5591.W5	Wine (Table KD4)
5593	Motor vehicle duties (Table KD3)
5595	Tobacco (Table KD3)
5597.A-Z	Other, A-Z
5597.A3	Admission to entertainment. Amusement
	Automobiles see KD5593
5597.C3	Candles
	Gambling see KD5597.W3
	Horse racing see KD5597.W3
5597.S4	Tax on servants
5597.W3	Wagering. Gambling. Horse racing
5600	Excise licenses
	Licenses to manufacture certain articles, to carry on certain trades and professions
	Cf. KD5750+ Fees. License fees. Local taxation licenses
	Taxes based on payroll or number of employees
5605	Selective Employment Tax
	Particular methods
	For assessment and collection of particular taxes, see these taxes, e.g. Income tax, Excise taxes
5612	Stamp duties (Table KD2)
5612.3	Capital duty (Table KD2)
5613	Other taxes. History

	Public finance
	National revenue
	Particular sources of revenue -- Continued
	Tariff. Customs duties
	For regional trade and tariff agreements, see the appropriate region
	For trade and tariff agreements not limited to a region see K4600+
	For foreign trade regulations see KD2460+
	For trade and tariff agreements with the United States see KF6668.A+
5641-5650	General (Table KD1)
	Particular tariffs
5655	General
5662.A-Z	Particular commodities, A-Z
5662.C6	Corn
5662.D7	Drugs
5662.I7	Iron
5662.M6	Molasses
5662.S3	Salt
5662.T4	Tea
	Customs administration
5681-5690	General. Customs service. Procedure. Remedies (Table KD1)
5692	Enforcement. Criminal law. Smuggling (Table KD3)
5694.A-Z	Special topics, A-Z
	Bonded warehouses see KD2530+
5694.B6	Bounties on import
	Local finance
5710	General (Table KD2)
5712	Budget. Expenditure control. Auditing and accounting (Table KD3)
5715	Local government debts. Municipal bonds
	Particular sources of revenue
	Taxation
5718	General. Tax powers of municipalities (Table KD3)
	Particular taxes
	Real property tax. Local rate. Poor rate
5721-5730	General. Rating and valuation (Table KD1)
5732.A-Z	Particular types of property, A-Z
5732.A9	Automotive service stations
5732.F3	Factories. Plants. Machinery
5732.L5	Licensed premises
5732.M5	Mines
5732.M6	Motion-picture theaters
5735	Exemptions from rating
	Relief from rates. Derating

	Public finance
	Local finance
	Particular sources of revenue
	Taxation
	Particular taxes
	Real property tax. Local rate. Poor rate
	Relief from rates. Derating -- Continued
5737	General
5738	Agricultural rating relief
5739	Industrial rating relief
5741	Appeal
5743	Special assessment
	Other sources of revenue
5750	Fees. License fees. Local taxation licenses
5752	Grants-in-aid
	National defense. Military law
6000	Comprehensive. General (Table KD2)
	Wartime and emergency legislation
	For wartime labor disputes see KD3086+
	For economic controls see KD5110+
6004	General (Table KD3)
6005	Through 1642 (Table KD3)
6006	1642-1660 (Civil War and Commonwealth) (Table KD3)
6007	1660-1914 (Table KD3)
6008	1914-1918 (Table KD3)
6010	1939-1945 (Table KD3)
6012	1945- (Table KD3)
	The military establishment. Armed Forces
6030	General
6032	Organization and administration. Ministry of Defense
	Armed Forces
	Comprehensive. General
	General works see KD6030
	Conscription. Draft
6040	General (Table KD2)
	Deferment. Exemptions
6042	General
6043.A-Z	Particular groups, A-Z
6043.C6	Conscientious objectors (Table KD4)
6045.A-Z	Special topics, A-Z
	Personnel. Services
6051	General (Table KD3)
6053	Enlistment. Recruiting. Impressment. Discharge
	Education. Training
6055	General
	Academies. Schools
6056	General

National defense. Military law
The military establishment. Armed Forces
Armed Forces
Comprehensive. General
Personnel. Services
General
Education. Training
Academies. Schools -- Continued

6057.A-Z   Particular schools, A-Z
                  Pay, allowances, benefits
6059   General (Table KD3)
6060   Retirement pensions (Table KD2)
                      For war veterans' pensions see KD6355
6061   Disability pensions and benefits (Table KD2)
                      Including survivors' pensions and benefits
6062   Service insurance. Indemnity
6063   Housing. Barracks
6065   Uniform regulations. Wearing of decorations and
                      medals
                      Class here service regulations only
6068   Officers (Table KD3)
                      Including commissions, promotions, retirement
6070   Enlisted personnel
6071   Reserves
6073   Women's services
                  Militia, volunteers see KD6114+
6076.A-Z   Special services, A-Z
6077   Equipment. Weapons. Plants. Supplies and stores
6078   Hospitals
                  Particular branches of service
                  Army
6086   Organization. Administration (Table KD2)
                  Personnel. Services
6091   General (Table KD3)
6093   Enlistment. Recruiting. Impressment. Discharge
                  Education. Training
6095   General
                  Academies. Schools
6096   General
6097.A-Z   Particular schools, A-Z
6097.S3   Royal Military College, Sandhurst
6097.W6   Royal Military Academy, Woolwich
                  Pay, allowances, benefits
6099   General (Table KD3)
6100   Retirement pensions (Table KD2)
                      For war veterans' pensions see KD6355

KD

National defense. Military law
The military establishment. Armed Forces
Armed Forces
Particular branches of service
Army
Personnel. Services
General
Pay, allowances, benefits -- Continued

6101	Disability pensions and benefits (Table KD2)
	Including survivors' pensions and benefits
6102	Service insurance. Indemnity
6103	Housing. Barracks
6105	Uniform regulations. Wearing of decorations and medals
	Class here service regulations only
6108	Officers (Table KD3)
	Including commissions, promotions, retirement
6110	Enlisted personnel
6111	Reserves
6113	Women's services
	Militia. Volunteers
	Including retirement pensions and other benefits
6114	General. Militia (Table KD2)
6115	Volunteers (Table KD3)
	Including Local Defense Volunteers, Home Guard, Territorial Army, Territorial and Army Volunteer Reserve, Imperial Yeomanry
6116.A-Z	Special services, A-Z
6116.M4	Medical Department
6116.V4	Veterinary corps
6117	Equipment. Weapons. Plants. Supplies and stores
6118	Hospitals
6120.A-Z	Colonial forces. By colony, A-Z
6120.E3	Egypt
6120.J3	Jamaica
6120.S8	Sudan
	Royal Navy
6128	Organization. Administration (Table KD2)
	Personnel. Services
6131	General (Table KD3)
6133	Enlistment. Recruiting. Impressment. Discharge
	Education. Training
6135	General
	Academies. Schools
6136	General
6137.A-Z	Particular schools, A-Z
	Pay, allowances, benefits

National defense. Military law
  The military establishment. Armed Forces
    Armed Forces
      Particular branches of service
      Royal Navy
        Personnel. Services
          General
            Pay, allowances, benefits -- Continued

6139	General (Table KD3)
6140	Retirement pensions (Table KD2)
	For war veterans' pensions see KD6355
6141	Disability pensions and benefits (Table KD2)
	Including survivors' pensions and benefits
6142	Service insurance. Indemnity
6143	Housing. Barracks
6145	Uniform regulations. Wearing of decorations and medals
	Class here service regulations only
6148	Officers (Table KD3)
	Including commissions, promotions, retirement
6150	Enlisted personnel
6151	Reserves
6153	Women's services
6156.A-Z	Special services, A-Z
6157	Equipment. Weapons. Plants. Supplies and stores
6158	Hospitals
	Royal Marine
6180	General. Organization. Administration
6182.A-Z	Special topics, A-Z
6182.E5	Enlistment. Recruiting
	Royal Air Force
6198	Organization. Administration (Table KD2)
	Personnel. Services
6201	General (Table KD3)
6203	Enlistment. Recruiting. Impressment. Discharge
	Education. Training
6205	General
	Academies. Schools
6206	General
6207.A-Z	Particular schools, A-Z
	Pay, allowances, benefits
6209	General (Table KD3)
6210	Retirement pensions (Table KD2)
	For war veterans' pensions see KD6355
6211	Disability pensions and benefits (Table KD2)
	Including survivors' pensions and benefits
6212	Service insurance. Indemnity

	National defense. Military law
	The military establishment. Armed Forces
	Armed Forces
	Particular branches of service
	Royal Air Force
	Personnel. Services
	General
	Pay, allowances, benefits -- Continued
6213	Housing. Barracks
6215	Uniform regulations. Wearing of decorations and medals
	Class here service regulations only
6218	Officers (Table KD3)
	Including commissions, promotions, retirement
6220	Enlisted personnel
6221	Reserves
6223	Women's services
6226.A-Z	Special services, A-Z
6227	Equipment. Weapons. Plants. Supplies and stores
6228	Hospitals
	Auxiliary services during war and emergency
	Merchant marine
6240	Organization. Administration
	Personnel. Services
6244	General
	Pay, allowances, benefits
6246	General
6248	Service insurance. Indemnity
6250	Military discipline
	Military criminal law and procedure
6270	General. Comprehensive (Table KD2)
	Criminal law
6275	General
6278.A-Z	Particular offenses, A-Z
6278.M8	Mutiny (Table KD4)
	Criminal procedure. Military justice
6290	General
	Courts-martial
6293	General (Table KD2)
6300	Evidence
	Particular branches of service
	Army
6310	General (Table KD2)
	Including evidence
	Trials
6315	Collections
6316.A-Z	Particular trials. By defendant, A-Z

National defense. Military law
  The military establishment. Armed Forces
    Military criminal law and procedure
      Criminal procedure. Military justice
        Courts-martial
          Particular branches of service -- Continued
          Navy

6320	General (Table KD2)
	Trials
6322	Collections
6323.A-Z	Particular trials. By defendant, A-Z
6326	Air Force
	Execution of sentence. Penalties. Punishment
6330	Military prisons (Table KD3)
6332	Corporal punishment. Flogging
6333	Capital punishment
6335	Civil status of members of the Armed Forces and auxiliary services. Civil law relating to soldiers, sailors, airmen, etc. (Table KD3)
	For re-employment rights see KD3098+
	For suffrage see KD4334
6338.A-Z	Other defense agencies, A-Z
6340	Civil defense
6350.A-Z	Other topics, A-Z
6350.S4	Security classification
6355	War veterans
	Including pensions, other benefits, and provisions for dependents
	For preferential employment see KD3098+
	For veterans' preference in civil service see KD4520
	Courts. Procedure
	History
	General works only
	For the history of a particular court or subject, see that court or subject
6850	General (Table KD3)
	By period
6853	Anglo-Saxon, to 1066
6854	From Norman Conquest to 1272
6857	From 1272
	Administration of justice. Courts and procedure before the Judicature Act of 1873
	For works covering this period and that after 1873 see KD7100+
	Superior courts
	Common-law courts and equity courts
6870	General. Courts (Table KD3)

Courts. Procedure
  Administration of justice. Courts and procedure before the
    Judicature Act of 1873
    Superior courts
      Common-law courts and equity courts -- Continued
        Civil procedure

6873   General (Table KD3)
6874   Pleading (Table KD3)
          Class here general pleading only
          For special pleadings, see relevant subject
      Common-law courts (Collective)
6878   General (Table KD2)
        Civil procedure
6881   General (Table KD2)
6883   Pleading (Table KD2)
          Class here general pleading only
          For special pleadings, see relevant subject
      Particular courts
6891   Curia regis
         For Curia regis civil rolls see KD190
        Primary jurisdiction
         King's (Queen's) Bench
6895   General. History. Organization (Table KD2,
           modified)
6895.A15   Directories
6896   Civil procedure (Table KD2)
          Including general pleading
          For particular subjects (e.g. Action, trial, evidence,
           etc.), see relevant subject with modern law
         Bail Court see KD7605
         Court of Common Pleas
6898   General. History. Organization (Table KD2)
6899   Civil procedure (Table KD2)
          Including general pleading
          For particular subjects (e.g. Action, trial, evidence,
           etc.), see relevant subject with modern law
         Court of Exchequer
6902   General. History. Organization (Table KD2)
6903   Civil procedure (Table KD2)
          Including general pleading
          For particular subjects (e.g. Action, trial, evidence,
           etc.), see relevant subject with modern law
6913   Assize Courts
         Including Courts of Nisi Prius, General Eyre, and
          itinerant justices
        Palatine courts
         Court of Common Pleas at Lancaster

Courts. Procedure
   Administration of justice. Courts and procedure before the
      Judicature Act of 1873
    Superior courts
     Common-law courts (Collective)
      Particular courts
       Primary jurisdiction
        Palatine courts
         Court of Common Pleas at Lancaster --
          Continued

6916	General (Table KD3)
6917	Civil procedure
6918	Session Court of Chester

       Courts of special jurisdiction
        Bankruptcy court see KD2153+
        Court of Divorce and Matrimonial Causes see
         KD751+
        Court of Probate see KD1518+
      Appellate jurisdiction

6925	Court of Exchequer Chamber

       Judicial Committee of the Privy Council (General)
        see KD7134+
       Judicial Committee of the Privy Council (Appellate
        procedure) see KD7634
       House of Lords (General) see KD7132+
       House of Lords (Appellate procedure) see KD7632
     Equity courts
      Primary jurisdiction
       Court of Chancery

6937	General. History. Organization (Table KD2)
6939	Equity practice and procedure (Table KD2)

         Including general pleading
         For particular subjects (e.g. Action, trial, evidence,
          etc.), see relevant subject with modern law

6940	Master of Chancery
6942	Court of Requests

       Palatine courts
        Chancery Court of Lancaster see KD7220+
      Appellate jurisdiction

6945	General. Lord High Chancellor
6947	Master of Rolls

     High Court of Admiralty. Admiralty proceedings see
      KD1832+
    Lower courts. Local courts. Lesser historical courts
     Class records of particular courts with such courts

6965	Court of Augmentations

     Manorial courts. Courts baron. Courts leet

KD

Courts. Procedure
  Administration of justice. Courts and procedure before the
    Judicature Act of 1873
    Lower courts. Local courts. Lesser historical courts
      Manorial courts. Courts baron. Courts leet -- Continued

6968	General (Table KD3)
6969.A-Z	Particular, A-Z
	County courts. Shire courts
	For modern county courts (since 1846) see KD7228+
6972	General
6973.A-Z	Particular, A-Z
6974	London Lord Mayor's Court (Table KD3)
	Hundred courts
6976	General
6977.A-Z	Particular, A-Z
6980	Court of Marshalsea
6981	Courts of Cinque Ports
6983	Court of Commissioners of Sewers
6985	Piepowder courts
6988	Courts of requests
6990	Courts of Stannaries (Devonshire and Cornwall). Court of the Vice Warden of the Stannaries
	Cf. KD2365.T5 Tin mining
6992	Courts of wards and liveries (Table KD3)
	Court of Chivalry see KD728
	Administration of justice. Courts and procedure since the Judicature Act of 1873
	Including works covering this period and that before 1873
7100	General (Table KD2)
	Law officers of the Crown. Attorney General. Solicitor General
7105	General
7105.5	Procedures for removal. Impeachment
	Including particular cases
7107	Lord Chancellor's Departments
	Court organization and procedure
7111	General (Table KD2)
	Special aspects
7117	Conduct of court proceedings. Decorum
	Contempt of court see KD8055
7119	Congestion. Delay
7121	Foreign judgments
7121.5	Judicial assistance (Table KD2)
	Administration and management
7122	General (Table KD2)
7122.5	Finance (Table KD2)
7123	Records management

Courts. Procedure
   Administration of justice. Courts and procedure since the
     Judicature Act of 1873
     Court organization and procedure -- Continued
       Particular courts and procedure (General) before such
         courts
         For particular subjects, e.g. actions, special pleading, trial
          evidence, see the subject
        Highest courts of appeals
         House of Lords

7132	General. History.
	Appellate procedure see KD7632
	Judicial Committee of the Privy Council
7134	General. History.
	Appellate procedure see KD7634
	Superior courts
	Supreme Court of Judicature
7139	General. History. Organization (Table KD2)
7141-7150	Civil procedure (Table KD1)
	Including general pleading
	For particular subjects, see the subject
	High Court of Justice
7154	General. History. Organization (Table KD2)
7156-7165	Civil procedure (Table KD1)
	Including general pleading
	For particular subjects, see the subject
7167	District registries and district registry practice
	King's (Queen's) Bench Division
7169	General. History. Organization (Table KD2)
7171-7180	Civil procedure (Table KD1)
	Including general pleading
	For particular subjects, see the subject
7182	Commercial Court
	Chancery Division
7184	General. History. Organization (Table KD2)
7186-7195	Equity practice and procedure (Table KD1)
	Including general pleading
	For particular subjects, see the subject
	Probate, Divorce, and Admiralty Division. Family Division
7210	General (Table KD1)
	Probate law and practice see KD1518+
	Divorce. Matrimonial causes see KD751+
	Admiralty proceedings see KD1832+
7216	Court of Appeal (Civil Division)
	Palatine courts
7220	Chancery Court of Lancaster (Table KD3)

Courts. Procedure
  Administration of justice. Courts and procedure since the
    Judicature Act of 1873
    Court organization and procedure
      Particular courts and procedure (General) before such
        courts -- Continued
        Lower courts. Local courts
          County courts since 1846 (Modern county courts)

7228	General. History. Organization (Table KD2, modified)
7228.A15	Directories
	Civil procedure
	Including general pleading
	For particular subjects, see the subject
7231-7240	General (Table KD1)
7241	Equity practice and procedure (Table KD3)
7242.A-Z	Particular county courts, A-Z
7246	Liverpool Court of Passage
	Mayor's and City of London Court
	Including the former Sheriff's Court of the city of London, the City of London Court, and the Mayor's Court
7248	General (Table KD2)
7249	Civil procedure (Table KD2)
	Magistrates' Courts. Justices of the peace
	General. Civil jurisdiction see KD7301+
	Criminal jurisdiction see KD8301+
	Courts of special jurisdiction
	Criminal courts see KD8240
	Consular courts
7260	General
7261.A-Z	By country, A-Z
	Restrictive Practices Court see KD2218+
	Court of Referees (on private bills in Parliament) see KD4370+
	Court of Claims see KD4456.C6
	Judicial officers. Court employees
7283	General
	Judges
7285	General (Table KD3)
7286.A-Z	Special topics, A-Z
	Continuing education for judges see KD435
7286.J8	Judicial ethics. Corruption
7286.R43	Referees, Official
7286.S3	Salaries. Pensions
	Others
7290	General. Collective (Table KD3)

Courts. Procedure
  Judicial officers. Court employees
    Others -- Continued
      Particular

7292	Bailiffs
7293	Clerks of court
7294	Constables (Table KD3)
	Cf. KD4831+ Police
	Cf. KD9140 Metropolitan Police
7296	Coroners. Medical examiners (Table KD2)
	For medical evidence see KD7523
	Cf. RA1001+ Medical jurisprudence
7298	Filacers

        Justices of the peace. Magistrates. Magistrates'
          Courts

7301-7310	General. Civil jurisdiction (Table KD1, modified)
7302.3	Directories
	Criminal jurisdiction see KD8301+
	Clerks of the Peace see KD7293
	Masters see KD7554+
	Masters in Chancery see KD6940
	Medical examiners see KD7296
	Notaries see KD470
7312	Sheriffs (Table KD3)
7314	Translators (Table KD3)

   Civil procedure

7325	General
	Including common law and equity
	For works on procedure and pleading in general before
	particular courts, see those courts

    Court rules
      Collections

7330.A19-.A199	Serials
7330.A2	Monographs. By date of publication
7330.A3-.A319	Particular rules
	Arrange chronologically by means of successive Cutter
	numbers, according to date of adoption or revision of
	rules
7440	Nisi prius procedure (Table KD2)
	Cf. KD7530.N5 Rules of evidence pertaining to
	particular proceedings
	Equity practice and procedure see KD7186+
7443	Jurisdiction. Venue (Table KD2)
	Actions
7445	General (Table KD3)
7448.A-Z	Particular actions, A-Z
	Assumpsit see KD1602

Courts. Procedure
  Civil procedure
    Actions
      Particular actions, A-Z -- Continued
7448.C3   Action on the case
               Conversion and trover see KD1970
               Replevin see KD1225
            Process and service
7451   General (Table KD3)
7451.5.A-Z   Particular subjects, A-Z
7451.5.O9   Outlawry in civil proceedings
          Pleading and motions
7453   General
               For pleading in general before particular court systems or
                  courts, see such courts
            Defenses and objections (Exceptions)
7455   Limitation of actions
7458   Counterclaims and cross claims
7460   Confession of judgment
          Parties
7463   General (Table KD3)
7463.5   Compulsory representation by counsel. Litigants in
               person (Table KD2)
7465   Interpleader
          Pretrial procedure
7470   General. Deposition and discovery. Interrogatories
               (Table KD3)
          Trial
7480   General
            Trial practice. Trial tactics
7483   General (Table KD3)
7486   Cross examination (Table KD2)
7487   Forensic psychology (Table KD2)
            Trial by jury see KD7540+
            Evidence
               For works on evidence pertaining to particular
                  proceedings see KD7530.A+
7491-7500   General (Table KD1)
            Burden of proof
7505   General (Table KD3)
7508.A-Z   Special topics, A-Z
7508.P7   Presumptions (Table KD4)
7508.P74   Proof of foreign law (Table KD4)
            Particular kinds

Courts. Procedure

  Civil procedure

    Trial

      Evidence

        Particular kinds -- Continued

7510   Circumstantial

            For techniques of identification (Criminology) see HV8073+

            For techniques of identification (Forensic medicine) see RA1001+

7512   Documentary

          Witnesses

7514   General

7514.5   Children as witnesses

7516   Oath and affirmation (Table KD3)

           Contempt of court see KD8055

           Privileged (confidential) communications

7518   General (Table KD2)

7519.A-Z   Particular relationships, A-Z

7519.A77   Attorney and client

7519.C6   Confessional

7519.P48   Physician and patient

         Expert evidence. Expert witnesses

7521   General (Table KD3)

           Particular kinds

7523   Medical evidence. Medical witnesses

7524   Psychiatric and psychological evidence (Table KD2)

           Particular groups of expert witnesses

7524.15   Accountants. Auditors (Table KD2)

            Medical personnel see KD7523

            Mental health personnel see KD7524

          Presumptions see KD7508.P7

         Admissibility and exclusion of evidence

7525   Hearsay

7530.A-Z   Rules of evidence pertaining to particular proceedings, A-Z

7530.N5   Nisi prius (Table KD4)

      Jury and jurors

7540   General (Table KD2)

7550   Instructions to juries

          For individual instructions see KD664

      Masters

7554   General

        By particular courts

         Masters in chancery see KD6940

7556   King's (Queen's) Bench masters (Table KD3)

	Courts. Procedure
	Civil procedure
	Trial -- Continued
7558	Judicial discretion
	Judgment
7562	General (Table KD3)
7564	Res judicata. Estoppel by judgment
	Costs. Fees
7566	General (Table KD3)
	For legal aid see KD512+
	Costs in special proceedings
	Arbitration see KD7647
7568.A-Z	By particular courts, A-Z
7568.C4	Court of chancery
7568.C6	County courts
	Divorce courts see KD751+
7568.E8	Exchequer
	High Court of Justice see KD7568.S82
	King's (Queen's) Bench Division see KD7568.S83
7568.L3	Chancery Court of Lancaster
7568.P7	Judicial Committee of the Privy Council
7568.S8	Supreme Court of Judicature
7568.S82	High court of Justice
7568.S83	King's (Queen's) Bench Division
7572	Summary judgment
7573	Declaratory judgments (Table KD2)
	Remedies and special proceedings
7576	General
7578	Injunctions. Provisional remedies (Table KD2)
7580	Ne exeat regno
	Interpleader see KD7465
	Possessory actions, ejectment see KD925
	Replevin see KD1225
	Receivers for debenture holders see KD2109
	Receivers for persons of unsound mind see KD741
	Receivers in bankruptcy see KD2155.R4
7584	Receivers in equity (Table KD3)
7586	Scire facias
	Execution of judgment
7590	General (Table KD3)
7592	Attachment. Garnishment (Table KD3)
7594	Writ of extent
7596	Imprisonment for debt (Table KD3)
7598	Wartime deferment of executions
	Including emergency powers of courts
7605	Bail Court. Practice Court. Bail in civil proceedings other than admiralty (Table KD3)

Courts. Procedure
 Civil procedure
  Remedies and special proceedings -- Continued
   Extraordinary remedies. Prerogative writs and orders
7610   General
    Particular remedies
7612   Habeas corpus
7613   Mandamus
7615   Quo warranto
   Appellate procedure
    Including older procedure
7630   General
7632   House of Lords
     Law reports see KD187.A+
7634   Judicial Committee of the Privy Council
      For Judicial Committee of the Privy Council as a
       court of appeal in ecclesiastical matters see
       KD8693
     Law reports see KD247+
7636   Proceedings by or against the Crown
    For crown proceedings see KD2004
   Proceedings relating to particular branches of the law or
    special subjects, or governed by special rules.
    Noncontentious (ex-parte) jurisdiction
7640   General
    Admiralty see KD1832+
    Bankruptcy see KD2141+
    Condemnation proceedings see KD1185+
    Crown proceedings see KD2004
    Lunacy proceedings see KD740+
    Matrimonial causes see KD751+
    Monopolies. Antitrust law see KD2218+
    Patent litigation see KD1411
    Probate see KD1518+
    Workers' compensation see KD3221+
7644 Negotiated settlement. Compromise (Table KD2)
  Arbitration and award. Commercial arbitration
7645   General (Table KD2)
7647   Costs
   Agricultural arbitration see KD908.A3
 Criminal law
   Cf. KD6270+ Military criminal law and procedure
   Cf. KD8471+ Juvenile criminal law and procedure
  History
7849   Sources
    For crown plea rolls see KD7864.8
7850   General works

KD

Criminal law
  History -- Continued
7852.A-Z   Special topics, A-Z
7852.B55   Black act
     Criminal laws against religious minorities see KD4100+
7852.D4   Depopulation
7852.S5   Slave trade
7852.W5   Witchcraft
7861-7870   General. Comprehensive (Table KD1, modified)
    Court decisions
7864.8   Crown plea rolls. By initial date of period covered and by editor
      For civil plea rolls see KD190
     Reports
      Crown cases (Several courts)
7865.A2   Serials
        e.g. Criminal Appeal Reports (1908-)
7865.A5-Z   Monographic collections
7865.2.A-Z   Particular courts, A-Z
7865.2.C4   Central Criminal Court
       Court of Quarter Sessions
7865.2.Q3   Collective. By date of publication
7865.2.Q32   Particular
         Arrange alphabetically by means of successive Cutter numbers according to place
7865.2.S7   Star Chamber
    Special topics
7872   Codification
7876   Administration of criminal justice. Reform of criminal law, enforcement, and procedure (Table KD2)
     Special aspects
7878   Speedy trial
7879   Crime and publicity. "Trial by newspaper" (Table KD3)
      Contempt of court see KD8055
    Punishment and penalties
     For theory and philosophy of criminal punishment see K5103
     Cf. HV6001+ Criminology
7882   General (Table KD3)
7883   Habitual criminals. Recidivists. Preventive detention (Table KD3)
7885.A-Z   Particular penalties, A-Z
7885.C3   Capital punishment (Table KD4)
      Cf. KD6333 Military criminal law
7885.C6   Corporal punishment (Table KD4)
7885.F5   Fines (Table KD4)
7885.H3   Hard labor (Table KD4)

	Criminal law
	Punishment and penalties
	Particular penalties, A-Z -- Continued
7885.I6	Imprisonment (Table KD4)
	Preventive detention see KD7883
	Penal institutions see KD8450+
	Criminology see HV6001+
	General principles
7888	Criminal jurisdiction (Conflict of criminal law) (Table KD3)
	Criminal liability
7890	General
7892	Culpability. Mens rea. Criminal intent. Criminal negligence
7892.5	Criminal liability of juristic persons (Table KD2)
	Exemption from liability. Defenses. Diminished responsibility
7896	General (Table KD3)
	Particular defenses
7897	Insanity (Table KD3)
7897.5	Drunkenness
7898	Husband's coercion
7899	Entrapment (Table KD3)
7900	Provocation (Table KD3)
7901	Double jeopardy (Table KD3)
7910	Parties to crimes. Principals and accessories
	Particular offenses
7950	General. Comprehensive
	Preliminary crimes. Inchoate offenses
7953	General (Table KD2)
7955	Conspiracy (Table KD3)
	Offenses against the person
7960	General (Table KD3)
	Homicide
7963	General
7964	Murder
7967	Infanticide
7969	Abortion. Procuring miscarriage
7972	Assault and battery
7973	Conjugal violence. Wife abuse. Husband abuse
7974	Child abuse (Table KD3)
7974.5	Stalking (Table KD3)
	Sexual offenses
7975	General (Table KD2)
	Including works on legal implications of sexual behavior in general
7976.A-Z	Particular offenses, A-Z
7976.P4	Pedophilia (Table KD4)

KD

Criminal law
  Particular offenses
    Offenses against the person
      Sexual offenses
        Particular offenses, A-Z -- Continued

7976.R3	Rape (Table KD4)
7976.S6	Sodomy (Table KD4)
	Offenses against reputation
7980	Libel. Slander. Defamation (Table KD3)
	Offenses against property
	Including works on white collar crime and offenses against the economic order in general
7990	General
	Larceny, theft, robbery, and cognate offenses
7992	General
7993	Burglary. Housebreaking
7994	Forcible entry (Table KD3)
7995	Receiving stolen goods
8000	Fraud. False pretenses (Table KD3)
8001	Insurance fraud
8002	Securities fraud (Table KD2)
	Threats. Extortion. Blackmail
8005	General (Table KD1)
8006	Racketeering. Organized crime (Table KD2)
	Crimes against the state and public order
	Crimes against the state
8020	General (Table KD2)
8022	Treason (Table KD3)
8024	Espionage. Illegal disclosure of official secrets (Table KD3)
8026	Sedition
8028.A-Z	Other, A-Z
	Offenses against public order. Breach of peace
8035	General (Table KD2)
8037	Riots
8039	Terrorism (Table KD3)
	Offenses against the public administration
8044	Contempt of Parliament
8045	Corruption and bribery
	Offenses against the administration of justice
8054	General (Table KD2)
8055	Contempt of court (Table KD3)
	Cf. KD7451.5.O9 Outlawry in civil proceedings
8057	Maintenance and champerty
8059	Perjury. Subornation of perjury
	Offenses against public convenience and morality. Crimes without victims

Criminal law
  Particular offenses
    Offenses against public convenience and morality. Crimes
      without victims -- Continued

8070	General (Table KD3)
8072	Betting. Gambling. Lotteries (Table KD3)
8073	Blasphemy (Table KD3)
8075	Obscenity (Table KD3)
8077	Prostitution. Procuring (Table KD2)
8079	Vagrancy

    Offenses against public property, public finance, and
      currency

8090	Counterfeiting. Forgery
	Customs crimes, smuggling see KD5692
	Tax evasion see KD5410

Criminal procedure
  History

8220	General
8225.A-Z	Special topics, A-Z
(8225.A7)	Right of asylum
	see KD4142
	Benefit of clergy see KD8607.B4
8225.T6	Torture
8225.W3	Wager of battle

  Older courts
    Assizes. Commissions of assize

8235	General (Table KD3)
8236.A-Z	Particular courts. By county, A-Z
	Including court records
8240	Courts of Oyer and Terminer and General Gaol
	Delivery
8242	Courts of Trailbaston
	Courts leet see KD6968+
8250	Court of High Commission
	Court of High Steward see KD8283
8253	Court of Star Chamber
	Courts of Quarter Session of the Peace see KD8294+
8256	Court of Crown Cases Reserved
8260	King's (Queen's) Bench (Crown side) (Table KD3)
8262	Crown Office. Crown Office rules

Criminal court organization and procedure

8276	General (Table KD3)
	For administration of criminal justice see KD7876
	Courts
8277	General
	Particular courts and procedure (general) before such
	courts

KD

Criminal procedure
  Criminal court organization and procedure
    Courts
      Particular courts and procedure (general) before such
        courts -- Continued
      House of Lords original jurisdiction
        For appellate jurisdiction see KD8429+
        Impeachment see KD4373

8283	Trial of peers. Lord High Steward (Table KD3)
	For trials of peers see KD376.A+
8285	King's (Queen's) Bench Division (Crown side)
8286	Crown Court
	Assizes
8287	General (Table KD3)
8289	Central Criminal Court (Old Bailey)
	Quarter Sessions
	Including both original and appellate jurisdiction
8292	General (Table KD3)
	County Quarter Sessions. Courts of Quarter Sessions of the Peace
8294	General
8295.A-Z	Particular courts. By county, A-Z
	Including court records
	Borough Quarter Sessions
8296	General
8297.A-Z	Particular courts. By borough, A-Z
	Magistrates' Courts (Courts of summary jurisdiction). Justices of the peace
8301-8310	General (Table KD1, modified)
8302.3	Directories
8312	Petty Sessions
8313.A-Z	Particular courts. By city, A-Z
	Juvenile courts and procedure see KD7876
	Procedure
8321-8330	General (Table KD1)
	For administration of criminal justice see KD7876
8335	Arrest and commitment. Warrant of arrest. Rights of suspects. Criminal investigation (Table KD2)
	Habeas corpus see KD7612
8338	Searches and seizures (Table KD3)
8340	Bail (Table KD3)
8344	Extradition
	Right to speedy trial see KD7878
	Indictment. Information. Public prosecutor
8348	General (Table KD3)
8348.5.A-Z	Indictment for particular types of offenses, A-Z
8348.5.L3	Larceny

Criminal procedure
  Criminal court organization and procedure
    Procedure
      Indictment. Information. Public prosecutor -- Continued
8350   Grand jury (Table KD3)
            For individual charges see KD664
          Preliminary examinations. Arraignment. Preparation for
            trial
8356   General
8358   Defense. Public defenders. Legal aid in criminal
              proceedings (Table KD3)
8360   Procedure without trial. Plea bargaining. Pleas of
              guilty. Nolo contendere (Table KD2)
          Trial
8362   General
8363   Custody of defendants. Dock (Table KD2)
8364   Trial practice
          Evidence
8371   General (Table KD2)
            Admission of evidence
8382   General
8384   Confession
8385   Means of identification. Fingerprints, footprints,
                toothprints, etc. (Table KD2)
8386   Self-incrimination
8388   Wiretapping. Electronic listening and recording
                devices
8391   Witnesses
8393   Expert evidence. Expert witnesses
8400   Jury (Table KD2)
8402   Instructions to jury
            For individual instructions see KD664
8406   Judgment. Sentence (Table KD2)
8409   New trial
8411   Costs (Table KD3)
        Appellate procedure. appellate jurisdiction
8420   General (Table KD3)
              For remedies and special proceedings see KD7576+
            Quarter Sessions see KD8292+
8424   King's (Queen's) Bench Division. Criminal Division
              (Table KD3)
              Class here works on both original and appellate jurisdiction
8427   Court of Criminal Appeal (Table KD3)
            House of Lords
8429   General. Appellate jurisdiction (Table KD3)
              Original jurisdiction
                For impeachment see KD4373

KD

	Criminal procedure
	Criminal court organization and procedure
	Appellate procedure. Appellate jurisdiction
	House of Lords
	Original jurisdiction
	Trial of peers. Lord High Steward see KD8283
8440	Pardon (Table KD2)
(8445)	Proceedings before juvenile courts
	see KD8471+
	Execution of sentence
	Imprisonment
8450	Prison administration. Prison discipline (Table KD3)
	Particular types of penal and correctional institutions
	Penitentiaries. Prisons. Institutions for criminal
	lunatics
8452	General
8454.A-Z	Particular institutions, A-Z
8454.B7	Broadmoor Institution
8454.N4	Newgate
8454.R4	Reading County Gaol
8454.W45	Whitecross Street Prison
	Juvenile detention homes see KD8492
	Preventive detention see KD7883
8458	Fines (Table KD2)
8460	Forfeitures. Political disabilities (Table KD2)
8462	Probation. Parole (Table KD3)
8463	Rehabilitation
8464	Judicial error. Compensation for judicial error
	Government compensation to victims of crimes see
	KD2007
8469	Judicial assistance in criminal matters (Table KD2)
	Extradition see KD8344
8470	Victims of crimes (Table KD2)
	Military criminal law and procedure see KD6270+
	Juvenile criminal law and procedure. Administration of juvenile
	justice
8471	General (Table KD2)
8473	Juvenile courts (Table KD2)
	Criminal procedure
8481	General (Table KD2)
	Execution of sentence
	Imprisonment
8492	Juvenile detention homes. Reformatories. Borstal
	institutions (Table KD2)

Ecclesiastical law. Canon law of the Church of England.
  Church and state
    For the periods of Roman Catholic canon law (to ca. 1559)
      in England see KBR1005.5+
    For English and Scottish canonists see KBR1820+
  Church of England

8600	Constitutional status. Church and state
8603	Royal supremacy. Royal prerogative in ecclesiastical matters

History
  General works

8605	Including periods of the Roman Catholic Church canon law (to 1559)

8607.A-Z	Special topics, A-Z
8607.B4	Benefices of the clergy

Discrimination against religious minorities see
  KD4100+
Sources

8620	Collections (General)

Including collections on all periods of the Church of
  England

8621	Abridgments. Digests

Particular kinds of sources
  Legislation of the Church (1559-   )

8624	Proposed codes (Table KD11)

Including the Reformatio legum ecclesiasticarum
  (1571)

8625	The constitutions and canons ecclesiastical (English Church canons) (1604) (Table KD11)

For the Provinciale, seu constitutiones Anglie
  (Constitutiones provinciales ecclesiae
  Anglicanae) see KBR1006.2
For the Constitutiones legitime seu legatine
  regionis Anglicane see KBR1006.22.L43

8627	Articles of religion (Table KD11)

Church Assembly Measures

8629	Collections. By date

Particular measures
  see the relevant subject
Prerogative instruments

8632	Injunctions of Edward VI and Elizabeth I (Table KD11)

Enactments of Parliament affecting the Church

8634	Collections. By date

Particular acts
  see the relevant subject

KD

Ecclesiastical law. Canon law of the Church of England.
  Church and state
Church of England
  Sources
    Particular kinds of sources -- Continued
      Ecclesiastical law reports and related materials
        For Admiralty and Ecclesiastical Precedents see
          KD245+
       Reports

8638.A2A-.A2Z	Serials
8638.A3	Monographs
	By date of publication
8639	Digests
	General and comprehensive works
8642	Treatises
8643	Compends. Minor works
	Government. Organization
8650	General
8652	Jurisdiction of the Church
	Particular bodies, A-Z
	Including Councils, Convocations, National Assembly, Church Assembly, Diocesan conferences, Boards of finance, etc.
8656	Church discipline
	Clergy
	Including salaries and pensions
8658	General (Table KD3)
8660.A-Z	Individual, A-Z
8660.B5	Bishops
8660.P3	Parish priests
8660.S7	Stipendiary curates
8664	Cathedral churches. Commissioners. Deans. Chapters
	Ecclesiastical courts. Practice and procedure
8680	General (Table KD3)
	Court organization and procedure
8682	History. Court of High Commission. Older courts
	Particular courts
	Archdeacon's Courts
8685	General (Table KD2)
8686.A-Z	Particular archdeaconries, A-Z
	Consistory Court (of the bishop of each diocese)
8687	General (Table KD2)
8688.A-Z	Particular consistory courts, A-Z
	Provincial Courts of the Archbishops
8690	Court of Arches (in the Province of Canterbury) (Table KD2)
8690.5	Prerogative Court of Canterbury (Table KD2)

Ecclesiastical law. Canon law of the Church of England.
Church and state
Church of England
Ecclesiastical courts. Practice and procedure
Court organization
Particular courts
Provincial Courts of the Archbishops -- Continued

8691	Chancery Court of York
8693	Judicial Committee of the Privy Council
8695	Practice and procedure (Table KD2)
8700	Parishes. Districts. Parochial councils
	Parochial officers
8705	General
8707.A-Z	Particular, A-Z
8707.C45	Church wardens
8712	Churches. Chapels (Table KD2)
8714	Ornaments
8716	Pews and pew rights
8718	Church rates
8725	Patronage. Advowson. Right of presentation
	Benefices
8730	General
	Special topics
8733	Dilapidation
8740	Church land. Lands of ecclesiastical corporations
	Special topics
	Pensions see KD8658+
8745	Queen Anne's Bounty
8747	Tithes (Table KD3)
	Cf. KD1016 Land charges
8749	Faculties (Church of England) (Table KD3)
	Sacraments. Rites
8751	General
	Particular
	Lord's Supper
8751.5	Reservation of the Sacrament
	Marriage see KD753+
8753	Ceremonies (Table KD3)
	Offenses against religion
8760	General
	Individual offenses
	Blasphemy see KD8073
8763	Heresy
8765	Simony
	Other churches and denominations
8785	Roman Catholic Church
8790	United Reformed Church

KD

	Local laws
	General see KD4746+
	England
8850.A-Z	Counties and shires, A-Z
	Subarrange each by Table KD5
	Cities, boroughs, and towns, etc.
	London
8860	Bibliography
	Sources
8862	Documents (Collections. Serials)
8864	Customs
	Ordinances and local laws. Charters
	Including codes
8866	Serials
8868	Other collections. By date
8870	Charters. By date
8872	Digests of local ordinances and local laws
8874	Reports of court decisions
8876	Collections of statutes affecting London
	Including indexes and other auxiliary materials
8878	Collections of decisions and rulings affecting London
	For decisions and rulings relative to a particular subject, see the subject
8882	History
<8884>	Periodicals
	see K1+
	Yearbooks. Judicial statistics. Surveys of local administration of justice
8886	General
8888	Criminal statistics
8890	Juvenile crime
8894.A-Z	Special topics, particular courts, A-Z
8896	General works. Treatises. Monographs
	Particular subjects
	For private law subjects see KD9090.A+
	Government
8910	General (Table KD12)
	Greater London Council
8913	General. Jurisdiction and powers. Organization and procedure (Table KD12 modified)
8913.A35	Standing orders, etc. By date
8915.A-Z	Special committees, commissions, boards, etc., A-Z
	London County Council
8920	General. Jurisdiction and powers. Organization and procedure (Table KD12 modified)
8920.A35	Standing orders, etc. By date

Local laws
England
Cities, boroughs, and towns, etc.
London
Particular subjects
Government
London County Council -- Continued

8922.A-Z	Special committees, commissions, boards, etc., A-Z
	Corporation of the City of London
8927	General. Court of Common Council (Table KD12 modified)
8927.A35	Standing orders, etc. By date
8929.A-Z	Special committees, commissions, boards, etc., A-Z
8931	Police and power of the police of the City of London (Table KD12)
	For Metropolitan Police see KD9140
	Public property
8950	General (Table KD12)
8952.A-Z	Particular topics, A-Z
8952.B8	Building (Table KD13)
8952.C5	City planning and redevelopment (Table KD13)
8952.H6	Housing (Table KD13)
8952.P3	Parks and recreation grounds. Open spaces (Table KD13)
	Municipal services. Public utilities
8960	General (Table KD12)
8962.A-Z	Particular, A-Z
8962.W3	Water (Table KD13)
	Transportation
8970	General. Local transit (Table KD12)
8972.A-Z	Particular types of carriers, A-Z
8972.A8	Autobuses (Table KD13)
8972.S7	Streetcars (Table KD13)
8972.T3	Taxicabs (Table KD13)
	Port of London authority see KD9120
	Regulation of industry, trade, and commerce. Occupational law
8980	General. Licensing (Table KD12)
	Trade regulations. Control of trade practices
8985	General (Table KD12)
8987.A-Z	Special topics, A-Z
8987.A3	Advertising (Table KD13)
	Trade and commerce
8990	General (Table KD12)
8992.A-Z	By commodity, A-Z

	Local laws
	England
	Cities, boroughs, and towns, etc.
	London
	Particular subjects
	Regulation of industry, trade, and commerce.
	Occupational law
	Trade and commerce
	By commodity, A-Z -- Continued
8992.C6	Coal (Table KD13)
	Social legislation
	Labor law
8996	General (Table KD12)
8998.A-Z	Special topics, A-Z
8998.W3	Wages. Minimum wages (Table KD13)
	Public welfare. Public assistance. Poor laws
9004	General (Table KD12)
9005.A-Z	Particular groups, A-Z
9005.O7	Orphans (Table KD13)
9006.A-Z	Special topics, A-Z
	Subarrange each by Table KD13
	Public health. Sanitation
9012	General (Table KD12)
9014.A-Z	Special topics, A-Z
9014.C6	Contagious and infectious diseases (Table KD13)
	Medical legislation
9018	General (Table KD12)
9020.A-Z	Special topics, A-Z
	Subarrange each by Table KD13
9024	Veterinary laws. Veterinary hygiene (Table KD12)
9028	Alcohol. Alcoholic beverages. Liquor laws (Table KD12)
	Public safety
9032	General (Table KD12)
9034.A-Z	Special topics, A-Z
9034.F5	Fire prevention and control (Table KD13)
	Control of social activities
9040	General (Table KD12)
9042.A-Z	Special topics, A-Z
9042.A3	Amusements (Table KD13)
9046	Education (Table KD12)
	Science and arts
9050	General (Table KD12)
	Performing arts
9052	General (Table KD12)
9054.A-Z	Special topics, A-Z

	Local laws
	England
	Cities, boroughs, and towns, etc.
	London
	Particular subjects
	Science and arts
	Performing arts
	Special topics, A-Z -- Continued
9054.M6	Motion pictures (Table KD13)
	Including censorship
	Public finance
9070	General (Table KD12)
	Taxation
9073	General (Table KD12)
	Particular taxes
9075	Real property taxes. Rating. Rating appeals (Table KD12)
9078	Special assessments (Table KD12)
	Local offenses (Violation of ordinances) and administration of criminal justice
9085	General (Table KD12)
9086.A-Z	Particular offenses and special topics, A-Z
	Subarrange each by Table KD13
9090.A-Z	Other subjects, A-Z
9090.I5	Inheritance and succession (Table KD13)
9090.N84	Nuisance (Table KD13)
	Special districts. Public securities. Joint boards
9120	Port of London Authority
9140	Metropolitan Police
	Under the direct administration of the Home Secretary
9142.A-Z	Greater London Boroughs, A-Z
	Subarrange each by Table KD5
	Including former administrative or political subdivisions
9150.A-Z	Other cities, boroughs, and towns, etc., A-Z
	Subarrange each by Table KD5
	For Greater London Boroughs see KD9142.A+
9310.A-Z	Manors, A-Z
9312.A-Z	Other, A-Z
	Subarrange each by Table KD5
9312.D4	Dean Forest
9312.R6	Romney Marsh
	Wales
9320.A-Z	Counties and shires, A-Z
	Subarrange each by Table KD5
9325.A-Z	Cities, boroughs, and towns, etc., A-Z
	Subarrange each by Table KD5
9350.A-Z	Manors, A-Z

Local laws
Wales -- Continued
9355.A-Z   Other, A-Z

	Law of Wales
	For material appliable to both England and Wales see KD1+
9400	Bibliography
9402	Documents (Collections. Serials)
	Customary law. Tribal law. Ancient law
9405	Custumals. Lawbooks. Codes
	Statutes
9407	Collections. By editor
	Law reports and related materials
9410	General
	Particular courts
9412	Court of Exchequer
9414	Court of Chancery
9417.A-Z	Other, A-Z
9420	Law dictionaries. Words and phrases
	Criminal trials
9423	Collections
	Including particular offenses
9424.A-Z	Particular trials. By defendant or by best known name, A-Z
	Including commentaries and stories on a particular trial.
	Includes records and briefs
9424.C35	Cardiff Explosives Trial, 1983
9430	History
	Particular subjects
9432	Persons (Table KD2)
	Building laws
9440	General
	Special buildings
9444	School buildings
9448	Health insurance. Friendly societies
9460	Education. Schools. Teachers
9462	Constitutional law (Table KD2)
9468	Local government (Table KD2)
	Courts and procedure
9480	General. Administration of justice (Table KD2)
	Particular courts
9482	Courts of Great Sessions
9484	Courts of Augmentation
9490	Criminal law and procedure
9492.A-Z	Other, A-Z
	Ecclesiastical law. The Welsh Church
9498	General
9500.A-Z	Particular topics, A-Z
	Local laws
	Counties see KD9320.A+
	Cities, boroughs, and towns, etc. see KD9325.A+
	Manors see KD9350.A+

Local laws -- Continued
Other see KD9355.A+

KDC

	Law of Scotland
	Bibliography
51	General
53	Library catalogs
	Official gazettes
56	Edinburgh Gazette
	Legislation
	Statutes
	Public general statutes
69	Serials
70	Sessional volumes
	By initial date of session
	General compilations. Collections
	Early and discontinued compilations
75	Serials
	By date of first publication
76	Monographs
	Arrange chronologically by initial date of period covered
78	Statutes revised
	By date of revision
	Current and continuing compilations
80	Serials
	e.g. Scottish Current Law Statutes. 1949-
81	Monographs
	Arrange chronologically by initial date of period covered
83	Statute law revision acts and reports
	By date of publication
86	Digests and abridgments of statutes
87	Citators to statutes
90	Indexes and tables to statutes
	Indexes and tables to particular publications are classed with the publication
	Law reports and related materials
	Including both authorized and collateral reports
	Class reports on particular subjects with the subject
	Highest courts of appeals
110	House of Lords (Table KD14)
	From 1850, House of Lords decisions are reported and bound in with the annual volumes of Session Cases
	Cf. KD275.2 The Law Reports. Appellate Series. Scotch Appeals
	Cf. KD275.4 The Law Reports. Appellate Series. Appeal Cases
113	Court of Session (Table KD14)
	High Court of Justiciary see KDC936+

Law reports and related materials -- Continued

116	Several courts (Table KD14)
	Including House of Lords, Court of Session, High Court of Justiciary, and Lower court decisions, combined
	Lower courts
	Trial courts
	Sheriff Court
121	General (Table KD14)
122.A-Z	Particular, A-Z
	Minor courts
125.A-Z	Municipal courts. By city, A-Z
	Older courts
130	Court of Exchequer (Table KD14)
133	Jury Court (Table KD14)
136	Privy Council (Table KD14)
	Special courts or reports on particular subjects
	see subject
140-140.Z	Digests and citators to various reports, A-Z
140.C8-.C84	Scottish Current Law
140.C8	Consolidation
140.C82	Yearbook
140.C84	Citator
150	Encyclopedias
152	Law dictionaries. Words and phrases
	For dictionaries on particular subjects, see the subject
	For bilingual and multilingual dictionaries see K50+
154	Legal maxims. Quotations
156	Form books
	Class here general works only
	For form books on a particular subject, see the subject
<157>	Periodicals
	see K1+
158	Yearbooks
	Class here only publications issued annually, containing information, statistics, etc. about the year just passed.
	Other publications appearing yearly are classed as periodicals in K1+
	Judicial statistics
161	General
162	Criminal statistics
165	Directories
170	Society and bar association journals
	Class here only journals restricted to society or bar association activities
	Journals devoted to legal subjects, either wholly or in part, are classed in K1+
	Collections

<table>
<tr><td></td><td>Collections -- Continued</td></tr>
<tr><td>175</td><td>Monographic series</td></tr>
<tr><td>176</td><td>Several authors. Festschriften</td></tr>
<tr><td>177</td><td>Minor collections. Anthologies</td></tr>
<tr><td>180.A-Z</td><td>Individual authors, A-Z</td></tr>
</table>

               Under each:

.x	*By date*
.xA-.xZ	*By editor, A-Z*

Trials
  Criminal trials and judicial investigations
    Collections

184	General
185.A-Z	Particular offenses, A-Z
185.M8	Murder
185.T7	Treason
185.W67	Witchcraft
186.A-Z	Particular trials. By defendant, A-Z

               Including commentaries and stories on a particular trial, and
                   including records and briefs

    Civil trials

187	Collections
188.A-Z	Particular trials. By plaintiff, A-Z

               Including commentaries and stories on a particular trial, and
                   including records and briefs

    Ecclesiastical trials see KDC963+

200	Legal research. Legal bibliography

               Class here works on methods of bibliographical research and how
                   to find the law

202	Legal composition and draftsmanship
	Legal education
210	General works. Standards. Criticism (Table KD3)
	Study and teaching
	General works see KDC210
215.A-Z	Particular law schools, A-Z
220.A-Z	Law societies, A-Z
220.J8	Juridical Society of Edinburgh
220.S6	Society of Advocates in Aberdeen
	Society of Clerks to His Majesty's Signet see KDC220.S65
220.S65	Society of Writers to Her Majesty's Signet
220.S7	Stair Society
	The legal profession
225	General. Law as a career
227	Advocates (Table KD3)
229	Solicitors. Writers. Law agents (Table KD3)
230	Notaries
	Practice of law
232	General (Table KD3)

	The legal profession
	Practice of law -- Continued
234	Legal ethics and etiquette. Professional discipline (Table KD3)
	Law office management
238	General
239	Attorneys' and legal secretaries' handbooks, manuals, desk-books, etc.
	The Scottish Bar. Solicitors' associations
245	Faculty of advocates
247	Law Society of Scotland
	Including predecessor associations, e.g. Incorporated Society of Law Agents in Scotland
260	Community legal services. Legal aid. Legal assistance to the poor (Table KD3)
	History
	For works on the history of a particular subject, see the subject
	Sources
270	General collections
272	Statutes and customs
275	Regiam Majestatem and Quoniam Attachiamenta
277	Collections of judgments
280	Registers of brieves (Writs)
282	Exchequer rolls
284.A-Z	Practicks. By compiler, A-Z
287	Privy Council records
290	Charters. Cartularies. Deeds
291	Other documents
296	Treatises. Monographs (Table KD3)
	Class treatises relating to a particular class of sources, e.g. Practicks, with those sources
	Biography
	Collective
310	General
311.A-Z	Local. By county, city, etc., A-Z
313.A-Z	Individual, A-Z
	Subarrange each by Table KD7
	Including criticism
	Particular aspects
315	Influence of foreign law
318	Jurisprudence and philosophy of Scottish law
320	Criticism. Legal reform. General administration of justice (Table KD2)
	Cf. KDC840 Judiciary
	Cf. KDC915 Administration of criminal justice
	General and comprehensive works
	Collections see KDC175+

	General and comprehensive works -- Continued
329	Cases. Readings
330	Treatises
331	Compends. Courses of study
332	Minor and popular works
333	Examination aids
334	Miscellaneous individual addresses and essays
	For collected essays see KDC175+
335.A-Z	Works for particular groups of users, A-Z
335.J68	Journalists
338	Equity
	Conflict of laws
340	General (Table KD3)
342.A-Z	Particular branches and subjects of the law, A-Z
342.M3	Marriage. Divorce. Marital property
	General principles and concepts
	Comprehensive works see KDC330
	Particular aspects
345	Stare decisis
347.A-Z	Concepts applying to several branches of law, A-Z
347.D3	Damages
347.E88	Estoppel
	Persons
350	General. Status. Capacity
	Natural persons
	Civil status
354	Absence and presumption of death (Table KD3)
	Capacity and disability
356	Women (Table KD3)
357	Infants. Pupils. Minors (Table KD3)
	Including liability
358	Mentally ill. People with mental or physical disabilities (Table KD2)
362	Recording and registration. Registers of births, marriages, and deaths. Birth and death certificates
	Corporations. Juristic persons see KDC556+
	Domestic relations. Family law
366	General (Table KD2)
	Marriage. Husband and wife
367	General (Table KD2)
370	Property relationships
372	Divorce. Separation
	Parent and child
374	General. Support (Table KD2)
376	Illegitimate children. Affiliation. Legitimation (Table KD2)
377	Adoption (Table KD2)
378	Guardian and ward. Judicial factors. Curators (Table KD2)

Property
390 General. Ownership
Real property. Land law
393 General (Table KD2)
Land tenure
395 General
397 Feudal law (Table KD3)
Ownership
399 General
400 Estates and interests. Freehold. Fee simple
402 Entails (Table KD3)
Future estates and interests
403 Rule against perpetuities
Concurrent ownership. Co-ownership
Including works on concurrent ownership in both real and
personal property
405 General
405.5.A-Z Particular topics, A-Z
405.5.H6 Housing cooperatives
Tenancy. Leaseholds. Landlord and tenant. Rent
412 General (Table KD2)
413 Rent control (Table KD3)
Particular kinds
415 Commercial leases
416 Farm tenancy. Agricultural holdings acts.
Allotments. Small holdings (Table KD2)
Rights and interests incident to ownership and
possession
420 General
421 Riparian rights. Water rights of individuals
Rights to use and profits of another's land
424 Easements. Servitudes
426.A-Z Particular topics, A-Z
426.P7 Prescription
Transfer of rights in land
Transfer inter vivos
430 General. Vendor and purchaser
Conveyances. Title investigation. Abstracts
433 General. Deeds (Table KD2)
435 Title investigation. Abstracts
436 Registration (Table KD2)
Transfer by will see KDC463
Intestate succession see KDC467
Unclaimed estates see KDC470
438 Mortgages. Pledges. Liens (Table KD2)
Public property. Public restraints on private property
440 General

Property
  Real property. Land law
    Public property. Public restraints on private property --
      Continued
    Roads
441   General. Highway law (Table KD3)
    Regional and city planning. Zoning. Building
446   General (Table KD3)
      Building laws
448   General (Table KD3)
449.A-Z   Particular types of buildings, A-Z
449.S3   School buildings
451   Dean of guild courts
452   Housing. City redevelopment
             Including housing finance
453   Eminent domain. Compulsory purchase (Table KD2)
455   Personal property (Table KD2)
460   Trusts and trustees
     Succession upon death
462   General (Table KD2)
       Testate succession. Wills. Probate law and practice
463   General. Probate courts (Table KD2)
465.A-Z   Special topics, A-Z
465.R5   Rights of spouses and children. Jus relictae. Legitim
467   Intestate succession (Table KD3)
468   Administration of decedents' estates. Personal
           representatives
470   Unclaimed estates. Heirless property. Bona vacantia
     Obligations
482   General
       Contracts
485   General and comprehensive works (Table KD2)
         General principles
487   Void and voidable contracts
         Particular contracts
495   Comprehensive. Commercial law. Mercantile
               transactions (Table KD2)
           Contract of service. Master and servant
498   General
             Local government employment see KDC796+
           Contract for work and labor (Contract for services).
               Independent contractors
500   General
             Particular types
501   Building and construction
505   Sale of goods
         Partnership see KDC554

Obligations
  Contracts
    Particular contracts -- Continued
510   Negotiable instruments
           Banking
513   General (Table KD3)
             Particular kinds of banks
515   Cooperative credit societies
517   Loan of money
520   Suretyship. Guaranty
           Secured transactions
522   General
             Particular transactions
523   Conditional sale. Installment sale. Hire-purchase
           Carriers. Carriage of goods and passengers
526   General. Liability
             Carriage by sea. Maritime (Commercial) law.
               Admiralty
530   General (Table KD3)
532   Admiralty proceedings
534   Insurance (Table KD2)
538   Quasi contracts
         Delictual and quasi delictual obligations. Torts
541   General. Reparation (Table KD2)
           Particular torts
542   Personal injuries. Death by wrongful act (Table KD3)
543   Libel and slander
545   Nuisance
           Strict liability. Llability without fault
546   General (Table KD2)
547   Products liability (Table KD2)
548   Agency (Table KD2)
         Associations
550   General. Comprehensive
             Including business enterprises in general, regardless of form of
               organization
           Unincorporated associations
552   General
554   Business associations. Partnership
           Corporations. Juristic persons
556   General
             Business corporations
557   General (Table KD3)
558   Disslution. Liquidation. Winding up (Table KD3)
         Insolvency and bankruptcy. Creditors' rights
560   General (Table KD3)
           Bankruptcy

	Insolvency and bankruptcy. Creditors' rights
	Bankruptcy -- Continued
561	General (Table KD3)
563	Assignments for benefit of creditors. Sequestration (Table KD3)
	Regulation of industry, trade, and commerce. Occupational law
570	General
	Primary production
	Agriculture. Forestry
580	General (Table KD3)
	Marketing regulations
582	General (Table KD3)
582.2.A-Z	By product, A-Z
582.2.G7	Grain (Table KD4)
	Including fiars prices
	Wildlife conservation
584	General
584.5	Game laws (Table KD3)
	Fishery
585	General (Table KD3)
586.A-Z	Particular fish or marine fauna, A-Z
586.S2	Salmon
588	Mining. Quarrying (Table KD2)
	Food processing industries
592	General
593.A-Z	Particular industries and products, A-Z
593.M4	Meat industry. Meat inspection
	Trade and commerce
	Service trades
597	General. Licensing (Table KD3)
598.A-Z	Particular trades, A-Z
	Transportation and communication
601	General
	Road traffic. Automotive transportation
604	General
607	Traffic regulations and enforcement
610	Carriage of passengers and goods
620	Railroads (Table KD3)
628	Press law (Table KD3)
	Social legislation
635	General
	Labor law
640	General
	Management-labor relations
642	General (Table KD2)
643.A-Z	Special topics, A-Z

	Social legislation
	Labor law
	Management-labor relations
	Special topics, A-Z -- Continued
643.I53	Industrial courts and tribunals (Table KD4)
	Labor standards
644	General. Labor conditions (Table KD3)
	Employment and dismissal
644.2	General (Table KD3)
	Discrimination in employment and its prevention
644.4	General. Racial discrimination (Table KD3)
644.5.A-Z	Particular groups, A-Z
644.5.W65	Women (Table KD4)
	Wages. Minimum wages
646	General
647.A-Z	Particular industries and groups of employees, A-Z
647.B3	Banking industry
647.C3	Carbonated beverage industry
647.C5	Clothing industry
647.D3	Dairy industry
647.H3	Hat industry
	Hours of labor
650	General
	Child labor see KDC655
	Woman labor see KDC656
	Protection of labor. Labor hygiene and safety
653	General
655	Child labor
	Including hours of child labor
656	Woman labor
	Including hours of woman labor
	Social insurance
662	General
	Particular branches
	Health insurance
664	General (Table KD3)
666	National Health Service. State medicine
	Public welfare. Public assistance. Poor laws
670	General (Table KD2)
	Particular groups
672	Children and young persons. Child welfare
674	Widows
680	Public health. Sanitation. Environmental pollution (Table KD3)
682	Disposal of the dead. Burial and cemetery laws
684	Water pollution. Drainage (Table KD3)
685	Air pollution. Control of smoke, noxious gases, etc.
	Medical legislation

	Medical legislation -- Continued
690	General
692	Hospitals and other medical institutions
694	The mentally ill (Table KD3)
695.A-Z	Disorders of character, behavior, and intelligence, A-Z
695.A5	Alcoholism (Table KD4)
	Food. Drugs
700	General
702	Drug laws
704	Alcohol. Alcoholic beverages. Liquor production. Liquor traffic (Table KD2)
	Education
	Education in general. Public education
715	General (Table KD3)
	Teachers
718	General
719	Education and training
720	Salaries, pensions, etc. (Table KD3)
	Elementary and secondary education
723	General
725	Evening and continuation schools (Table KD3)
728	Higher education. Colleges and universities
	Science and the arts. Research
732	General
	The arts
735	Motion pictures
	Constitutional law
750	History (Table KD3)
	For the history of a particular subject of constitutional law, see the subject
752	Constitutional law in general (Table KD3)
	Individual and state
758	Civil and political rights and liberties (Table KD2)
	Church and state. Church of Scotland see KDC958+
	The Parliament
762	History
	Peerage. Peerage claims
764	General
764.5	Peerage claims
766	General. Legislative process
768	Private bill legislation (Table KD3)
	Election law
771	General (Table KD2)
772	Registration (Table KD3)
773	Election districts. Apportionment (Table KD3)
774	Local elections
774.5	Corrupt practices

Constitutional law -- Continued
  The Crown and the Central Government (Executive branch)
777   General (Table KD3)
779   Succession to the throne
781   The Scottish Office. Scottish government departments
783   Judiciary. Judicial power (Table KD3)
785   Decorations of honor. Awards of honor. Dignities
    Local government
788   General (Table KD2)
        Municipal government. Municipal services
790   General. Municipal corporations (Table KD3)
792   Charters. Ordinances. Local laws
794   County (Shire) government
        Local government officials and employees
796   General
797   Salaries. Retirement. Pensions (Table KD3)
798   Police and power of the police (Table KD3)
801   Administrative law. Administrative organization and procedure
802   Judicial review (Table KD2)
804   Government measures in time of war, national emergency, or
        economic crisis. Emergency economic legislation
        For rent control see KDC413
    Public finance
807   General
      Particular sources of revenue
        Taxation
810   General
812   Tax administration. Procedure and practice
          Particular taxes
            Property taxes. Taxation of capital
            Real property taxes
816   General (Table KD3)
817   Land valuation. Real property assessment (Table
                KD3)
819   Betterment levy
821   Estate, inheritance, and gift taxes
823   Tariff. Customs duties (Table KD3)
825   Local finance (Table KD3)
835   National defense. Military law (Table KD3)
    Courts. Procedure
840   Administration of justice. Organization of the judiciary
      Court organization and procedure
842   General
843   Judicial assistance (Table KD2)
        Particular courts
          Including procedure in general before such courts
        Court of Session

Courts. Procedure
  Administration of justice. Organization of the judiciary
  Court organization and procedure
    Particular courts
     Court of Session -- Continued

844   General. Organization. History
846   Procedure (Table KD2)
        For appellate procedure before the Inner House
          see KDC902.4
849   Bill Chamber
850   The Teind Court
        For tithes see KDC972
     Sheriff Court
852   General. Organization. History
853   Procedure (Table KD2)
855.A-Z   Particular courts. By sheriffdom, A-Z
     Justices of the Peace
860   General (Table KD3)
        Including procedure
860.5.A-Z   Particular courts, A-Z
        Including court records
     Dean of Guild Courts see KDC451
     Older courts
863   Court of Exchequer
      Courts baron. Regality courts. Heritable jurisdictions
865   General
866.A-Z   Particular, A-Z
         Including court records
    Judicial officers. Court employees
868   General. Collective
869.A-Z   Particular officers or employees, A-Z
869.C6   Constables
      Justices of the Peace see KDC860+
869.M3   Messengers-at-arms
      Notaries see KDC230
   Civil procedure
    General
     Court rules. Acts of Sederunt
      General. Comprehensive
875.A2   Collections. By date of publication

Courts. Procedure
Civil procedure
General
Court rules. Acts of Sederunt
General. Comprehensive -- Continued
875.A3-.A319   Particular rules
Arrange chronologically by means of successive Cutter
numbers according to date of adoption, revision, or
consolidation of rules
Under each:
.xA2   *Unannotated texts. By date of*
publication
.xA3-.xZ7   *Annotated editions. Commentaries.*
By author of commentary or
annotation, A-Z
.xZ8-.xZ89   *Digests*
Particular courts
For court rules of a particular court, see the court
878   General works (Table KD3)
879   Jurisdiction. Venue (Table KD3)
880   Actions. Process and service
883   Pleading and motions (Table KD3)
Trial. Trial practice
885   General (Table KD3)
Evidence
888   General (Table KD3)
Particular kinds
889   Witnesses
891   Jury and jurors (Table KD3)
893   Costs. Fees
Remedies and special proceedings
895   General (Table KD3)
896   Injunctions. Interdict
898   Execution of judgment. Diligence
899   Arrest of debtors meditating flight (meditatio fugae)
Appellate procedure
902   General (Table KD2)
902.4   Court of Session, Inner House
902.6   House of Lords
904   Arbitration and award
Criminal law
Cf. KDC951+ Juvenile criminal law and procedure
History
910   General
911.A-Z   Special topics, A-Z
911.W5   Witchcraft
913   General. Comprehensive (Table KD2)

	Criminal law -- Continued
915	Administration of criminal justice. Reform of criminal law, enforcement, and procedure
	Punishment and penalties
917	General
918	Habitual criminals. Recidivists
920.A-Z	Particular offenses, A-Z
920.C65	Contempt of court
920.I55	Inchoate offenses
920.O44	Offenses against the person
920.S4	Sexual offenses
920.T7	Treason
	Criminal procedure
930	General (Table KD3)
930.5	Arrest and commitment. Warrant of arrest. Rights of suspects. Criminal investigation (Table KD3)
931	Bail (Table KD3)
933	Indictment. Information. Public prosecutor (Table KD3)
	Trial
934	General (Table KD2)
934.5	Evidence (Table KD2)
935	Judgment. Sentence (Table KD2)
	Execution of sentence
935.6	General works
935.7	Forfeitures. Political disabilities (Table KD2)
	Courts
935.8	General (Table KD3)
	Particular courts and procedure before such courts
	High Court of Justiciary
936	General (Table KD2, modified)
936.A545	Court records. By initial date of period covered
938.A-Z	By circuit, etc., A-Z
941	Magistrates' courts. Summary proceedings
945	Appeal (Table KD3)
	Proceedings before juvenile courts see KDC951+
948	Probation
	Juvenile criminal law and procedure. Administration of juvenile justice
951	General (Table KD3)
952	Juvenile courts (Table KD3)
	Ecclesiastical law. Church of Scotland
	Church of Scotland
	For sources of Roman Catholic canon law (before 1560) see KBR1006.3 and KBR1820-1822.4
958	Constitutional status. Church and state
960	Acts of the General Assembly
	By initial date of period covered

	Ecclesiastical law. Church of Scotland
	Church of Scotland
	Acts of the General Assembly -- Continued
961	Abridgments
	Trials
963	Collections
963.5.A-Z	Particular trials. By defendant, A-Z
965	General and comprehensive works (Table KD3)
966	Ecclesiastical courts. Practice and procedure (Table KD3)
968	Parishes. Parochial clergy. Parochial officers (Table KD3)
969	Church land
971	Patronage
972	Tithes. Teinds
	For the Court of Teinds see KDC850
	Marriage see KDC367+
974.A-Z	Other subjects, A-Z
	Local laws
980.A-Z	Counties (Shires), A-Z
	Subarrange each by Table KD5
985.A-Z	Cities, burghs, towns, parishes, A-Z
	Subarrange each by Table KD5
990.A-Z	Other, A-Z

KDC

KDE

Law of Northern Ireland
    For the law of Ireland (as a whole) before division in 1922
        see KDK21+
21   Bibliography
            Official gazettes
24   The Belfast Gazette
            Parliamentary publications see J307.5
                Both Houses
<26>   Papers by command
                        If collected, otherwise by subject
                    Senate
<28>   Proceedings
<29>   Journals
<30>   Debates
                    House of Commons
<33>   Proceedings
<34>   Journals
<35>   Debates
<36>   Bills and reports
            Legislation
                Statutes
                    Public general acts
                        Sessional or annual volumes
                            Including local and private acts, and orders in councils
42   Serials
43   Monographs
                                By date of session or of initial session
                        General compilations. Collections
44   The Statutes Revised
47   Chronological tables and indexes
                    Subordinate [Delegated] legislation
49   Statutory rules and orders of Northern Ireland
50   Indexes
            Law reports and related materials
55   General reports
                    e. g. Northern Ireland Reports (1925-   )
                    For decisions of the courts of Ireland before 1922 see
                        KDK61+
                    For reports of Northern Ireland court decisions for 1922-
                        1924 (Law reports (Ireland)) see KDK63
58   Digests
59   Indexes. Tables
60   Records and briefs
            Collections

Collections -- Continued
70   Individual authors
              Under each:
              .x   *By date*
              .xA-.xZ   *By editor, A-Z*
              Including collected opinions, instructions to juries, and charges
                to grand juries
            Criminal trials and judicial investigations
72   Collections
74.A-Z   Particular trials or investigations
              By defendant or best known name, A-Z
            The legal profession. Practice of law
75   General
            Special topics
77   Fees
80   Bar associations. Solicitors' associations
87   Criticism. Legal reform. General administration of justice
              (Table KD3)
            General and comprehensive works
88   Treatises
88.5.A-Z   Works for particular groups of users, A-Z
88.5.B86   Businesspeople. Foreign investors
              Foreign investors see KDE88.5.B86
            Persons
            Natural persons
90   General. Status. Capacity
92   Infants. Minors (Table KD2)
                Including liability
              Domestic relations
94   General. Comprehensive
98.A-Z   Particular subjects, A-Z
98.A34   Adoption
98.D58   Divorce
98.I4   Illegitimate children. Affiliation. Legitimation
            Corporations see KDE220
            Property
110   General
            Real property
112   General
              Land tenure
113   General
113.5   Feudal tenure
120   Tenancy. Leaseholds. Land purchase acts
              Transfer of rights in land
121   General
122   Registration of title
            Public property. Public restraints on private property

KDE

131

Property
  Real property
    Public property. Public restraints on private property --
      Continued
125   General
131   Eminent domain. Compulsory acquisition
      Regional and city planning. Zoning. Building
135   General
137   Building laws
138   Housing (Table KD2)
  Trusts and trustees
140   General
142.A-Z   Special topics, A-Z
142.C4   Charitable trusts
  Succession upon death
145   General
149   Probate law and practice
151   Administration of decedents' estates. Executors and
      administrators
  Contracts
155   General
    Particular contracts
170   Banking
  Torts
194   General
    Particular torts
195   Personal injuries
210   Compensation to victims of crimes. Reparation (Table KD3)
      Including injuries to both person and property, and compensation
        by government
220   Corporations. Business corporations (Table KD3)
230   Insolvency and bankruptcy
  Regulation of industry, trade, and commerce. Occupational
    law
235   General
    Food processing industries
250.A1A-.A1Z   General
250.A5-Z   Particular products, A-Z
250.D3   Dairy products. Milk production and distribution
    Trade and commerce
260   Retail trade
    Transportation
280   General
282   Ratemaking
  Social legislation
320   General
    Labor law

Social legislation
Labor law -- Continued
322   General
324   Labor-management relations. Labor unions. Trade
                                unions. Collective labor agreements
                            Labor standards
326   General
                                Employment and dismissal
327   General
327.5   Discrimination in employment and its prevention (Table
                                        KD3)
                                    Wages. Minimum wage
328   General
330.A-Z   Particular industries and groups of employees, A-Z
330.B3   Baking industry
330.B6   Boot and shoe workers
330.B7   Broom and brush industry
330.C5   Clothing industry
                                            Dressmakers see KDE330.C5
330.L3   Laundry workers
330.P3   Paper bag and box industry
330.R6   Ropemakers
                                            Tailors see KDE330.C5
330.T4   Textile industry. Linen industry
330.W3   Waste products industry
                                    Protection of labor. Labor hygiene and safety. Employee
                                        rules
333   General
335   Child labor (Table KD3)
                                            Including hours of child labor
                            Social insurance
340   General (Table KD3)
                                Particular branches
342   Health insurance
344   Workers' compensation
346   Social security. Retirement. Old age and disability
                                        pensions. Survivors' benefits. Widows' and orphans'
                                        pensions
348   Unemployment insurance (Table KD3)
                    Public health. Sanitation. Environmental pollution
355   General (Table KD3)
360   Environmental pollution (Table KD3)
378   Alcohol. Alcoholic beverages. Liquor laws (Table KD3)
                    Control of social activities
380   General
382   Lotteries. Games of chance. Gambling
                    Education

	Education -- Continued
392	General
	Students. Compulsory education
394	General
395.A-Z	Particular subjects, A-Z
395.S7	Student aid. Scholarships
	Constitutional law
	Sources
410	General
412	Texts of the constitution
415	Constitutional law in general (Table KD3)
	Including constitutional history
	Individual and state
420	Civil and political rights and liberties (Table KD3)
	Control of individuals
423	Internal security. Control of subversive activities (Table KD3)
	Election law
425	General
427	Election districts. Apportionment
430	Corrupt practices. Personation at elections
	Legislation
	Parliament
440	General
445	Senate
	House of Commons
450	General
452	Rules and practice. Standing orders
	The executive branch
455	General
460	Civil service
	Including salaries, retirement and pensions
462	Police and power of the police
478	Administrative law. Administrative organization and procedure (Table KD2)
	Public finance
480	General
	National revenue
482	General
	Taxation
484	General
	Particular taxes
487	Estate, inheritance, and gift taxes
	National defense. Military law
505	Comprehensive. General
	The military establishment. Armed Forces
506	General (Table KD3)

National defense. Military law
 The military establishment. Armed Forces -- Continued
507   Military criminal law and procedure (Table KD3)
Courts. Procedure
510   General
 Courts
515   General
  Particular courts
521   Supreme Court of Judicature of Northern Ireland (Table KD3)
523   Lower courts. Local courts (Table KD3)
  Judicial officers. Court employees
524   General (Table KD3)
524.5   Judges
524.7.A-Z   Others, A-Z
524.7.C65   Coroners. Medical examiners (Table KD4)
     Medical examiners see KDE524.7.C65
 Civil procedure
525   Court rules
527   General and comprehensive works
530.A-Z   Particular subjects, A-Z
530.J8   Jury and jurors
540   Criminal law
  Cf. KDE561+ Juvenile criminal law and procedure
 Criminal procedure
550   General
552   Defense
  Proceedings before juvenile courts see KDE561+
557   Execution of sentence. Imprisonment. Prison administration
 Juvenile criminal law and procedure. Administration of juvenile justice
561   General (Table KD3)
562   Juvenile courts (Table KD3)
 Local laws
570.A-Z   Counties, A-Z
   Subarrange each by Table KD5
580.A-Z   Cities, boroughs, towns, parishes, A-Z
   Subarrange each by Table KD5

	Law of Isle of Man. Channel Islands
	Isle of Man
	Legislative documents
	see J305.5
<21>	Debates
<22>	Proceedings
<24>	Committees
	Legislation
	Statutes
26.A-Z	Serials. By title or editor, A-Z
26.2	Monographs. By initial date of period covered
26.3	Indexes
	Law reports and related materials
	Manx law reports
27.A5-.A519	Serials
27.A52A-.A52Z	Monographic collections. By date of publication
	History
28	Sources
28.2	General works
29	General works
31.A-Z	Works for particular groups of users, A-Z
31.B87	Businesspeople. Foreign investors
	Foreign investors see KDG31.B87
	Property
33	General
33.2	Real property. Land law
	Contracts
35	General
	Particular contracts
35.2	Banking
42	Associations. Business associations. Partnership.
	Corporations (Table KD3)
	Social legislation
50	General
50.2	Labor law
50.3	Social insurance
	Including health insurance, workers' compensation, social security, etc.
60	Constitutional law
64	Local government
	Public finance
70	General
	National revenue
	Taxation
70.2	General
70.4.A-Z	Particular taxes, A-Z
70.4.I5	Income tax

	Isle of Man
	Public finance
	National revenue -- Continued
70.6	Tariff. Trade agreements. Customs duties
75	Courts. Civil procedure. Administration of justice (Table KD3)
85	Criminal law (Table KD3)
	Channel islands
120	Law reports and related materials
	Including court rolls
130	General and comprehensive works
138	Contracts. Commercial law (Table KD3)
	Public finance
160	General
	Taxation
162	General
164.A-Z	Particular taxes, A-Z
164.I5	Income tax
170	Criminal law
	Jersey
	Statutes and administrative regulations
	Statutes
220.A-Z	Serials. By title or editor, A-Z
221	Monographs
	By initial date of period covered
225	Regulations and orders
226	Indexes, tables, etc.
228	Customary law
	For the ancient laws and customs of the Duchy of Normandy see KD562
	Law reports and related materials
	Royal Court
232.A5-.A519	Serials
232.A52	Monographic collections. By date of publication
	Criminal trials and judicial investigations
240	Collections
242.A-Z	Particular trials or investigations. By defendant, A-Z
243	The legal profession
	History
245	Sources
246	General works (Table KD3)
	Biography
247	Collective
248.A-Z	Individual, A-Z
	Subarrange each by Table KD7
250	General and comprehensive works
	Persons

	Channel islands
	Jersey
	Persons -- Continued
260	General. Status. Capacity
261.A-Z	Particular subjects, A-Z
261.R4	Recording and registration. Registers of birth, marriages, and deaths
	Domestic relations. Family law
263	General
265.M3	Marriage. Husband and wife
	Property
268	General
	Real property
269	General
	Public property. Public restraint of private property
276	General
279	Housing
281	Trusts and trustees
284	Succession upon death
290	Associations. Business associations. Partnership. Corporations (Table KD3)
296	Insolvency and bankruptcy. Creditors' rights (Table KD3)
	Regulation of industry, trade, and commerce. Occupational law
300	General
	Food processing industries
310	Meat industry. Meat inspection
	Transportation and communication
320	General
	Aviation
323	General
324	Airports
	The professions
328.A3A-.A3Z	General
328.A4-Z	Particular professions, A-Z
328.D4	Dentists and dental specialists
	Social legislation
329	General
329.2	Labor law
329.3	Social insurance
	Including health insurance, workers' compensation, social security, etc.
331	Public health. Sanitation
337	Liquor laws
	Science and arts. Research
342	General
344	Libraries

	Channel islands
	Jersey -- Continued
351	Constitutional law
	Public finance
356	General
	Taxation
358	General
	Particular taxes
	Excise taxes. Taxes on transactions
363	General
	Particular commodities, services, transactions
	Alcoholic beverages. Liquor taxes
366	General
367.A-Z	Particular beverages, A-Z
367.B4	Beer
368.A4-Z	Other, A-Z
368.A5	Amusements
368.E7	Essences
368.T6	Tobacco
	Courts. Civil procedure
375	General
380.A-Z	Particular subjects, A-Z
380.E9	Execution of judgment
	Guernsey
	Statutes and administrative regulations
	Statutes
421.A-Z	Serials. By title or editor, A-Z
422	Monographs
	By initial date of period covered
425	Regulations and orders
428	Customary law
	Law reports and related materials
429.A5-.A519	Serials
429.A52	Monographic collections
	Each divided by date of publication
430	History
435	General and comprehensive works
440.A-Z	Particular subjects, A-Z
440.C56	Constitutional law
440.C6	Contracts. Commercial law
	Copyright see KDG440.I5
440.C7	Criminal law
440.I5	Intellectual and industrial property
	Patent law see KDG440.I5
440.P7	Property. Real property
440.T38	Taxation
	Trademarks see KDG440.I5

	Law of Ireland (Éire)
	Including works on Ireland as a whole before division in 1922
	Bibliography
21	General
22	Library catalogs
23	Indexes to periodical literature
	Official gazettes
25	Dublin Gazette (to 1937), Iris Oifigiuil (1937-)
<28-36>	Parliamentary publications
	see J307+
	Senate. Seanad
<28>	Proceedings
<29>	Journals
<30>	Debates
<31>	Bills
	House of representatives. Dáil
<33>	Proceedings
<34>	Journals
<35>	Debates
<36>	Bills
	Legislation
	Statutes
	Session laws. Statutes at large
38	Serials
39	Monographs
	By date of session or of initial session
	Collections. Revised editions
40.A-Z	Serials. By title, A-Z
41	Monographs. By date
43	Digests of statutes
	Indexes
44	General
45	Indexes to British statutes applicable in Ireland
46	Tables and other bibliographic aids
	Subordinate legislation
48	Statutory Rules, Orders, and Regulations
49	Indexes
50	Statutory instruments
51	Indexes
	Law reports and related materials
	For reports relating to particular subjects, see subject
	Highest court
	Including older courts
61	Irish House of Lords (Table KD14)
	Final court of appeals from 1783 to 1801. Reports cover the period from 1784 to 1796

KDK

	Law reports and related materials -- Continued
63	Several courts (Table KD14)
	Including highest court and lower courts, law courts and equity courts combined
	e.g. Law Reports (Ireland), 1878-1893, Law Reports, New Series, 1894-
	Superior courts
65	Circuit cases (Table KD14)
66	Court of Chancery (Table KD14)
67	Rolls Courts (Table KD14)
69	Court of Common Pleas (Table KD14)
70	King's (Queen's) Bench (Table KD14)
72	Court of Exchequer (Table KD14)
74	Nisi prius courts (Table KD14)
	Special courts and reports on particular subjects
	see the subject
	Crown (Criminal) cases see KDK1750+
	Ecclesiastical reports see KDK1860+
	Registration cases see KDK1287
78	Selective reports (Table KD14)
80	Digests of various reports
84	Law dictionaries. Words and phrases
	For bilingual and multilingual dictionaries see K50+
85	Form books
	Class here general works only
	For form books on a particular subject, see the subject
<87>	Periodicals
89	Judicial statistics
91	Directories
93	Society and bar association journals
	Class here only journals restricted to society or bar association activities
	For journals devoted to legal subjects, either wholly or in part see K1+
	Collections
95	Monographic series
96	Several authors. Festschriften
97	Minor collections. Anthologies
98	Individual authors
	Under each:
	.x By date
	.xA-.xZ By editor, A-Z
	Including collected opinions, instructions to juries, and charges to grand juries
	Trials
	Criminal trials and judicial investigations
	Collections

	Trials
	Criminal trials and judicial investigations
	Collections -- Continued
102	General
103.A-Z	Particular offenses, A-Z
103.M8	Murder
103.T7	Treason
104.A-Z	Particular trials. By defendant, A-Z
	Including commentaries and stories on a particular trial, and including records and briefs
	Civil trials
105	Collections
106.A-Z	Particular trials. By plaintiff, A-Z
	Including commentaries and stories on a particular trial, and including records and briefs
110	Legal research. Legal bibliography
	Legal education
	Including standards and criticism
113	General works (Table KD3)
115.A-Z	Particular law schools, A-Z
	The legal profession
120	General. Law as a career
121.7	Notaries (Table KD3)
	Practice of law
122	General (Table KD3)
	Biography of lawyers see KDK160+
	Economics of law practice
126	General
126.3	Fees
128	Attorneys' and legal secretaries' handbooks, manuals, desk-books, etc.
	Bar associations. Solicitors' associations
130	General
	For monographs and publications on particular subjects, see the subject
	For membership directories see KDK91
	For bar association and Law Society serial publications see KDK93
	Particular types of organizations
	National
	Barristers
132	King's Inns, Dublin
	Solicitors
134	Incorporated Law Society of Ireland
137	Legal aid (Table KD3)
	History
	For works on the history of a particular subject, see the subject

KDK

History -- Continued
  General
    Sources
141   General collections
145   Ancient laws. Brehon law
148   Judicial sources
             e.g. Calendar of the Justiciary Rolls (1295-1314), 1905-
                 1914, 1956; Calendar of the Patent and Close Rolls of
                 Chancery in Ireland (1514-1602, 1625-1633, 1861-
                 1863
150   Extracts. Readings
156   General works (Table KD3)
       Biography
160   Collective
161.A-Z   Individual, A-Z
             Subarrange each by Table KD7
166   Criticism. Legal reform. General administration of justice
           Cf. KDK1580 Judiciary
           Cf. KDK1752 Administration of criminal justice
       General and comprehensive works
         Collections see KDK95+
170   Treatises
171   Compends
172   Minor and popular works
173   Examination aids
174   Miscellaneous individual addresses and essays
             For collected essays see KDK95+
175.A-Z   Works for particular groups of users, A-Z
175.A43   Aged. Older people. Retired persons
175.B87   Businesspeople. Foreign investors
             Foreign investors see KDK175.B87
             Older people see KDK175.A43
175.P64   Police
             Retired persons see KDK175.A43
177.A-Z   Works on diverse legal aspects of a particular subject and
               falling within several branches of the law, A-Z
177.P82   Public interest law
       English law in Ireland see KDK141+
178   Equity
       Conflict of laws
179   General (Table KD3)
180.A-Z   Particular branches and subjects of the law, A-Z
180.M37   Marriage. Divorce. Marital property
180.P47   Persons
       General principles and concepts
181   Stare decisis
       Persons

Persons -- Continued
185 General. Status. Capacity
Natural persons
186 Civil status
Capacity and disability
188 General
189 Minors
Including liability
191 Persons of unsound mind. Mentally disordered
persons. Lunacy proceedings
195 Recording and registration. Registers of births,
marriages, and deaths. Vital statistics. Birth and
death certificates
Corporations. Juristic persons see KDK496+
Domestic relations. Family law
200 General (Table KD2)
201 Domestic relations courts and procedure (Table KD2)
For decisions of ecclesiastical courts see KDK1860
Marriage. Husband and wife
203 General (Table KD3)
203.6 Void and voidable marriage. Nullity (Table KD3)
204 Marriage settlements. Antenuptial contracts (Table KD2)
205 Divorce. Separation (Table KD2)
For decisions of ecclesiastical courts see KDK1860
Parent and child
207 General. Support (Table KD2)
209 Illegitimate children. Affiliation (Table KD2)
210 Adoption (Table KD2)
Property
215 General. Ownership
Real property. Land law
217 General (Table KD2)
Land tenure
Ownership and possession
219 General
Tenancy. Leaseholds. Landlord and tenant
222 General (Table KD2)
223 Rent. Rent control (Table KD2)
Particular kinds of leaseholds
225 Agricultural tenancy. Farm tenancy (Table KD2)
Including Land Law acts and Land Purchase acts
227 Ecclesiastical leases (Table KD3)
229 Town tenancy (Table KD3)
Rights and interests incident to ownership and
possession
235 Actions to recover the possession of land. Ejectment
240.A-Z Special topics, A-Z

KDK

	Property
	Real property. Land law
	Land tenure
	Ownership and possession
	Rights and interests incident to ownership and possession
	Special topics, A-Z -- Continued
	Burning of land see KDK572
240.E27	Easements. Servitudes
	Servitudes see KDK240.E27
	Tithes see KDK1880
240.W3	Water rights. Riparian rights
	Transfer of rights in land
	Transfer inter vivos
245	General. Vendor and purchaser. Real estate transactions
	Conveyances. Title investigation. Registration of title
247	General (Table KD3)
249	Registration of title (Table KD3)
251	Landed Estates Court (Table KD3)
	Including procedure
	Transfer by will see KDK360+
	Intestate succession see KDK360+
	Public property. Public restraints on private property
270	General
	Regional and city planning. Zoning. Building
275	General (Table KD3)
	Building laws
278	General (Table KD2)
280	Plumbing
	Housing
283	General (Table KD3)
286	Housing finance
290	Eminent domain. Compulsory purchase (Table KD3)
	Personal property
300	General
	Special kinds of property
	Intangible. Choses in action
	Intellectual and industrial property
315	General (Table KD3)
320	Copyright (Table KD2)
330	Patent law (Table KD3)
345	Trademarks. Marks of origin
	Trusts and trustees
350	General (Table KD3)
354	Charitable trusts (Table KD3)
	Succession upon death

Succession upon death -- Continued

360   General
365   Probate law and practice. Probate courts (Table KD2)
                For probate decisions of ecclesiastical courts see
                    KDK1860
367   Administration of decedents' estates (Table KD2)
            Contracts
370   General (Table KD2)
            Void and voidable contracts
374   General
375   Lack of genuine consent
                Including duress, undue influence, mistake, fraud,
                    misrepresentation
            Particular contracts
378   Comprehensive. Commercial law. Mercantile transactions
                (Table KD2)
380   Contract of service. Master and servant
            Contract for work and labor (Contract for services).
                Independent contractors
381   General (Table KD3)
382.A-Z   Particular types of contracts, A-Z
                Package tours see KDK382.T72
382.T72   Transportation contracts
                    Including travel contracts and package tours
                Travel contracts see KDK382.T72
384   Bill of sale (Table KD3)
405   Banking
            Particular kinds of banks
407   Building societies (Table KD2)
            Loan of money. Debtor and creditor. Interest. Usury
412   General (Table KD3)
414   Pawnbroking
417   Secured transactions (Table KD2)
420   Marketing of securities. Investments. Stock-exchange
                transactions (Table KD2)
            Carriers. Carriage of goods and passengers
430   General. Liability
            Carriage by sea. Maritime (Commercial) law. Admiralty
435   General (Table KD3)
437   High Court of Admiralty. Admiralty proceedings (Table
                    KD2)
440   Insurance (Table KD2)
                Including regulation of insurance business
            Torts
450   General
            Particular torts
452   Personal injuries. Death by wrongful act (Table KD2)

KDK

	Torts
	Particular torts -- Continued
453	Violation of privacy
454	Libel and slander (Table KD2)
	Negligence
460	General
461	Liability for condition and use of land (Table KD3)
462	Malpractice (Table KD2)
	For malpractice and tort liability of particular professions, see the profession
463.A-KD463.Z	Particular types of accidents, A-Z
463.T7	Traffic accidents. Automobile accidents
	Strict liability. Liability without fault
467	General
469	Damage caused by animals. Distress. Impounding distress
	Liability for torts of others. Vicarious liability
470.5	Employers' liability
470.7	Government torts (Table KD2)
471	Compensation to victims of crimes. Reparation (Table KD3)
	Including injuries to both person and property, and compensation by government
	Associations
490	General
	Corporations. Juristic persons
496	General
	Nonprofit corporations
498	General
	Particular types
	Foundations. Endowments see KDK354
	Business corporations. Companies
502	General (Table KD2)
	Particular subjects
504	Management
	Including board of directors and corporate officers
520	Dissolution. Liquidation. Winding up (Table KD3)
	Insolvency and bankruptcy. Creditors' rights
530	General (Table KD2)
533	Bankruptcy courts and procedure (Table KD2)
540	Composition. Receivership to avoid bankruptcy. Deeds of arrangement (Table KD3)
	Economic policy. Economic planning
	For economic emergency legislation see KDK1400+
543	General (Table KD2)
545	Foreign investment (Table KD2)
	Regulation of industry, trade, and commerce. Occupational law

	Regulation of industry, trade, and commerce. Occupational law -- Continued
550	General
	Trade regulations. Control of trade practices. Consumer protection
552	General. Unfair trade practices (Table KD3)
	Primary production. Extractive industries
	Agriculture. Forestry
570	General (Table KD3)
572	Conservation of agricultural and forest lands. Soil conservation. Burning of land
	Wildlife conservation
580	General
582	Game laws (Table KD3)
	Fishery
590	General (Table KD3)
591.A-Z	Particular fish or marine fauna, A-Z
	Including conservation, control, and regulation of industry
591.S3	Salmon
	Mining. Quarrying
610	General
615.A-Z	Particular mineral resources, A-Z
615.P4	Peat
	Manufacturing industries
	Textile industry
630	General
635.A-Z	Particular products, A-Z
635.L55	Linen fabrics
	Food processing industries
645	General
650	Diary industry. Dairy products industry
	Trade and commerce
670	General
	Retail trade
680	General (Table KD2)
685.A-Z	Particular products, A-Z
685.G74	Groceries (Table KD4)
	Service trades
690	General. Licensing
691.A-Z	Particular trades, A-Z
691.D39	Day care centers. Nursery schools
691.H6	Hotels. Inns. Restaurants
	Public utilities
695	General (Table KD2)
	Particular utilities
697	General (Table KD2)
698	Electricity (Table KD2)

KDK

	Regulation of industry, trade, and commerce. Occupational law -- Continued
	Transportation and communication
705	General
	Road traffic. Automotive transportation
710	General (Table KD3)
	Traffic regulations and enforcement
712	General (Table KD2)
713	Criminal provisions. Traffic violations. Drunk driving (Table KD2)
	Railroads
730	General
748	Local transit. Streetcar lines. Tramways
	Water transportation. Navigation and shipping
750	General (Table KD2)
764	Navigation and pilotage (Table KD3)
	Harbors and ports
768	General
769.A-Z	Particular harbors and ports, A-Z
769.D8	Dublin
774	Press law (Table KD2)
	Telecommunication
775	General works (Table KD2)
780	Radio and television broadcasting (Table KD2)
	Social legislation
800	General
	Labor law
802	General (Table KD2)
	Management-labor relations
804	General. Labor Court (Table KD2)
807	Labor unions. Trade unions
	Labor standards
815	General. Labor conditions
	Employment and dismissal
816	General (Table KD2)
820	Dismissal. Resignation. Job security (Table KD2)
	Wages. Minimum wage
830	General
840.A-Z	Particular industries and groups of employees, A-Z
840.B6	Boot and shoe workers
840.B7	Broom and brush industry
840.B8	Button industry
840.C3	Canning and preserving industry
840.C35	Carbonated beverage industry
840.C5	Clothing industry
840.D3	Dairy industry. Milk distribution
840.L5	Linen industry

	Social legislation
	Labor law
	Labor standards
	Wages. Minimum wage
	Particular industries and groups of employees, A-Z -- Continued
840.P3	Paper bag and box industry
	Shirtmaking industry see KDK840.C5
	Tailoring see KDK840.C5
840.T3	Tobacco manufacture
840.W3	Waste products industry
850	Hours of labor. Nightwork
857	Protection of labor. Labor hygiene and safety
860.A-Z	Labor law of particular industries or types of employment, A-Z
860.A3	Agricultural laborers
	Social insurance
870	General
	Particular branches
873	Health insurance (Table KD3)
878	Workers' compensation (Table KD2)
885	Social security. Retirement. Old age and disability pensions. Survivors' benefits
895	Public welfare. Public assistance. Poor laws (Table KD2)
	Public health. Sanitation. Environmental pollution
910	General (Table KD3)
	Contagious and infectious diseases
918	General
919.A-Z	Particular diseases, A-Z
919.T8	Tuberculosis
	Environmental pollution
920	General (Table KD3)
924.A-Z	Other public health hazards and measures, A-Z
924.R44	Refuse disposal (Table KD4)
	Medical legislation
926	General
928	Hospitals and other medical institutions
931	The mentally ill (Table KD3)
	For lunacy proceedings see KDK191
932.A-Z	Disorders of character, behavior, and intelligence, A-Z
932.A5	Alcoholism (Table KD4)
940	Food law
952	Alcohol. Alcoholic beverages. Liquor laws (Table KD3)
	Control of social activities
975	General
978	Games of chance. Gambling. Lotteries
	Education

KDK

	Education -- Continued
1050	General (Table KD3)
1070	Teachers (Table KD3)
	Science and arts. Research
1090	General
1092	Historic buildings and monuments. Architectural landmarks (Table KD2)
	Including preservation of cultural property
1100	Archives. Historical documents. Record management
1101	Access to public records. Freedom of information (Table KD2)
	Including databases and data protection
	Constitutional law
	Sources
1200	Collections
	Particular sources
1201	Individual sources other than constitutions
	Arrange chronologically
1203	Particular constitutions. By date of constitution

Under each:

.A15	*Collections*
.A2	*Proceedings. Debates*
.A25-.A259	*Drafts of constitution*
	Arranged chronologically
.A28	*Miscellaneous documents*
.A285	*Contemporary criticism. Private proposals and drafts*
.A29	*Works on the legislative history (origin and making) of the constitution*
.A3-.A39	*Texts of the constitution*
	Arranged chronologically

	History
1205	General (Table KD3)
	By period
1210	To the Act of Union, 1800
1215	From 1800 to 1920
1220	Recent history, since 1920
1225	Constitutional law in general (Table KD3)
	Constitutional principles
1227	Separation of powers. Delegation of powers (Table KD2)
	Sources and relationships of law
1227.5	International and municipal law. Treaties and agreements
1228	Statutory law and delegated legislation. Ordinances. Rules. Select Committee on Statutory Instruments (Table KD2)

Constitutional law -- Continued
  Individual and state
1250   Nationality and citizenship
    Civil and political rights and liberties
1255   General (Table KD2)
      Discrimination
1258   General
1259   Sex discrimination (Table KD2)
1260.A-Z   Discrimination against particular groups, A-Z
1260.C45   Catholics (Table KD4)
    Particular political rights and liberties
1261   Linguistic rights. Bilingualism (Table KD2)
1262   Freedom of expression. Censorship. Freedom of the press
    Control of individuals
1270   Aliens (Table KD2)
      Including immigration
  Church and state see KDK1850
  Organs of the government
    The people
      Election law
1285   General (Table KD2)
1287   Suffrage. Registration (Table KD3)
1288   Election districts. Apportionment (Table KD3)
1295   Local elections
1298   Corrupt practices
    The legislature
      The Parliament. Oireachtas
1305   History (Table KD3)
1306   General. Organization
1308   Rules and procedure. Standing orders (Table KD3)
    Legal status of legislators
1310   General
1312   Salaries, pensions, etc.
    Contested elections
1315   General
      Cases
1316   Collections. By date
1317.A-Z   Particular cases. By incumbent, A-Z
    The Senate. Seanad Éireann
1320   General
1322   Rules and procedure (Table KD2)
    House of Representatives. Dáil Éireann
1330   General
1332   Rules and procedure (Table KD2)
    The executive branch
1340   General. Executive power

KDK

	Constitutional law
	Organs of the government
	The executive branch -- Continued
1342	The President
1344	The Prime Minister and the Cabinet
1346	Executive departments. Boards
	Prefer classification by subject
1348	Advisory committees. Commissions of inquiry
1350	Civil service
	Local government
1365	General (Table KD3)
1367	Municipal government. Municipal corporations (Table KD3)
1375	Police and power of the police
	Administrative organization and procedure
1380	General. Administrative law (Table KD2)
1382	Judicial review
	Government measures in time of war, national emergency, or
	economic crisis. Emergency economic legislation
1400	General (Table KD3)
	Rent control see KDK223
	Public finance
1430	General (Table KD3)
1432	Money. Currency. Coinage
1434	Foreign exchange regulations
1438	Public debts. Loans. Bond issues
	National revenue
1440	General
	Particular sources of revenue
	Taxation
1443	General (Table KD2)
	Tax administration and procedure
1445	General
1448	Double taxation
	Particular taxes
	Income tax
1452	General (Table KD2)
1458	Payroll deduction. Withholding tax (Table KD2)
	Income of business organizations
1460	General. Corporation income tax (Table KD3)
1462	Corporation profits tax
	Property taxes. Taxation of capital
1467	General (Table KD3)
1468	Wealth tax (Table KD3)
1480	Estate duty. Legacy and succession duty
	Excise taxes. Taxes on transactions
1490	General
1491	Value-added tax (Table KD2)

Public finance
National revenue
General
Particular sources of revenue
Taxation
Particular taxes
Excise taxes. Taxes on transactions -- Continued
1492.A-Z   Particular commodities, services, transactions, A-Z
1492.A5   Alcoholic beverages. Liquor taxes
Particular methods of assessment and collection
For assessment and collection of particular taxes, see the taxes, e.g. Income tax
1494   Stamp duties (Table KD3)
Tariff. Trade agreements. Customs duties
For regional trade and tariff agreements, see the appropriate region
For trade and tariff agreements not limited to a region see K4600+
For trade and tariff agreements with the United States see KF6668.A+
1510   General (Table KD3)
Trade agreements. Particular tariffs
1512   General
1514.A-Z   Particular commodities, A-Z
1514.C5   Clothing
1516   Customs administration
Local finance
1520   General
Taxation
1523   General
Particular taxes
1526   Real property taxes. Poor rate
National defense. Military law
1540   Comprehensive. General
The military establishment. Armed Forces
1545   Armed Forces
Military criminal law and procedure
1560   General. Comprehensive
1562   Criminal law (Table KD3)
Courts. Procedure
1580   Administration of justice. Organization of the judiciary (Table KD3)
1582   Judiciary Committee
Court organization and procedure
1586   General (Table KD2)
1588.A-Z   Special aspects, A-Z

Courts. Procedure
  Court organization and procedure -- Continued
    Courts before 1924
1590   General. Comprehensive (Table KD3)
      Particular courts
        Including procedure in general before such courts
        Superior courts
          Superior courts preceding the Supreme Court of
            Judicature (Ireland) Act, 1877
1595-1597   Court of Chancery (Table KD15)
           Court of Exchequer
1600-1602   General (Table KD15)
1603   Equity side (Table KD3)
           Court of Matrimonial Causes and Matters see
             KDK201
1605-1607   The Supreme Court of Judicature (Table KD15)
        Lower courts. Local courts. Lesser historical courts
1610-1612   Justices of the Peace. Courts of Quarter Sessions.
            Petty Sessions (Table KD15)
            Cf. KDK1820 Criminal procedure. Summary
              conviction
          Manorial courts. Courts baron. Courts leet
1613   General (Table KD3)
1614.A-Z   Particular, A-Z
1615-1617   County courts (Table KD15)
1620   Courts of the assistant barrister. Civil Bill Courts
    Courts since 1924
1625   General. Collective (Table KD2)
1627   Attorney General (Table KD2)
      Particular courts
        Including procedure in general before such courts
        Court of final appeal
          Supreme Court
           For appeals see KDK1713
        Courts of first instance
1630-1632   High Court (Table KD15)
1635-1637   Circuit Courts (Table KD15)
1640-1642   District courts (Table KD15)
        Courts of special jurisdiction
          Bankruptcy courts see KDK533
          Domestic relations courts see KDK201
          High Court of Admiralty see KDK437
          Labor Court see KDK804
          Landed Estates Court see KDK251
          Probate court see KDK365
    Judicial officers. Court employees
1650   General

	Courts. Procedure
	Court organization and procedure
	Judicial officers. Court employees -- Continued
1652	Judges
	Other
1655	General. Collective
1656.A-Z	Particular, A-Z
1656.C5	Clerks of court. Administrative officers
	Justices of the Peace see KDK1610+
	Justices of the Peace (Criminal jurisdiction) see
	KDK1820
1656.S4	Sheriffs
	Civil procedure
	General
	Legislation
	Statutes
1660.A3	Collections
	By date of publication
1660.A4-.A419	Particular acts
	Arrange chronologically by means of successive Cutter
	numbers, according to date of original enactment
	or revision of law
	Court rules
	For court rules of a particular court, see the court
	General. Comprehensive
1661.A3	Collections
	By date of publication
1661.A4-.A419	Particular rules
	Arrange chronologically by means of successive
	Cutter numbers, according to date of adoption,
	revision, or consolidation of rules
1666	General works (Table KD2)
1668	Nisi prius procedure
	Actions
1672	General
1674	Process and service (Table KD3)
1676	Pleading and motions (Table KD3)
	For pleading in general before particular court systems or
	courts, see the courts
	Pretrial procedure
1680	General. Deposition and discovery. Interrogatories
	(Table KD3)
	Trial
1685	General
1688	Evidence (Table KD3)
	Jury and jurors
1691	General (Table KD3)

	Courts. Procedure
	Civil procedure
	Trial
	Jury and jurors
	General -- Continued
	Special aspects
1692	Women jurors
	Judgment
1694	General
1695	Costs. Fees (Table KD3)
	Remedies and special proceedings
1698	General
1700	Receivers in equity
	Possessory actions, ejectment see KDK235
1702	Execution of judgment (Table KD3)
	Appellate procedure
1710	General (Table KD2)
1711	Intermediate appeals
1713	Appeals to Supreme Court
1745	Arbitration and award. Commercial arbitration (Table KD2)
	Criminal law
	Cf. KDK1560+ Military criminal law and procedure
	Cf. KDK1836+ Juvenile criminal law and procedure
1750	General. Comprehensive (Table KD2)
1752	Administration of criminal justice. Reform of criminal law, enforcement, and procedure
	Criminal liability
1760	General (Table KD3)
	Exemption from liability. Defenses. Diminished responsibility
1763	General (Table KD3)
	Particular defenses
1764	Insanity (Table KD3)
	Particular crimes
	Offenses against the person
1770	General (Table KD2)
1771.A-Z	Particular offenses, A-Z
1771.A25	Abortion (Table KD4)
1771.S49	Sexual offenses (Table KD4)
	Offenses against property
1773	General (Table KD2)
1774.A-Z	Particular offenses, A-Z
1774.F73	Fraud (Table KD4)
1774.L37	Larceny (Table KD4)
	Offenses against government and public order
1775	Political offenses
	Offenses against the administration of justice

Criminal law
  Particular crimes
    Offenses against the administration of justice -- Continued
1780   Contempt of court
    Offenses against public convenience and morality. Crimes without victims
1786   General (Table KD3)
1787.A-Z   Particular offenses, A-Z
1787.B42   Blasphemy (Table KD4)
1787.O3   Obscenity (Table KD4)
  Criminal procedure
1800   General (Table KD2)
1806   Information. Indictment. Public prosecutor. Grand jury (Table KD3)
     For collected instructions see KDK98
     For individual instructions see KDK174
1807   Discovery (Table KD3)
   Trial
1810   General
1815   Evidence
1820   Proceedings before justices of the peace and magistrates' courts. Summary conviction (Table KD3)
   Proceedings before juvenile courts see KDK1836+
1825   Appeals. Appellate procedure
   Execution of sentence
1831   Imprisonment. Prison administration. Prison discipline
     Particular types of penal and correctional institutions
      Juvenile detention homes see KDK1840
1833   Forfeitures (Table KD3)
   Government compensation to victims of crimes see KDK471
  Military criminal law and procedure see KDK1560+
  Juvenile criminal law and procedure. Administration of juvenile justice
1836   General (Table KD3)
1837   Juvenile courts (Table KD3)
   Criminal procedure
1839   General (Table KD3)
    Execution of sentence
     Imprisonment
1840   Juvenile detention homes. Reformatories. Borstal institutions (Table KD3)
Ecclesiastical law
1850   General. Church and state
   Sources
1855   Enactments of Parliament affecting the Church
    Ecclesiastical law reports and related materials
1860   Reports

KDK

	Ecclesiastical law
	General. Church and state -- Continued
1865	General works (Table KD3)
	Particular subjects
	Benefices. Church property. Tithes
1875	General
1878	Church property
	For ecclesiastical leases see KDK227
1880	Tithes (Table KD3)
	Discrimination on the grounds of religion see KDK1260.A+
	Particular churches and denominations
	The Church of Ireland
1890	General (Table KD2)
1892.A-Z	Particular topics, A-Z
1895	The Methodist Church in Ireland
	Local laws
1910.A-Z	Counties, A-Z
	Subarrange each by Table KD5
1930.A-Z	Cities, boroughs, towns, parishes, A-Z
	Subarrange each by Table KD5
1950.A-Z	Other, A-Z

1	Bibliography
(1.5)	Surveys of legal research
	The Library of Congress discontinued use of this form subdivision in 2008
	see KD1 2 or KD1 9.A7+
2	Periodicals
	Class here periodicals consisting primarily of informative materials (newsletters, bulletins, etc.) relating to a particular subject, and annuals containing information about the year past, such as statistics, etc.
	For periodicals consisting predominantly of legal articles, regardless of subject matter and jurisdiction, see K1+
(2.1)	Yearbooks. Statistics
	The Library of Congress discontinued use of this form subdivision in 2008
	see KD1 2
(2.3)	Society publications
	The Library of Congress discontinued use of this form subdivision in 2008
	see KD1 2 or KD1 9.A7+
(2.5)	Congresses and conferences. By date
	The Library of Congress discontinued use of this form subdivision in 2008
	see KD1 9.A2
	Legislative documents
(3)	Bills. By date
	The Library of Congress discontinued use of this form subdivision in 2008
	see KD1 3.5
(3.2)	Reports of Parliamentary committees
	The Library of Congress discontinued use of this form subdivision in 2008
	see KD1 3.5
(3.4)	Other documents, such as reports of Royal commissions, departmental committees, law reform committees, staff reports, etc.
	The Library of Congress discontinued use of this form subdivision in 2008
	see KD1 3.5
3.5	Reports of Parliamentary committees, Royal commissions, Departmental committees, law reform committees, staff reports, and bills
	Statutes. Regulations. Orders. Rules of practice, etc.
	Statutes
	Collections. Compilations
	Including collections consisting of both statutes and regulations
3.99	Serials

TABLES

	Statutes. Regulations. Orders. Rules of practice, etc.
	Statutes
	Collections. Compilations -- Continued
4	Monographs. By date of publication
(4.5-.579)	Particular acts

         The Library of Congress discontinued use of this span of numbers in 2008

         see KD1 4.58\<date>

4.58\<date>   Particular acts

         Arrange chronologically by appending the date of original enactment or total revision of the law to this number and deleting any trailing zeros. If more than one law is enacted in a single year, append a lowercase letter to the year (b, c, d, etc.) for each subsequent law

         Under each:

	Legislative history
.A15	*Compilations of documents. Treatises. By date of publication*
(.A16)	*Treatises see .A15, above*
	Texts
	Including official editions, with or without annotations, and annotated editions and commentaries
(.A2)	*Serials*
	Serial editions are classed in the number for Serials under "Collections. Compilations," above
.A3	*Monographs. By date of publication*
(.A5-.Z)	*Annotated editions. Commentaries. By author of commentary or annotations see .A3, above*

         Including collections consisting of an individual act and its associated regulations

    Regulations. Orders. Rules of practice, etc. (Subordinate legislation. Prerogative instruments)

      Collections. Compilations

         For collections consisting of both statutes and regulations see KD1 3.99+

         For collections consisting of an individual act and its associated regulations see KD1 4.58\<date>

4.599   Serials

         Including serial editions of individual regulations

	Statutes. Regulations. Orders. Rules of practice, etc.
	Regulations. Orders. Rules of practice, etc. (Subordinate legislation. Prerogative instruments)
	Collections. Compilations
4.6	Monographs. By date of publication
(4.7-.719)	Particular regulations, orders, rules of practice, etc. (or groups of regulations, etc. adopted as a whole)

4.6   Monographs. By date of publication

(4.7-.719)   Particular regulations, orders, rules of practice, etc. (or groups of regulations, etc. adopted as a whole)
The Library of Congress discontinued use of this span of numbers in 2008
see KD1 4.72

4.72   Particular regulations, orders, rules of practice, etc. (or groups of regulations, etc. adopted as a whole). By date of adoption or promulgation
Including both official and unofficial editions, with or without annotations
For rules of practice before a separately classed agency, see the issuing agency

(4.73)   Digests of statutes and regulations
The Library of Congress discontinued use of this form subdivision in 2008
see KD1 4.79

(4.75)   Citators for statutes and regulations
The Library of Congress discontinued use of this form subdivision in 2008
see KD1 4.79

(4.77)   Indexes. By date
The Library of Congress discontinued use of this form subdivision in 2008
see KD1 4.79

(4.78)   Collections of summaries of legislation
The Library of Congress discontinued use of this form subdivision in 2008
see KD1 4.79

4.79   Finding aids for statutes and regulations
Including digests, citators, indexes, and summaries
Class citators for both cases and legislation with citators for court decisions or decisions of regulatory agencies

   Court decisions
    Reports

5.A2   Serials
5.A5-Z   Monographic collections
5.3   Digests of reports (Case finders)
5.5   Citators
Including citators for both cases and statutes
5.7   Indexes
   Decisions of regulatory agencies. Rulings
    Reports

TABLES

	Decisions of regulatory agencies. Rulings
	Reports -- Continued
6.A2	Serials
6.A5-Z	Monographic collections
6.2	Digests of reports (Case finders)
6.25	Citators
6.28	Indexes
(6.3.A-Z)	Collections of summaries of cases ("Digests" of cases decided by courts or regulatory agencies). By editor, A-Z
	The Library of Congress discontinued use of this form subdivision in 2008
	see KD1 5.3 or KD1 6.2
(6.5)	Encyclopedias
	The Library of Congress discontinued use of this form subdivision in 2008
	see KD1 7.5
7	Form books
7.5	Dictionaries. Encyclopedias
(8)	Casebooks. Readings
	The Library of Congress discontinued use of this form subdivision in 2008
	see KD1 9.A7+
	General works
(9.A1)	Collections. Monographic series
	The Library of Congress discontinued use of this form subdivision in 2008
	see KD1 2 or KD1 9.A7+
9.A2	Congresses. Symposia. Collected papers and essays
(9.A3-.A499)	Official reports and monographs
	The Library of Congress discontinued use of this form subdivision in 1994. After 1994, official reports and monographs are classed as periodicals or general works
9.A7-Z	Treatises. Monographs
(9.3)	Compends. Outlines. Minor works
	The Library of Congress discontinued use of this form subdivision in 2008
	see KD1 9.6
(9.4)	Examination aids
	The Library of Congress discontinued use of this form subdivision in 2008
	see KD1 9.6
(9.5)	Popular works
	The Library of Congress discontinued use of this form subdivision in 2008
	see KD1 9.6

General works -- Continued

9.6   Examination aids. Popular works

                            Including compends, outlines, and works for particular classes of users

(9.7.A-Z)   Foreign language treatises. By language, A-Z

                            The Library of Congress discontinued use of this form subdivision in 2008

                            see KD1 9.A7+

TABLES

.A1	Bibliography
.A13	Periodicals
	Class here periodicals consisting primarily of informative material (newsletters, bulletins, etc.) relating to a particular subject, and annuals containing information about the year past, such as statistics, etc.
	For periodicals consisting predominantly of legal articles, regardless of subject matter and jurisdiction, see K1+
(.A152)	Yearbooks. Statistics
	The Library of Congress discontinued use of this form subdivision in 2008
	see KD2 .A13
(.A16)	Society publications
	The Library of Congress discontinued use of this form subdivision in 2008
	see KD2 .A13 or KD2 .A9+
(.A17)	Congresses and conferences. By date
	The Library of Congress discontinued use of this form subdivision in 2008
	see KD2 .A75
	Legislative documents
(.A2)	Bills. By date
	The Library of Congress discontinued use of this form subdivision in 2008
	see KD2 .A26
(.A22)	Reports of Parliamentary committees
	The Library of Congress discontinued use of this form subdivision in 2008
	see KD2 .A26
(.A25)	Other documents, such as reports of Royal commissions, departmental committees, law reform committees, staff reports, etc.
	The Library of Congress discontinued use of this form subdivision in 2008
	see KD2 .A26
.A26	Reports of Parliamentary committees, Royal commissions, Departmental committees, law reform committees, staff reports, and bills
	Statutes. Regulations. Orders. Rules of practice, etc.
	Statutes
	Collections. Compilations
	Including collections consisting of both statutes and regulations
.A29	Serials
.A3	Monographs. By date of publication

	Statutes. Regulations. Orders. Rules of practice, etc.
	Statutes
(.A31-.A328)	Particular acts
	The Library of Congress discontinued use of this span of numbers in 2008
	see KD2 .A328<date>
.A328<date>	Particular acts
	Arrange chronologically by appending the date of original enactment or total revision of the law to this number and deleting any trailing zeros. If more than one law is enacted in a single year, append a lowercase letter to the year (b, c, d, etc.) for each subsequent law

Under each:

	Legislative history
.xA15	*Compilations of documents. Treatises. By date of publication*
(.xA16)	*Treatises see .xA15, above*
	Texts
	Including official editions, with or without annotations, and annotated editions and commentaries
(.xA2)	*Serials*
	Serial editions are classed in the number for Serials under "Collections. Compilations," above
.xA3	*Monographs. By date of publication*
(.xA5-.xZ)	*Annotated editions. Commentaries. By author of commentary or annotations see .xA3, above*

	Including collections consisting of an individual act and its associated regulations
	Regulations. Orders. Rules of practice, etc. (Subordinate legislation. Prerogative instruments)
	Collections. Compilations
	For collections consisting of both statutes and regulations see KD2 .A29+
	For collections consisting of and individual act and its associated regulations see KD2 .A328<date>
.A329	Serials
	Including serial editions of individual regulations
.A33	Monographs. By date of publication

                                    Statutes. Regulations. Orders. Rules of practice, etc.

Regulations. Orders. Rules of practice, etc. (Subordinate legislation. Prerogative instruments)

(.A35-.A369) Particular regulations, orders, rules of practice, etc. (or groups of regulations, etc. adopted as a whole)

The Library of Congress discontinued use of this span of numbers in 2008

see KD2 .A3692

.A3692 Particular regulations, orders, rules of practice, etc. (or groups of regulations, etc. adopted as a whole). By date of adoption or promulgation

Including both official and unofficial editions, with or without annotations

For rules of practice before separately classed agency, see issuing agency

(.A3698) Indexes. By date

The Library of Congress discontinued use of this form subdivision in 2008

see KD2 .A4

.A37-.A379 Collections of summaries of legislation

The Library of Congress discontinued use of this form subdivision in 2008

see KD2 .A4

.A4 Finding aids for statutes and regulations

Including digests, citators, indexes, and summaries

Class citators for both cases and legislation with citators for court decisions or decisions of regulatory agencies

Court decisions

Reports

.A5-.A519 Serials

.A52 Monographic collections

.A53 Digests of reports (Case finders)

.A535 Citators

Including citators for both cases and statutes

.A54 Indexes

Decisions of regulatory agencies. Rulings

Reports

.A55-.A559 Serials

.A56 Monographic collections

.A57 Digests of reports (Case finders)

.A575 Citators

.A58 Indexes

(.A59A-.A59Z) Collections of summaries of cases ("Digests" of cases decided by courts or regulatory agencies). By editor, A-Z

The Library of Congress discontinued use of this form subdivision in 2008

see KD2 .A53 or KD2 .A57

(.A6)	Encyclopedias
	The Library of Congress discontinued use of this form subdivision in 2008
	see KD2 .A68
.A65	Form books
.A68	Dictionaries. Encyclopedias
(.A7)	Casebooks. Readings
	The Library of Congress discontinued use of this form subdivision in 2008
	see KD2 .A9+
	General works
(.A73)	Collections. Monographic series
	The Library of Congress discontinued use of this form subdivision in 2008
	see KD2 .A13 or KD2 .A9+
.A75	Congresses. Symposia. Collected papers and essays
(.A8-.A89)	Official reports and monographs
	The Library of Congress discontinued use of this form subdivision in 1994. After 1994, official reports and monographs are classed as periodicals or general works
.A9-.Z8	Treatises. Monographs
(.Z9)	Compends. Outlines. Minor works
	The Library of Congress discontinued use of this form subdivision in 2008
	see KD2 .A9+

TABLES

.A1	Bibliography
.A13	Periodicals
	Class here periodicals consisting primarily of informative material (newsletters, bulletins, etc.) relating to a particular subject
	For periodicals consisting predominantly of legal articles, regardless of subject matter and jurisdiction, see K1+
.A25	Legislative documents. By date
	Statutes. Regulations. Orders. Rules of practice, etc.
	Statutes
	Including collections consisting of both statutes and regulations
.A29	Serials
.A3	Monographs. By date of publication
	Regulations. Orders. Rules of practice, etc. (Subordinate legislation. Prerogative instruments)
	For collections consisting of both statutes and regulations see KD3 .A29+
.A329	Serials
.A33	Monographs. By date of publication
	Court decisions
	Reports
.A38	Serials
.A4	Monographic collections
	Decisions of regulatory agencies. Rulings
	Reports
.A44	Serials
.A45	Monographic collections
.A59	Collections of summaries of cases ("Digests" of cases decided by courts or regulatory agencies). By editor, A-Z
.A65	Form books
.A68	Dictionaries
(.A7)	Casebooks. Readings
	The Library of Congress discontinued use of this form division in 2008
	see KD3 .A9+
	General works
(.A73)	Collections. Monographic series
	The Library of Congress discontinued use of this form division in 2008
	see KD3 .A13 or KD3 .A9+
.A75	Congresses. Symposia. Collected papers and essays
(.A8-.A89)	Official reports and monographs
	The Library of Congress discontinued use of this form subdivision in 1994. After 1994, official reports and monographs are classed as periodicals or general works
.A9-.Z8	Treatises. Monographs

General works -- Continued
(.Z9)   Compends. Outlines. Minor works
The Library of Congress discontinued use of this form division in
2008
see KD3 .A9+

.xA15-.xA199	Periodicals
	Including gazettes, bulletins, circulars, etc.
.xA2	Legislative documents. By date
.xA3	Treaties. Statutes. Statutory orders (Collective or individual).
	By date
.xA52	Cases. Decisions (Collective or individual). By date
.xA7-.xZ9	General works. Treatises

.xA15	Bibliography. Checklists. Sales catalogs
	Documents
	Class documents relating to a particular subject with the subject
.xA2-.xA24	Serials
.xA25	Monographs. By date of publication
.xA27	Statutes affecting counties, cities, etc. By date
	Collections of charters, ordinances, and local laws
.xA3-.xA34	Serials
.xA35	Monographs
	By date of publication
	Local law reports. Collections of decisions and rulings
	Class decisions and rulings relating to a particular subject with the subject
.xA4-.xA44	Serials
.xA45	Monographs
	By date of publication
	Yearbooks. Statistics. Surveys of local administration of justice
.xA6-.xA62	Serials
.xA63	Monographs
	By date of publication
	General works. Local legal history
.xA8-.xA84	Sources
.xA85-.xZ	Treatises. Monographs
.x2A-.x2Z	Particular subjects, A-Z
	Each subject arranged alphabetically by author
	Building see KD5 .x2Z6+
	City government see KD5 .x2G6+
	City planning and redevelopment see KD5 .x2Z6+
.x2C6-.x2C69	Correctional and penal institutions
	County government see KD5 .x2G6+
.x2C7-.x2C79	Criminal offenses (Violations of local law) and local administration of criminal justice
.x2E4-.x2E49	Education. Teachers. Schools
.x2F54-.x2F549	Finance. Taxation
.x2F55-.x2F559	Fire prevention and control
.x2G6-.x2G69	Government
.x2H3-.x2H39	Health regulations
.x2L6-.x2L69	Lodging houses
.x2M5-.x2M59	Mining. Quarrying
.x2M8-.x2M89	Municipal services
	Penal institutions see KD5 .x2C6+
.x2P65-.x2P659	Police
.x2P68-.x2P689	Power supply
.x2P74-.x2P749	Property
.x2P915-.x2P9159	Public baths
	Public finance. Taxation see KD5 .x2F54+
	Public health see KD5 .x2H3+

TABLES

	Particular subjects, A-Z -- Continued
.x2P92-.x2P929	Public property
.x2P93-.x2P939	Public safety
	Public welfare see KD5 .x2S6+
	Schools see KD5 .x2E4+
.x2S6-.x2S69	Social legislation. Public welfare
	Taxation see KD5 .x2F54+
	Teachers see KD5 .x2E4+
.x2T6-.x2T69	Traffic regulation
.x2T7-.x2T79	Transportation. Local and metropolitan transit
	Water supply see KD5 .x2M8+
.x2Z6-.x2Z69	Zoning. Building. City planning and redevelopment

.xA2-.xA29	Reports
	Arranged chronologically
.xA3-.xA49	Abridgments. Digests
.xA5-.xA69	Indexes. Tables

TABLES

.xA3	Autobiography. By date
	Letters. Correspondence
.xA4	General collections
	By date of publication
.xA41-.xA49	Collections of letters to particular individuals
	By correspondent, alphabetically
	Correspondence on a particular subject is classed with the subject
.xA5-.xZ	Biography and criticism

| .x | General |
| .x1.A-Z | Particular cases. By employer, A-Z |

TABLES

| .A2A-.A2Z | Sources |
| .A3-.Z | Treatises. Monographs |

1	General (Table KD3)
1.2	Requisitioned land and war works
1.3	Control of manpower
	Enemy property. Alien property
	see KD813
	Trading with the enemy
	see KD1607
	Debtors' relief
1.4	General moratorium (Table KD3)
	Deferment of executions
	see KD7598
	Insolvent debtors' wartime relief
	see KD2168
	Rationing
2	General (Table KD3)
2.1.A-Z	By commodity or service, A-Z
	Price control. Profiteering
2.4	General
2.5.A-Z	By commodity or service, A-Z
	Rent
	see KD902
	Wage control
	see KD3120
	Industrial priorities and allocations. Commodity control
3	General (Table KD2)
3.1.A-Z	By industry or commodity, A-Z
3.6	War damage compensation. Foreign claims settlement (Table KD3)
4.A-Z	Other, A-Z

TABLES

.A2	Unannotated texts. By date of publication
.A3-.Z	Annotated editions. Commentaries
	By author of annotation or commentary

.A2-.A29   Legislative documents
                            Legislation
.A295-.A299   Serials
.A3   Monographs. By date
.A5-.A59   Decisions. By court, agency, etc.
.A7-.A79   Miscellaneous documents
.A8-.Z   General works. Treatises. Monographs

TABLES

.xA2-.xA29	Legislative documents
	Legislation
.xA295-.xA299	Serials
.xA3	Monographs. By date
.xA5-.xA59	Decisions. By court, agency, etc.
.xA7-.xA79	Miscellaneous documents
.xA8-.xZ	General works. Treatises. Monographs

0	Reports. By initial date of period covered	
	Under each:	
	.A2A-.A2Z	*Serials. By compiler, editor, or title, A-Z*
	.A3-.Z	*Monographs. By compiler, editor, or title, A-Z*
0.1	Abridgments. Digests	
	By editor, or title	
0.2	Indexes. Tables	
	Indexes relating to a particular publication, reporter system, or digest (e.g. descriptive-word indexes) are classed with that publication	
0.4	Records and briefs. By citation or docket number	

TABLES

0	General (Table KD3)
	Civil procedure
	Court rules
1.A3	Collections. By date of publication
1.A4-.A419	Particular rules
	Arrange chronologically by means of successive Cutter numbers according to date of adoption, revision, or consolidation of rules
2	General works (Table KD3)
	Including general pleading

A

Abbreviations: KD400
Abortion: KD7969
  Ireland (Éire): KDK1771.A25
Absence, Leaves of
  Labor law: KD3142
Absence, missing persons, and
  presumption of death: KD729
  Scotland: KDC354
Absentee voting: KD4342
Abstracts of title: KD971+
Access to children: KD779+
Access to public records: KD3756
  Ireland (Éire): KDK1101
Accident control
  Public safety: KD3508+
Accident insurance: KD1874+
Accidents, Marine
  Liability: KD1825+
Accidents, Traffic
  Ireland (Éire): KDK463.T7
Accord and satisfaction: KD1594
Accountants
  Expert witnesses: KD7524.15
  Regulation of profession: KD2974
  Works for: KD665.A25
Accounting: KD2042
  Corporations: KD2098
  Decedents' estates: KD1530.A3
  Law office management: KD495.A3
  Local finance: KD5712
  Public finance: KD5295
  Trustees: KD1495
Acquisition of personal property:
  KD1214+
Act of State: KD4450
Action on the case
  Civil procedure: KD7448.C3
Actions
  Civil procedure: KD7445+
  Ireland (Éire): KDK1672+
Acts of Sederunt
  Scotland: KDC875.A+
Acts of the General Assembly
  Ecclesiastical law
  Scotland: KDC960

Administration of courts: KD7122.5
Administration of criminal justice:
  KD7876, KD8471+
  Ireland (Éire): KDK1752
  London: KD9085+
  Northern Ireland: KDE561+
  Scotland: KDC915
Administration of decedents' estates:
  KD1528+
  Ireland (Éire): KDK367
  Northern Ireland: KDE151
  Scotland: KDC468
Administration of justice: KD654
  Courts and procedure: KD6870+
  Ireland (Éire): KDK1580
  Isle of Man: KDG75
  North Ireland: KDE87
  Scotland: KDC320
  Wales: KD9480
Administration of juvenile justice:
  KDC951+
  Ireland (Éire): KDK1836+
Administrative and constitutional law:
  KD3930+
Administrative organization and
  procedure: KD4871+
  Ireland (Éire): KDK1380+
  Northern Ireland: KDE478
  Scotland: KDC801
Administrative tribunals: KD4890
Administrators, Arts
  Works for: KD665.A77
Admiralty and ecclesiastical precedents
  Law reports: KD245+
Admiralty proceedings: KD1833
  Ireland (Éire): KDK437
  Scotland: KDC532
Admissibility and exclusion of evidence:
  KD7525+
Admission of evidence
  Criminal procedure: KD8382+
Admission to entertainment tax:
  KD5597.A3
Admission to law school: KD444
Admission to practice law: KD476
Adoption: KD777
  Ireland (Éire): KDK210

Adoption
  Northern Ireland: KDE98.A34
  Scotland: KDC377
Adulteration of food: KD3455
Adverse possession: KD989
Advertisements, Legal
  Bankruptcy: KD2146.4
Advertising
  Legal ethics: KD482.A4
  Restrictions on public property:
    KD1045
  Trade regulations: KD2206+
Advertising, Disparagement in
  Unfair competition: KD2226.D5
Advertising, Legal: KD703.N6
Advisory committees
  Civil service: KD4479+
Advocates
  Scotland: KDC227
Advocates, Faculty of
  Scotland: KDC245
Advocates in Aberdeen, Society of:
  KDC220.S6
Affiliation of children: KD775
  Ireland (Éire): KDK209
  Northern Ireland: KDE98.I4
  Scotland: KDC376
Affirmation and oath
  Witnesses: KD7516
Affreightment: KD1811+
Agency: KD2020+
  Scotland: KDC548
Agents, Estate: KD2517.E7
Agents, Insurance: KD1862
Agents, Real estate: KD2517.E7
Agricultural arbitration
  Farm tenancy: KD908.A3
Agricultural cooperative credit
  associations: KD1723
Agricultural economic assistance:
  KD2245+
Agricultural holdings acts: KD907+
  Scotland: KDC416
Agricultural laborers
  Health insurance: KD3207.A4
  Labor law
    Ireland (Éire): KDK860.A3

Agricultural land, Conservation of
  Ireland (Éire): KDK572
Agricultural marketing agreements:
  KD2250
Agricultural marketing controls: KD2250
Agricultural products industry: KD2408+
Agricultural rating relief: KD5738
Agricultural tenancy
  Ireland (Éire): KDK225
Agriculture: KD2241+
  Ireland (Éire): KDK570+
  Labor hygiene and safety:
    KD3172.A4
  Scotland: KDC580+
  Wages: KD3126.A4
AIDS (Disease): KD3368.A54
Air and light easements: KD940
Air, Carriage by: KD1804
Air pollution: KD3378
  Ireland (Éire): KDK910+
  Scotland: KDC685
Air safety: KD2723
Air traffic rules: KD2723
Airlines: KD2732
Airmen
  Civil status: KD6335
Airports
  Jersey: KDG324
Airworthiness: KD2723
Alcohol: KD3466+
  Ireland (Éire): KDK952
  Northern Ireland: KDE378
  Scotland: KDC704
  Taxation: KD5590+
Alcoholic beverages: KD3466+
  Ireland (Éire): KDK952
  Northern Ireland: KDE378
  Scotland: KDC704
  Taxation: KD5590+
    Ireland (Éire): KDK1492.A5
    Jersey: KDG366+
Alcoholism
  Medical legislation: KD3413.A4
    Ireland (Éire): KDK932.A5
    Scotland: KDC695.A5
Aleatory contracts: KD1920+
Alien property: KD813

Aliens
  Capacity and disability: KD744.A5
  Control of: KD4130+
  Income tax: KD5494.A4
  Ireland (Éire): KDK1270
Alimony
  Domestic relations: KD769
  Income tax: KD5483.A4
Allotments
  Land tenure: KD907+
    Scotland: KDC416
Allowances
  Foreign Service: KD4477
  Income tax: KD5450+
Almshouses: KD3310
Alteration of area
  Municipal government: KD4776.A5
Ambulance chasing (Legal ethics):
  KD482.A6
Ambulance service: KD3405.E45
Amusement
  Taxation: KD5597.A3
Amusements
  Regulation: KD3523
  Taxation
    Jersey: KDG368.A5
Ancient law
  Wales: KD9405+
Ancient laws
  Ireland (Éire): KDK145
Ancient lights (Easements): KD940
Anglo-American law: KD1+
Anglo-Norman period: KD570+
Anglo-Saxon dooms: KD543
Animal experimentation and research:
  KD3426
Animal protection: KD3424+
Animal rights: KD3424+
Animal welfare: KD3424+
Animals
  Legal aspects: KD667.A5
  Tort liability: KD1985
    Ireland (Éire): KDK469
Annexation
  Municipal government: KD4776.A5
Annuities
  Income tax: KD5473

Annuities
  Personal property: KD1240
Antenuptial contracts: KD762
  Marriage law
    Ireland (Éire): KDK204
Antitrust laws: KD1361+, KD2218+
Apiculture: KD2285
Appellate jurisdiction
  Criminal courts: KD8420+
Appellate procedure
  Administrative: KD4902
  Civil: KD7630+
    Ireland (Éire): KDK1710+
    Scotland: KDC902+
  Criminal: KD8420+
    Ireland (Éire): KDK1825
    Scotland: KDC945
  Taxation: KD5401
Apportionment
  Election law: KD4346
    Ireland (Éire): KDK1288
    Northern Ireland: KDE427
    Scotland: KDC773
Apprentices
  Labor law: KD3165
Arbitration
  Labor disputes: KD3071
    Civil service: KD4524+
    Maritime laborers: KD1839
Arbitration and award: KD7645+
  Scotland: KDC904
Archdeacon's Courts: KD8685+
Architects: KD2978
Architectural landmarks: KD3740
  Ireland (Éire): KDK1092
Archives: KD3753+
  Ireland (Éire): KDK1100
Armed Forces: KD6039.2+
  Ireland (Éire): KDK1545
  Northern Ireland: KDE506+
Army: KD6086+
  Courts-martial: KD6310+
Arraignment: KD8356+
Arrest and commitment: KD8335
  Criminal procedure
    Scotland: KDC930.5

Arrest of debtors meditating flight
  Scotland: KDC899
Art, Works of
  Copyright: KD1320+
Articled clerks: KD468
Articles of religion
  Ecclesiastical law: KD8627
Artificial flower industry
  Wages: KD3126.F4
Artificial insemination
  Medical legislation: KD3415
Artificial islands: KD2798
Arts administrators
  Works for: KD665.A77
Arts, The: KD3720+
Assault and battery: KD7972
Assaying of gold and silver: KD2231.G6
Assembly and association, Freedom of:
  KD4117
Assessment
  Income tax: KD5490+
  Real property tax
    Scotland: KDC817
Assignment of contracts: KD1574
Assignments for benefit of creditors:
  KD2172.A7
  Scotland: KDC563
Assignments, Patent: KD1401
Assistant barrister, Courts of
  Ireland (Éire): KDK1620
Assize Courts
  Common-law courts: KD6913
  Criminal procedure: KD8287+
  Older courts: KD8235+
Associations: KD2040+
  Ireland (Éire): KDK490+
  Isle of Man: KDG42
  Jersey: KDG290
  Scotland: KDC550+
Associations, Law student: KD448.A+
Associations, Legal education:
  KD430.A+
Associations, Medical: KD2950+
Associations, Trade: KD2228
Assumpsit: KD1602
Asylum seekers
  Aliens: KD4142

Atomic power
  Public safety: KD3497
  Public utilities: KD2560
Attachment and garnishment: KD7592
Attorney and client: KD485+
  Privileged communications:
    KD7519.A77
Attorney General
  Ireland (Éire): KDK1627
Attorneys' and legal secretaries'
  handbooks, manuals, desk-books, etc:
  KD493
  Ireland (Éire): KDK128
  Scotland: KDC239
Attorney's lien: KD490
Attorneys, Patent: KD1413
Auction sales
  Contracts: KD1660
  Land transfer: KD990
Auctioneers: KD2517.E7
Auditing: KD2042
  Corporations: KD2098
  Local finance: KD5712
  Public finance: KD5295
Auditors: KD2974+
  Expert witnesses: KD7524.15
Author and publisher: KD1340
Automation
  Law office management: KD495.A87
Automobile accidents: KD1980.A8
  Ireland (Éire): KDK463.T7
Automobile industry
  Labor disputes: KD3091.A9+
Automobile insurance: KD1892
Automobile service stations
  Local taxation: KD5732.A9
Automobile trade: KD2510.A8
Automotive transport workers:
  KD3177.H5
Automotive transportation: KD2591+
  Ireland (Éire): KDK710+
  Scotland: KDC604+
Auxiliary services during war and
  emergency: KD6240+
Aviation: KD2720+
  Jersey: KDG323+
Aviation, Commercial: KD2720+

Aviation insurance: KD1886
Awards of honor: KD4656+
  Scotland: KDC785
Awards to inventors: KD1394

B

Bag and sack industry
  Wages: KD3126.S3
Bail
  Criminal procedure: KD8340
    Scotland: KDC931
Bail bonds: KD1902
Bail Court: KD7605
Bailiffs: KD7292
Bailment
  Contracts involving bailments:
    KD1679+
  Personal property: KD1222
  Securities: KD1681.5
Baking industry
  Hours of labor: KD3140.B3
  Regulation: KD2408
  Wages: KD3126.B3
    Northern Ireland: KDE330.B3
Bank secrets: KD1737.R43
Banking: KD1715+
  Ireland (Éire): KDK405
  Northern Ireland: KDE170
  Scotland: KDC513+
Banking contracts
  Isle of Man: KDG35.2
Banknotes: KD5284+
Bankruptcy courts: KD2153+
  Ireland (Éire): KDK533
Bankruptcy lawyers: KD472.B35
Banks
  Scotland: KDC515+
  Tort liability: KD1990.5.B35
Banks of issue: KD1718
Bar association journals: KDC170
  Ireland (Éire): KDK93
Bar associations: KD498+
  Ireland (Éire): KDK130+
  Journals: KD345
  Northern Ireland: KDE80
  Scotland: KDC245+

Barnard's Inn: KD505.B37
Barracks
  Armed Forces: KD6063
  Army: KD6103
  Royal Air Force: KD6213
  Royal Navy: KD6143
Barristers: KD463+
  Scottish Bar: KDC245+
Battery
  Criminal law: KD7972
Battle, Wager of
  Criminal procedure: KD8225.W3
Beauty shops: KD2517.B4
Beef
  Import trade: KD2475.B4
  Standards and grading: KD2260.C3
Beekeeping: KD2285
Beer
  Liquor laws: KD3477.B4
  Taxation: KD5591.B4
    Jersey: KDG367.B4
Belfast Gazette: KDE24
Benefices
  Ecclesiastical law: KD8730+
    Ireland (Éire): KDK1875+
Benefices of the clergy
  Church of England: KD8607.B4
Bequests: KD1515.L4
Betrothal: KD754
Betterment levy: KD5539
  Scotland: KDC819
Beverage industry: KD2430.A+
Bible in English law: KD540.5.R4
Bible reading in schools: KD3632
Bibliography: KDC51+
Bicycles: KD2611.B5
Bilingualism
  Ireland (Éire): KDK1261
Bill drafting: KD4238
Bill of sale: KD1683
  Ireland (Éire): KDK384
Bills of attainder: KD4244
Bills of exchange: KD1696+
Bills of lading: KD1664
  Ocean bills of lading: KD1827
Biomedical engineering
  Medical legislation: KD3407+

Biotechnology
  Patent law: KD1387.B55
Biotechnology industries: KD2398.B56
Bird protection: KD2290+
Birth certificates: KD746
  Ireland (Éire): KDK195
  Scotland: KDC362
Birth control: KD3340
Bishops: KD8660.B5
Black act: KD7852.B55
Blackmail: KD8005+
Blasphemy
  Criminal law: KD8073
  Ireland (Éire): KDK1787.B42
Blind persons
  Public welfare: KD3315
Board of directors
  Ireland (Éire): KDK504
Board of Inland Revenue: KD5377
Board of Trade: KD2201
Boards of education: KD3611
Boards of finance
  Ecclesiastical law: KD8652.A+
Boats
  Sales contracts: KD1657.B6
Boats, Small
  Safety regulations: KD2768.P5
Bona vacantia: KD1534
  Scotland: KDC470
Bond issues: KD5300
  Ireland (Éire): KDK1438
Bonded warehouses: KD2530
Bonding: KD1902+
Bonds
  Corporations: KD2108
Bonds, Municipal: KD5715
Bonus system
  Labor law: KD3124.P7
Book industries and trade: KD2398.B6
Boot and shoe workers
  Wages: KD3126.B65
    Ireland (Éire): KDK840.B6
Boot and shoe workers (Wages)
  Northern Ireland: KDE330.B6
Borough boundaries
  Municipal government: KD4776.A5

Boroughs
  Local government: KD4770
  Local laws
    England: KD8860+
    Ireland (Éire): KDK1930.A+
    Northern Ireland: KDE580.A+
    Wales: KD9325.A+
Borstal institutions: KD8492
  Ireland (Éire): KDK1840
Bottomry and respondentia: KD1834.B6
Bounties on imports: KD5694.B6
Boycotts: KD3076+
Bracton, H.: De legibus et
  consuetudinibus Angliae libri quinque
  (1248-1258): KD600.B73
Breach of contract: KD1600+
Breach of peace: KD8035+
Breach of promise: KD754
Breach of trust: KD1493
Bread
  Weights and measures: KD2231.B7
Brehon law
  Ireland (Éire): KDK145
Brevia
  Anglo-Norman legal sources: KD576
Brewing industry
  Income tax: KD5526.B6
Bribery: KD8045
Bribes
  Unfair competition: KD2226.S4
Bristol (England), Port of: KD2796.B7
Broadmoor Institution: KD8454.B7
Brokers: KD2024.B7
Brokers, Insurance: KD1862
Brokers, Ship: KD2024.S4
Broom and brush industry
  Northern Ireland: KDE330.B7
  Wages: KD3126.B7
    Ireland (Éire): KDK840.B7
Budget
  Local finance: KD5712
  Public finance: KD5292
Building accidents: KD1980.B84
Building and construction industry
  Bankruptcy: KD2163.C65
  Contracts: KD1641
    Government contracts: KD1615+

Building and construction industry
  Contracts
    Scotland: KDC501
  Labor disputes: KD3091.B9+
  Labor hygiene and safety:
    KD3172.C6
Building laws: KD1125+
  Ireland (Éire): KDK275+, KDK278+
  London: KD8952.B8
  Northern Ireland: KDE135+, KDE137
  Scotland: KDC446+, KDC448+
  Wales: KD9440+
Building ownership
  Income tax: KD5471
Building societies: KD1726
  Ireland (Éire): KDK407
Building valuation
  Real property taxes: KD5534
Burden of proof
  Civil procedure: KD7505+
Burgage: KD836.B8
Burghs
  Local laws
    Scotland: KDC985.A+
Burglary: KD7993
Burial and cemetery laws: KD3365
  Scotland: KDC682
Burial insurance: KD1877
Burning of land
  Ireland (Éire): KDK572
Bus lines: KD2632
Business associations: KD2049+
  Isle of Man: KDG42
  Jersey: KDG290
  Scotland: KDC554
Business corporations: KD2071+
  Ireland (Éire): KDK502+
  Northern Ireland: KDE220
  Scotland: KDC557+
Business enterprises: KD2040
  Scotland: KDC550
Business insurance: KD1879
Business interruption insurance:
  KD1887.B8
Business names: KD1450
Business organizations
  Income tax: KD5501+

Business organizations
  Income tax
    Ireland (Éire): KDK1460+
Business records: KD2043
Business secrets: KD2226.T7
Business tenancies: KD905
Businesspeople
  Works for: KD665.B86
    Ireland (Éire): KDK175.B87
    Isle of Man: KDG31.B87
    Northern Ireland: KDE88.5.B86
Button industry
  Wages: KD3126.B8
    Ireland (Éire): KDK840.B8
Bylaws
  Business corporations: KD2085
Bylaws, Model building: KD1152

C

Calendar
  Regulation: KD2233
Calendar of the Justiciary Rolls:
  KDK148
Calendar of the Patent and Close Rolls
  of Chancery in Ireland: KDK148
Canals
  Navigation and pilotage: KD2784+
Candles
  Taxation: KD5597.C3
Canning and preserving industry
  Wages
    Ireland (Éire): KDK840.C3
Canon law of the Church of England:
  KD8600+
Canons
  Church of England: KD8625
Capacity and disability: KD732+
  Ireland (Éire): KDK188+
  Jersey: KDG260
  Northern Ireland: KDE90
  Scotland: KDC356+
Capital
  Corporate finance: KD2094+
Capital allowances
  Income tax: KD5452
Capital duty: KD5612.3

INDEX

Capital gains tax: KD5550
Capital investment
  Income tax: KD5475+
Capital punishment
  Criminal law: KD7885.C3
  Military law: KD6333
Caravan sites: KD2517.T7
Caravan sites development
  Public land law: KD1107.T7
Carbonated beverage industry
  Regulation: KD2430.C3
  Wages: KD3126.C3
    Ireland (Éire): KDK840.C35
    Scotland: KDC647.C3
Cardiff Explosives Trial, 1983:
  KD9424.C35
Carriage by air: KD1804
Carriage by land: KD1802
Carriage by sea: KD1811+
  Ireland (Éire): KDK435+
  Scotland: KDC530+
Carriers
  Contracts: KD1800+
    Ireland (Éire): KDK430+
    Scotland: KDC526+
  London transportation: KD8972.A+
Cartularies
  Norman period: KD564
  Scottish legal history: KDC290
Casebooks: KD658
Casket and coffin industry
  Wages: KD3126.C64
Casualty insurance: KD1890+
Cathedral churches
  Ecclesiastical law: KD8664
Catholics
  Civil and political rights: KD4102.C3
  Discrimination
    Ireland (Éire): KDK1260.C45
Cattle: KD2267+
  Standards and grading: KD2260.C3
Cattle raising: KD2267+
Celluloid industry: KD2376.C4
Censorship
  Constitutional law: KD4110+
    Ireland (Éire): KDK1262
  Motion pictures: KD3731

Censorship
  Motion pictures
    London: KD9054.M6
  Theater and theaters: KD3726
Central banks: KD1718
Central catalogs: KD56
Central Criminal Court: KD8289
  Reports: KD7865.2.C4
Central government and local
  government: KD4765
Cereal products industry: KD2408+
Ceremonies
  Ecclesiastical law: KD8753
Champerty: KD8057
Chancery and Equity Series (The Law
  Reports): KD276+
Chancery Court of Lancaster: KD7220
  Costs: KD7568.L3
Chancery Court of York: KD8691
Chancery Division
  High Court of Justice: KD7184+
  The Law Reports: KD276.3
Chancery records: KD574
Channel Islands: KDG21+, KDG120+
Chapels: KD8712
Charitable trusts: KD1487+
  Ireland (Éire): KDK354
  Northern Ireland: KDE142.C4
Charter parties
  Maritime law: KD1834.C5
Charter rolls: KD588
Chartered companies: KD2117
Charters
  Anglo-Norman period: KD571
  Scottish legal history: KDC290
Charters of feoffment: KD590
Chattel mortgages: KD1757
Chattels
  Transfer of properrty: KD685.T7
Chattels, Torts affecting: KD1970
Checklists of law reports: KD54
Checklists of statutes: KD53
Checks: KD1699
Checkweighting: KD3124.C45
Chemical industries: KD2375+
Chemicals
  Patent law: KD1387.C4

Chemists: KD2990.C4
Chester, Session Court of: KD6918
Child abuse: KD7974
Child labor: KD3159
  Northern Ireland: KDE335
  Scotland: KDC655
Child support
  Domestic relations: KD780
Child welfare: KD3305
  Scotland: KDC672
Children
  Capacity and disability: KD735
    Ireland (Éire): KDK189
    Scotland: KDC357
  Child labor: KD3159
    Scotland: KDC655
  Liability: KD735
    Ireland (Éire): KDK189
    Northern Ireland: KDE92
    Scotland: KDC357
  Northern Ireland: KDE92
  Public welfare: KD3305
    Scotland: KDC672
Children, Access to: KD779+
Children as witnesses: KD7514.5
Children's rights
  Scotland: KDC465.R5
Chivalry, Court of: KD728
Choses in action: KD1238+
  Ireland (Éire): KDK315+
Choses in possession: KD1220
Church and education: KD3605
Church and Parliament: KD8634
  Ireland (Éire): KDK1855
Church and state: KD8600+
  Ireland (Éire): KDK1850+
  Scotland: KDC958+, KDC958
Church Assembly
  Ecclesiastical law: KD8652.A+
Church Assembly Measures: KD8629+
Church discipline: KD8656
Church land: KD8740
  Ireland (Éire): KDK1878
  Scotland: KDC969
Church of England: KD8600+
Church of Ireland: KDK1890+
Church of Scotland: KDC958+

Church property: KD8740
  Ireland (Éire): KDK1878
  Scotland: KDC969
Church rates: KD8718
Church wardens: KD8707.C45
Churches: KD8712
C.I.F. clause: KD1673
Cinque Ports, Courts of: KD6981
Circuit Courts
  Ireland (Éire): KDK1635+
    Law reports: KDK65+
Circumstantial evidence: KD7510
Cities
  Local government: KD4770+, KD4770
  Local laws
    England: KD8860+
    Ireland (Éire): KDK1930.A+
    Northern Ireland: KDE580.A+
    Scotland: KDC985.A+
    Wales: KD9325.A+
City of London Court: KD7248+
City redevelopment: KD1171+
  London: KD8952.C5
  Scotland: KDC452
Civil Bill Courts
  Ireland (Éire): KDK1620
Civil defense: KD6340
Civil law: KD720+
Civil rights: KD4080+
  Ireland (Éire): KDK1255+
  Northern Ireland: KDE420
  Scotland: KDC758
Civil service
  Executive branch
    Ireland (Éire): KDK1350
    Northern Ireland: KDE460
  Local government: KD4805+
Civil Service
  Executive branch: KD4467+
Civil Service Commission: KD4510
Civil service examinations: KD4513
Civil status
  Natural persons
    Ireland (Éire): KDK186
    Scotland: KDC354+
Civil trials: KD378+
  Ireland (Éire): KDK105+

Civil trials
  Scotland: KDC187+
Civilian awards: KD4656
Claims, Court of: KD4456.C6
Claims, Priority of: KD2160
Clement's Inn: KD505.C5
Clergy
  Ecclesiastical law: KD8658+
Clergy, Benefices of the
  Church of England: KD8607.B4
Clergy, Parochial
  Scotland: KDC968
Clerks, Articled: KD468
Clerks of court: KD7293
  Ireland (Éire): KDK1656.C5
Clerks to Her Majesty's Signet, Society
  of: KDC220.S65
Client and attorney: KD485+
  Privileged communications:
    KD7519.A77
Clifford's Inn: KD505.C55
Close companies: KD2115
Clothing
  Tariff
    Ireland (Éire): KDK1514.C5
Clothing industry
  Regulation: KD2385+
  Wages: KD3126.C5
    Ireland (Éire): KDK840.C5
    Northern Ireland: KDE330.C5
    Scotland: KDC647.C5
Clubs: KD2047.C6
Clubs, Lawyers': KD510.A+
Co-ownership
  Land tenure: KD878+
    Scotland: KDC405+
Coal
  London trade and commerce:
    KD8992.C6
  Weights and measures: KD2231.C6
Coal mining industry
  Hours of labor: KD3140.C6
  Labor disputes: KD3091.C6+
  Labor hygiene and safety:
    KD3172.M53
  Regulation: KD2350+
Coastwise navigation: KD2780

Coats of arms: KD728
Codification: KD700
  Criminal law: KD7872
Coercion, Husband's
  Criminal liability: KD7898
Coffin industry
  Wages: KD3126.C64
Coinage: KD5284+
  Ireland (Éire): KDK1432
Collection agencies: KD2517.C6
Collection laws: KD1734
Collective bargaining: KD3062+
Collective labor agreements: KD3062+
  Maritime unions: KD1839
  Northern Ireland: KDE324
College students: KD3688
Colleges and universities: KD3680+
  Scotland: KDC728
Collisions at sea: KD1825
Colonial forces: KD6120.A+
Commercial arbitration: KD7645+
Commercial aviation: KD2732
Commercial Court (High Court of
  Justice): KD7182
Commercial crime: KD7990
  False pretenses: KD8000
  Fraud: KD8000
Commercial espionage: KD2226.T7
Commercial law: KD1621+
  Channel Islands: KDG138
  Guernsey: KDG440.C6
  Directories: KD340.C65
  Ireland (Éire): KDK378
  Scotland: KDC495
Commercial leases: KD905
  Scotland: KDC415
Commission merchants: KD2024.B7
Commissioners of Sewers, Court of:
  KD6983
Commissions
  Armed Forces
    Officers: KD6068
  Army
    Officers: KD6108
  Royal Air Force
    Officers: KD6218

Commissions
  Royal Navy
    Officers: KD6148
Commissions, Secret
  Unfair competition: KD2226.S4
Commitment
  Criminal procedure: KD8335
    Scotland: KDC930.5
Committees
  House of Commons: KD4358+
  House of Lords: KD4280+
  Legislative process: KD4235
Common law: KD671
  Anglo-Norman period: KD570+
Common Pleas at Lancaster, Court of:
  KD6916+
Commons and inclosures: KD952
Commonwealth and Empire: KD5020+
Communication: KD2571+
  Ireland (Éire): KDK705+
  Jersey: KDG320+
  Scotland: KDC601+
Communication, Radio: KD2900+
Communications, Confidential:
  KD7518+
Communications, Privileged: KD7518+
Community legal services: KD512+
  Scotland: KDC260
Companies: KD2071+
  Ireland (Éire): KDK502+
Companies, Family: KD2115
Companies, Investment: KD1782
Companies, Trust: KD1491
Compensation for judicial error:
  KD8464
Competition
  Retail trade: KD2492+
Competition, Unfair: KD2225+
Composition
  Bankruptcy: KD2170
    Ireland (Éire): KDK540
Compromise: KD7644
Compulsory education: KD3624+
  Northern Ireland: KDE394+
Compulsory representation by counsel:
  KD7463.5
Computation of time: KD703.T5

Computer contracts: KD1642.C65
Computer programs
  Copyright: KD1303.C65
Computers
  Legal aspects: KD667.C65
Computers and privacy: KD1957.C65
Conciliation
  Labor disputes: KD3071
    Civil service: KD4524
Concurrent ownership: KD878+
  Scotland: KDC405+
Conditional sale: KD1759
  Scotland: KDC523
Conduct of court proceedings: KD7117
Conduits, Electric
  Building laws: KD1160
Confession
  Criminal procedure: KD8384
Confession of judgment: KD7460
Confessional
  Privileged communications:
    KD7519.C6
Confidential communications: KD7518+
Conflict of criminal law: KD7888
Conflict of interests
  Constitutional law: KD4005
Conflict of laws: KD680+
  Ireland (Éire): KDK179+
  Scotland: KDC340+
Conflicts
  Conflict of laws: KD685.C6
Conjugal violence: KD7973
Conscience and religion, Freedom of:
  KD4100+
Conscientious objectors: KD6043.C6
Conscription
  Armed Forces: KD6040+
Consent, Lack of genuine
  Void and voidable contracts:
    KD1582+
    Ireland (Éire): KDK375
Conservation of natural resources
  Agriculture: KD2241+
  Forestry: KD2241+
    Ireland (Éire): KDK572
  Public property: KD1035

Consistory Court
  Ecclesiastical law: KD8687+
Consolidation and merger of
  corporations: KD2127
Conspiracy
  Criminal law: KD7955
Constables: KD7294
  Scotland: KDC869.C6
Constitutional and administrative law:
  KD3930+
Constitutional history
  Northern Ireland: KDE415
Constitutional law: KD3931+
  Guernsey: KDG440.C56
  Ireland (Éire): KDK1200+
  Isle of Man: KDG60
  Jersey: KDG351
  Northern Ireland: KDE410+
  Sark: KDG540.C65
  Scotland: KDC750+
  Wales: KD9462
Constitutions and canons ecclesiastical
  Church of England: KD8625
Construction and interpretation,
  Statutory: KD691
Construction companies
  Business insurance: KD1879
Construction industry: KD3177.C65
Consular courts: KD7260+
Consumer credit: KD1755
Consumer protection: KD2204+
  Ireland (Éire): KDK552+
Consumers, Works for: KD665.C6
Contagious and infectious diseases:
  KD3367+
  Ireland (Éire): KDK918+
  London: KD9014.C6
Container industry
  Wages: KD3126.C65
Containers: KD2230+
Contempt of court: KD8055
  Ireland (Éire): KDK1780
  Scotland: KDC920.C65
Contempt of Parliament: KD8044
Contested elections: KD4380+
  Ireland (Éire): KDK1315+

Contingent remainders
  Future estates and interests: KD867
Contraband trade: KD5692
Contract for services: KD1638+
  Scotland: KDC500+
Contract for work and labor: KD1638+,
  KDK381+
  Scotland: KDC500+
Contract of service: KD1634+
  Ireland (Éire): KDK380
  Scotland: KDC498+
Contractors
  Building and construction industry:
    KD2435
Contractors, Independent: KD1638+
Contractors' liens: KD1640
Contracts: KD1554+
  Channel Islands: KDG138
  Guernsey: KDG440.C6
  Conflict of laws: KD685.C6
  Ireland (Éire): KDK370+
  Isle of Man: KDG35+
  Northern Ireland: KDE155+
  Scotland: KDC485+
Contracts, Aleatory: KD1920+
Contracts and war: KD1607
Contracts, Banking
  Isle of Man: KDG35.2
Contracts, Defense: KD1613
Contracts, Engineering: KD1641
Contracts, Government: KD1610+
Contracts, Municipal: KD1611
Contracts, Public: KD1610+
Contracts under seal: KD1568
Contracts, Unlawful: KD1578+
Contracts, Wagering: KD1920+
Contracts, War: KD1613
Contributions
  Social security: KD3252
Contributory negligence: KD1976
Control of individuals
  Constitutional law: KD4122+
    Northern Ireland: KDE423+
  Ireland (Éire): KDK1262.12+
Control of social activities: KD3521+
  Ireland (Éire): KDK975+
  London: KD9040+

Control of social activities
  Northern Ireland: KDE380+
Control of subversive activities: KD4160
  Northern Ireland: KDE423
Control of trade practices: KD2204+
  Ireland (Éire): KDK552+
  London: KD8985+
Controls on employment
  Immigration law: KD4141
Conversion
  Torts: KD1970
Conversion, Equitable
  Land tenure: KD858
Conveyances: KD971+
  Ireland (Éire): KDK247+
  Scotland: KDC433+
Conveyances, Fraudulent: KD2162
Conveyancing costs (Land transfer):
  KD986
Convocations
  Ecclesiastical law: KD8652.A+
Cooperative credit associations,
  Agricultural: KD1723
Cooperative credit societies
  Scotland: KDC515
Cooperative societies
  Banking: KD1722
  Corporations: KD2120+
Cooperatives
  Income tax: KD5523
Copyholds
  Feudal tenure: KD838.M3
Copyright: KD1281+
  Guernsey: KDG440.I5
  Income tax: KD5483.I53
  Ireland (Éire): KDK320
Corn laws: KD5662.C6
Coronation
  Constitutional law: KD4456.C6
Coroners: KD7296
  Northern Ireland: KDE524.7.C65
Corporal punishment
  Criminal law: KD7885.C6
  Military law: KD6332
Corporate finance: KD2094+
Corporate officers
  Ireland (Éire): KDK504

Corporate practice lawyers: KD472.I5
Corporate reorganization
  Taxation: KD5528.C65
Corporate shares: KD2100+
Corporation of the City of London:
  KD8927+
Corporations: KD2057+, KD2057
  Income tax: KD5504+
    Ireland (Éire): KDK1460+
  Ireland (Éire): KDK496+
  Isle of Man: KDG42
  Jersey: KDG290
  Northern Ireland: KDE220
  Scotland: KDC556+
  Tort liability: KD1990+
Corporations, Family
  Income tax: KD5524
Corporations, Public: KD4481+
Corporations, Publicly chartered:
  KD2117
Correality and solidarity: KD1571
Correctional institutions: KD8452+
Corrupt practices
  Election law: KD4349
    Ireland (Éire): KDK1298
    Northern Ireland: KDE430
    Scotland: KDC774.5
Corruption
  Criminal law: KD8045
Corruption, Judicial: KD7286.J8
Corset industry
  Wages: KD3126.C67
Cosmetics: KD3450+
Costs
  Arbitration: KD7647
  Civil procedure: KD7566+
  Conveyancing: KD986
  Courts
    Bankruptcy: KD2155.C5
    Civil procedure
      Ireland (Éire): KDK1695
      Scotland: KDC893
    Domestic relations: KD751+
Cotton fabric industry: KD2383.C6
Cotton-waste industry
  Wages: KD3126.C68

Councils
  Ecclesiastical law: KD8652.A+
Counterclaims
  Civil procedure: KD7458
Counterfeiting: KD8090
Counties
  Local laws
    England: KD8850.A+
    Ireland (Éire): KDK1910.A+
    Northern Ireland: KDE570.A+
    Scotland: KDC980.A+
    Wales: KD9320.A+
County civil service: KD4816+
County council: KD4785
County courts
  Costs: KD7568.C6
  Ireland (Éire): KDK1615+
  Law reports: KD228+
  Modern: KD7228+
  Old: KD6972+
County government: KD4785+
  Scotland: KDC794
Court administration
  Data processing: KD394.5.C67
Court costs: KD7566+
  Ireland (Éire): KDK1695
  Scotland: KDC893
Court employees: KD7283+
  Ireland (Éire): KDK1650+
  Northern Ireland: KDE524+
  Scotland: KDC868+
Court fees: KD7566+
  Ireland (Éire): KDK1695
  Scotland: KDC893
Court of Appeal (Civil Division)
  Supreme Court of Judicature:
    KD7216
Court of Appeal in ecclesiastical
  matters: KD8693
Court of Arches (in the Province of
  Canterbury)
  Ecclesiastical law: KD8690
Court of Augmentation
  Wales: KD9484
Court of Augmentations: KD6965

Court of chancery
  Law reports
    Ireland (Éire): KDK66
Court of Chancery: KD6937+
  Costs: KD7568.C4
  Ireland (Éire): KDK1595+
  Law reports: KD232+
    Wales: KD9414
Court of Chivalry: KD728
Court of Claims: KD4456.C6
Court of Commissioners of Sewers:
  KD6983
Court of Common Pleas: KD6898+
  Law reports: KD203+
    Ireland (Éire): KDK69
Court of Common Pleas at Lancaster:
  KD6916+
Court of Criminal Appeal: KD8427
Court of Crown Cases Reserved:
  KD8256
Court of Divorce and Matrimonial
  Causes: KD751+
Court of Exchequer: KD6902+
  Costs: KD7568.E8
  Ireland (Éire): KDK1600+
  Law reports
    Ireland (Éire): KDK72
    Law: KD208+
    Scotland: KDC130
    Wales: KD9412
  Scotland: KDC863
Court of Exchequer Chamber: KD6925
Court of Exchequer (Equity)
  Law reports: KD236+
Court of General Eyre: KD6913
Court of High Commission
  Ecclesiastical law: KD8682
Court of High Steward: KD8283
Court of itinerant justices: KD6913
Court of Marshalsea: KD6980
Court of Protection: KD740+
Court of Referees: KD4370
Court of Requests: KD6942
  Law reports: KD240+
Court of Session: KDC844+
  Law reports: KDC113

Court of Star Chamber
  Criminal law reports: KD7865.2.S7
  Criminal procedure: KD8253
Court of the Vice Warden of the
  Stannaries: KD6990
Courts and procedure
  Before 1873: KD6870+
    Common law and equity courts:
      KD6870+
    Common law (Collective): KD6878+
      Particular courts: KD6891+
    Equity courts: KD6937+
    Inferior courts: KD6965+
  Civil procedure in general: KD7325+
  Criminal procedure
    Scotland: KDC935.8+
  History: KD6850+
  Ireland (Éire): KDK1580+
  Isle of Man: KDG75
  Northern Ireland: KDE510+
  Scotland: KDC840+
  Since 1873: KD7100+
    Courts of special jurisdiction:
      KD7259.2+
    Highest courts of appeal: KD7132+
    Lower courts and local courts:
      KD7228+
    Superior courts: KD7139+
  Wales: KD9480+
Courts baron: KD6968+
  Ireland (Éire): KDK1613+
  Scotland: KDC865+
Courts leet: KD6968+
  Ireland (Éire): KDK1613+
Courts-martial: KD6293+
Courts of Cinque Ports: KD6981
Courts of first instance
  Ireland (Éire): KDK1630+
Courts of Great Sessions: KD9482
Courts of Quarter Sessions
  Criminal law reports: KD7865.2.Q3+
  Criminal procedure: KD8294+
  Ireland (Éire): KDK1610+
Courts of requests: KD6988
Courts of special jurisdiction:
  KD7259.2+

Courts of Stannaries (Devonshire and
  Cornwall): KD6990
Courts of summary jurisdiction
  Criminal procedure: KD8301+
  Matrimonial causes: KD752
Courts of the assistant barrister
  (Éire): KDK1620
Courts of Trailbaston: KD8242
Courts of wards and liveries: KD6992
Courts Oyer and Terminer and General
  Gaol Delivery: KD8240
Covenants not to compete
  Labor law: KD3101
Covenants running with the land:
  KD954
Credit, Consumer: KD1755
Credit insurance: KD1904
Credit, Letters of: KD1735
Credit societies, Cooperative
  Scotland: KDC515
Creditors' rights: KD2139+
  Ireland (Éire): KDK530+
  Jersey: KDG296
  Scotland: KDC560+
Crime and publicity: KD7879
Crimes against the state and public
  order: KD8020+
Crimes without victims: KD8070+
  Ireland (Éire): KDK1786+
Criminal Appeal, Court of: KD8427
Criminal courts and procedure:
  KD8220+
  Ireland (Éire): KDK1800+
  Northern Ireland: KDE550+
  Scotland: KDC930+
  Wales: KD9490
Criminal intent: KD7892
Criminal investigation: KD8335
  Criminal procedure
    Scotland: KDC930.5
Criminal jurisdiction: KD7888
Criminal law: KD7849+
  Channel Island
    Guernsey: KDG440.C7
  Channel Islands: KDG170
  Customs: KD5692
  Ireland (Éire): KDK1750+

Criminal law
  Isle of Man: KDG85
  Northern Ireland: KDE540
  Scotland: KDC910+
  Taxation: KD5410
  Wales: KD9490
Criminal laws against religious
  minorities: KD4100+
Criminal liability: KD7890+
  Ireland (Éire): KDK1760+
Criminal liability of juristic persons:
  KD7892.5
Criminal lunatics, Institutions for:
  KD8452+
Criminal negligence: KD7892
Criminal statistics: KD330
  London: KD8888
  Scotland: KDC162
Criminal trials: KD370+
  Ireland (Éire): KDK102+
  Jersey: KDG240+
  Northern Ireland: KDE72+
  Scotland: KDC184+
  Wales: KD9423+
Cross claims
  Civil procedure: KD7458
Cross examination: KD7486
Crown and the Central Government:
  KD4430+
  Scotland: KDC777+
Crown Cases Reserved, Court of:
  KD8256
Crown Court: KD8286
Crown lands: KD1102
Crown Office: KD8262
Crown privilege: KD4010
Crown proceedings
  Torts: KD2004
Cruelty to animals, Prevention of:
  KD3424+
Culpability
  Criminal law: KD7892
Cultural exchanges: KD3758
Cultural property, Preservation of
  Ireland (Éire): KDK1092
Curates, Stipendiary: KD8660.S7
Curia regis: KD6891

Curia regis
  Civil rolls: KD190
Currency: KD5284+
  Ireland (Éire): KDK1432
Curricula
  Educational law: KD3652+
Curtesy: KD1523.D6
Custody of children: KD779+
Custody of defendants: KD8363
Custom and usage: KD693
Customary law
  Guernsey: KDG428
  Jersey: KDG228
  London: KD8864
  Wales: KD9405+
Customs administration: KD5681+
  Ireland (Éire): KDK1516
Customs and statutes
  Scottish legal history: KDC272
Customs crimes: KD5692
Customs duties: KD5641+
  Ireland (Éire): KDK1510+
  Isle of Man: KDG70.6
  Scotland: KDC823
Customs, Municipal and mercantile
  Anglo-Norman period: KD597
Custumals
  Anglo-Norman period: KD572
  Anglo-Saxon period: KD544
  Wales: KD9405
Cutlery industry
  Wages: KD3126.C8
Cy pres doctrine: KD1488

D

Dáil Éireann: KDK1330+
Dairy industry
  Ireland (Éire): KDK650
  Regulation: KD2423
  Wages: KD3126.D3
    Ireland (Éire): KDK840.D3
    Scotland: KDC647.D3
Dairy products industry
  Ireland (Éire): KDK650
  Regulation: KD2423
    Northern Ireland: KDE250.D3

Dairy products industry
  Standards and grading: KD2423
Damages: KD703.D3
  Contracts: KD1602
  Income tax: KD5483.D35
  Scotland: KDC347.D3
  Torts: KD1941+
Dams: KD1071
Data protection
  Public records: KD3756
    Ireland (Éire): KDK1101
Databases
  Public records: KD3756
    Ireland (Éire): KDK1101
Day care centers
  Ireland (Éire): KDK691.D39
Dean Forest: KD9312.D4
Dean of Guild Courts: KDC451
Death by wrongful act: KD1954
  Ireland (Éire): KDK452
  Scotland: KDC542
  Torts: KD1954
Death certificates: KD746
  Ireland (Éire): KDK195
  Scotland: KDC362
Death penalty: KD7885.C3
Debentures
  Corporations: KD2108
Debt, Imprisonment for: KD7596
Debtor and creditor: KD1740
  Conflict of laws: KD685.C6
  Ireland (Éire): KDK412+
Debtors' relief: KD2166+
Decedents' estates, Administration of
  Ireland (Éire): KDK367
Deceit
  Torts: KD1963
Declaratory judgments: KD7573
Decorations of honor: KD4656+
  Scotland: KDC785
Decorum in court: KD7117
Deductions
  Income tax: KD5450+
Deeds
  Land transfer: KD971+
  Scottish legal history: KDC290

Deeds of arrangement
  Bankruptcy: KD2170
    Ireland (Éire): KDK540
Defenders, Public: KD8358
Defense
  Criminal procedure: KD8358,
    KDE552
Defense, Civil: KD6340
Defense contracts: KD1613
Defenses
  Criminal law: KD7896+
    Ireland (Éire): KDK1763+
Defenses and objections
  Civil procedure: KD7455+
Deferment
  Military service: KD6042+
Deferment of executions, Wartime:
  KD7598
Delegation of powers: KD4000
  Ireland (Éire): KDK1227
Delicts
  Scotland: KDC541+
Demurrage
  Maritime law: KD1834.D4
Denominational schools: KD3605
Dental specialists: KD2965.D4
  Jersey: KDG328.D4
Dentists: KD2965.D4
  Jersey: KDG328.D4
Depopulation
  Criminal law: KD7852.D4
Deposit of goods: KD1681
Deposition: KD7470
  Ireland (Éire): KDK1680
Deposits
  Banking: KD1733
Depreciation allowances
  Income tax: KD5452
Derating
  Real property tax: KD5737+
Derivative securities: KD1777.D47
Desertion
  Domestic relations: KD780
Design protection: KD1345
  Copyright: KD1325
  Patent law: KD1398

Designs and models
  Copyright: KD1325
  Patent law: KD1398
Detention, Preventive: KD7883
Development gains tax: KD5539
Dialogus de Scaccario: KD600.D5
Digest, The: KD296.E5
Dignities: KD4656+
  Scotland: KDC785
Dikes: KD1071
Dilapidation
  Ecclesiastical law: KD8733
Diminished responsibility
  Criminal liability: KD7896+
    Ireland (Éire): KDK1763+
Diocesan conferences
  Ecclesiastical law: KD8652.A+
Diplomata
  Anglo-Norman period: KD590
  Norman period: KD564
Direct selling: KD2500.3
Directories
  General: KD336+
  Ireland (Éire): KDK91
  Law schools: KD422
  Patent attorneys: KD1413.3
  Scotland: KDC165
Disability pensions: KD3241+
  Armed Forces: KD6061
  Army: KD6101
  Ireland (Éire): KDK885
  Northern Ireland: KDE346
  Royal Air Force: KD6211
  Royal Navy: KD6141
Discharge
  Armed Forces: KD6053
  Army: KD6093
  Royal Air Force: KD6203
  Royal Navy: KD6133
Discharge of contract: KD1588+
Discipline, Ecclesiastical: KD8656
Discipline, Employment
  Civil service: KD4515+
Discipline, Labor: KD3146+
Discipline, Military: KD6250
Discipline, Professional
  Legal profession: KD479+

Disclosure requirements
  Stock transfers: KD2101
Discovery: KD7470
  Criminal procedure
    Ireland (Éire): KDK1807
  Ireland (Éire): KDK1680
Discrimination
  Constitutional law: KD4095
  Employment: KD3102+
    Northern Ireland: KDE327.5
    Scotland: KDC644.4+
  Housing: KD1184
  Ireland (Éire): KDK1258+
Diseases, Occupational
  Workers' compensation: KD3235
Dismissal of employees: KD3096+,
  KD3110+, KDK820
  Northern Ireland: KDE327+
  Scotland: KDC644.2+
Dismissal pay: KD3111
Disparagement in advertising
  Unfair competition: KD2226.D5
Disposal of the dead: KD3365
  Scotland: KDC682
Dissection
  Animals: KD3426
Dissemination
  Copyright
    Literary copyright: KD1305.2
Dissenters
  Civil rights: KD4102.D5
Dissolution
  Corporations: KD2125
    Ireland (Éire): KDK520
    Scotland: KDC558
Distress
  Landlord and tenant: KD910
  Torts
    Ireland (Éire): KDK469
District courts
  Ireland (Éire): KDK1640+
District registries
  High Court of Justice: KD7167
Dividends
  Corporate law: KD2094+
  Income tax: KD5477

Diving operations
  Labor hygiene and safety:
    KD3172.D58
Divorce
  Conflict of laws: KD685.M3
    Ireland (Éire): KDK180.M37
    Scotland: KDC342.M3
  Domestic relations: KD764+
    Ireland (Éire): KDK205
    Northern Ireland: KDE98.D58
    Scotland: KDC372
Divorce and Matrimonial Causes, Court
  of: KD751+
Divorce costs: KD751+
Dock
  Criminal procedure: KD8363
Doctors' Commons: KD507
Doctrines
  Anglo-American law: KD640+
  English legal institutions: KD640+
Documentary evidence: KD7512
Documents of title: KD1663+
Dogs
  Legal aspects: KD667.D6
Domain, Public
  National revenue: KD5323+
Domesday Book: KD582
Domestic relations: KD750+
  Ireland (Éire): KDK200+
  Jersey: KDG263+
  Northern Ireland: KDE94+
  Scotland: KDC366+
Domestic relations courts: KD751+
  Ireland (Éire): KDK201
Domicile
  Civil status: KD725
  Double taxation: KD5382
  Public welfare: KD3311
Donation of organs, tissues, etc:
  KD3409
Double jeopardy
  Criminal liability: KD7901
Double taxation: KD5380+
  Ireland (Éire): KDK1448
Dower: KD1523.D6
Draft
  Armed Forces: KD6040+

Drainage
  Public health: KD3375
    Scotland: KDC684
  Public land law: KD1095+
Drains
  Building laws: KD1162
Dressmakers
  Wages: KD3126.D7
    Northern Ireland: KDE330.C5
Drivers' licenses: KD2607
Drug addiction
  Medical legislation: KD3413.N3
Drug laws: KD3460+
  Scotland: KDC702
Drugs: KD3450+
  Products liability: KD1988.D78
  Scotland: KDC700+
  Trade agreements: KD5662.D7
Drum and keg industry
  Wages: KD3126.K4
Drunk driving: KD2618
  Ireland (Éire): KDK713
Drunkenness
  Criminal liability: KD7897.5
Dublin harbor: KDK769.D8
Due process of law: KD4106
Dumping
  Unfair competition: KD2226.D8
Duress: KD1582
  Ireland (Éire): KDK375
Dyes and dyestuffs industry:
  KD2376.D9

E

Easements: KD936+
  Ireland (Éire): KDK240.E27
  Scotland: KDC424
Ecclesiastical and admiralty precedents
  Law reports: KD245+
Ecclesiastical courts: KD8680+
  Scotland: KDC966
Ecclesiastical discipline: KD8656
Ecclesiastical law: KD8600+
  Ireland (Éire): KDK1850+
  Law reports: KD8638+
    Ireland (Éire): KDK1860+

Ecclesiastical law
  Scotland: KDC958+
  Wales: KD9498+
Ecclesiastical leases
  Ireland (Éire): KDK227
Economic assistance
  Agriculture and forestry: KD2245+
Economic planning: KD2185+
  Ireland (Éire): KDK543+
Economic policy: KD2185+
  Ireland (Éire): KDK543+
Economics, Medical: KD2960.F4
Economics of law practice: KD488+
  Ireland (Éire): KDK126+
Edinburgh Gazette: KDC56
Education: KD3600+
  Armed Forces: KD6055+
  Army: KD6095+
  Ireland (Éire): KDK1050+
  Labor hygiene and safety:
    KD3172.E38
  London: KD9046
  Northern Ireland: KDE392+
  Royal Air Force: KD6205+
  Royal Navy: KD6135+
  Scotland: KDC715+
  Wales: KD9460
Education and church: KD3605
Education, Legal: KD417+
  Ireland: KDK113+
  Scotland: KDC210+
Education, Medical: KD2960.E4
Education, Prelaw-school: KD444
Education, Private: KD3670
Education, Technical: KD3662
Education, Vocational: KD3660+
Educational exchanges: KD3758
Educational vouchers: KD3617
Ejectment: KD925
  Ireland (Éire): KDK235
Election
  Wills: KD1515.E5
Election districts: KD4346
  Ireland (Éire): KDK1288
  Northern Ireland: KDE427
  Scotland: KDC773
Election law: KD4321+

Election law
  Ireland (Éire): KDK1285+
  Northern Ireland: KDE425+
  Scotland: KDC771+
Electric conduits
  Building laws: KD1160
Electric industries
  Collective labor agreements:
    KD3064.E4
Electric installations
  Building laws: KD1160
Electric utilities: KD2545+
  Ireland (Éire): KDK698
Electronic data processing
  Legal research: KD394+
Electronic funds transfer
  Banking law: KD1737.E44
Electronic listening and recording
  devices
  Criminal procedure: KD8388
Elementary and secondary education:
  KD3648+
  Scotland: KDC723+
Emblem, National: KD4650
Emergence medical services:
  KD3405.E45
Emergency powers: KD4440
  Courts: KD7598
Eminent domain: KD1185+
  Ireland (Éire): KDK290
  Northern Ireland: KDE131
  Real property taxes: KD5534
  Scotland: KDC453
Employee participation in management
  and planning: KD3045
Employees' inventions: KD1390+
Employees, Resignation of: KD3110+
Employers' liability: KD2002
  Ireland (Éire): KDK470.5
Employment: KD3096+
  Northern Ireland: KDE327+
Employment agencies: KD3273
Employment, Controls on
  Immigration law: KD4141
Employment discipline
  Civil service: KD4515+
Employment discrimination: KD3102+

Employment discrimination
  Scotland: KDC644.4+
Enameled ware industry: KD2398.E6
Encyclopedias
  Scotland: KDC150
Endowments
  Income tax: KD5500
Enemy property: KD813
Engineering contracts: KD1641
Engineers: KD2980
Engineers, Works for: KD665.E5
English and Empire Digest: KD296.E5
English law in Ireland
  History: KDK141+
Enlisted personnel
  Armed Forces: KD6070
  Army: KD6110
  Royal Air Force: KD6220
  Royal Navy: KD6150
Enlistment
  Armed Forces: KD6053
  Army: KD6093
  Royal Air Force: KD6203
  Royal Marine: KD6182.E5
  Royal Navy: KD6133
Enrichment, Unjust: KD1924
Entailed interests: KD854
Entails
  Scotland: KDC402
Entrapment
  Criminal law: KD7899
Environmental damages
  Torts: KD1989+
Environmental impact charges
  Public health: KD3382.E58
Environmental pollution: KD3351+,
  KD3372+
  Ireland (Éire): KDK910+, KDK920+
  Northern Ireland: KDE355+
  Scotland: KDC680
Environmental taxes
  Public health: KD3382.E58
Equipment
  Armed Forces: KD6077
  Army: KD6117
  Royal Air Force: KD6227
  Royal Navy: KD6157

Equitable conversion
  Land tenure: KD858
Equitable interests: KD845+
Equitable ownership: KD858
Equity: KD674
  Ireland (Éire): KDK178
  Scotland: KDC338
Equity courts, practice, and procedure:
  KD6870+, KD6937+, KD7220
  Ireland (Éire): KDK1595+
  Law reports: KD231.2+, KD276+
    Ireland (Éire): KDK66
    Wales: KD9414
Espionage: KD8024
Espionage, Industrial: KD2226.T7
Essences
  Taxation
    Jersey: KDG368.E7
Estate agents: KD2517.E7
Estate duty
  Ireland (Éire): KDK1480
Estate management, Rural: KD1020.4
Estate management, Urban: KD1020.6
Estate planning: KD1497
Estate tax: KD5560+
  Northern Ireland: KDE487
  Scotland: KDC821
Estates and interests
  Real property: KD841+
    Ireland (Éire): KDK222+
    Scotland: KDC400
Estoppel: KD703.E7
  Scotland: KDC347.E88
Estoppel by judgment: KD7564
Ethics in government: KD4005
Ethics, Judicial: KD7286.J8
Ethics, Legal: KD479+
Etiquette, Legal: KD479+
Eugenics: KD3417
Euthanasia
  Medical legislation: KD3410.E88
Evening schools
  Educational law
    Scotland: KDC725
Evidence
  Civil procedure: KD7491+
    Ireland (Éire): KDK1688

Evidence
  Civil procedure
    Scotland: KDC888+
  Courts-martial: KD6300
  Criminal procedure: KD8371+
    Ireland (Éire): KDK1815
    Scotland: KDC934.5
Evidence, Circumstantial: KD7510
Evidence, Documentary: KD7512
Evidence, Hearsay: KD7525+
Evidence, Medical
  Civil procedure: KD7523
Examination aids: KD663
Examinations, Civil service: KD4513
Exceptions
  Civil procedure: KD7455+
Excess profits tax: KD5511+
Exchanges, Educational: KD3758
Exchequer Chamber, Court of: KD6925
Exchequer rolls
  Anglo-Norman period: KD586
  Norman period: KD558
  Scottish legal history: KDC282
Exchequer, The: KD5282
Excise licenses: KD5600
Excise taxes: KD5588+
  Ireland (Éire): KDK1490+
  Jersey: KDG363+
Exclusion of evidence: KD7525+
Execution of judgment: KD7590+
  Ireland (Éire): KDK1702
  Jersey: KDG380.E9
  Scotland: KDC898
Execution of sentence
  Criminal procedure: KD8450+
    Ireland (Éire): KDK1831+
    Military law: KD6330+
    Northern Ireland: KDE557
    Scotland: KDC935.6+
  Juvenile criminal law: KD8492+
    Ireland (Éire): KDK1840+
Executions, Wartime deferment of:
  KD7598
Executive branch: KD4430+
  Ireland (Éire): KDK1340+
  Northern Ireland: KDE455+
  Scotland: KDC777+

Executive departments
  Ireland (Éire): KDK1346
Executive privilege: KD4010
Executors and administrators: KD1528+
  Northern Ireland: KDE151
  Scotland: KDC468
Executory devices
  Future estates and interests: KD867
Exemption
  Criminal liability: KD7896+
    Ireland (Éire): KDK1763+
  Military service: KD6042+
  Real property tax: KD5735
Expenditure control
  Local finance: KD5712
  Public finance: KD5295
Expenses
  Income tax: KD5460+
Expert evidence
  Civil procedure: KD7521+
  Criminal procedure: KD8393
Expiring law continuance legislation:
  KD146
Explosives
  Public safety: KD3498
  Shipping: KD2770.E9
Export trade: KD2463+
Extortion: KD8005+
Extractive industries: KD2241+
  Ireland (Éire): KDK570+, KDK572
Extradition
  Criminal procedure: KD8344
Extraordinary remedies: KD7610+

F

Factories
  Local taxation: KD5732.F3
Factors
  Agency: KD2024.B7
Factory inspection: KD3170
Faculties
  Church of England: KD8749
Faculty of advocates
  Scotland: KDC245
Fair and unfair labor practices: KD3095

Fairs
  Retail trade: KD2500
False pretenses: KD8000
Family companies: KD2115
Family corporations
  Income tax: KD5524
Family Division, High Court of Justice:
  KD7210
  The Law Reports: KD279.4
Family law: KD750+
  Ireland (Éire): KDK200+
  Jersey: KDG263+
  Scotland: KDC366+
Family planning: KD3340
Family provisions
  Succession upon death: KD1515.F3
Farm crops
  Standards and grading: KD2257.A+
Farm marketing cooperatives: KD2254
Farm producers' cooperatives: KD2254
Farm tenancy: KD907+
  Ireland (Éire): KDK225
  Scotland: KDC416
Farmers
  Income tax: KD5494.F37
  Works for: KD665.F3
Feather industry
  Wages: KD3126.F4
Fee simple: KD845+
  Scotland: KDC400
Fee tail: KD854
Feeding stuffs industry: KD2376.F4
Fees
  Local finance: KD5750
  National revenue history: KD5329
Fees, License: KD5750
Fees, Medical: KD2960.F4
Fellow servant rule: KD2002
Fences
  Real property: KD921
Fertilizer industry: KD2376.F4
Feudal tenure: KD834+
  Northern Ireland: KDE113.5
  Scotland: KDC397
Fiars prices
  Scotland: KDC582.2.G7

Field crops
  Standards and grading: KD2257.A+
Filacers: KD7298
Finance
  Higher education: KD3685
Finance, Court: KD7122.5
Finance, Wartime: KD5336+
Financial statements: KD2042
  Corporations: KD2098
Fine rolls: KD588
Fines
  Criminal law: KD7885.F5
  Criminal procedure: KD8458
  Land transfer: KD992
  National revenue history: KD5329
Fingerprints
  Criminal procedure: KD8385
Fire departments: KD3516
Fire fighters: KD3516
Fire insurance: KD1885
Fire prevention and control: KD3515+
  London: KD9034.F5
Firearms
  Public safety: KD3492
Firearms industry
  Labor disputes: KD3091.F5+
First instance, Courts of
  Ireland (Éire): KDK1630+
Fish protection: KD2290+
Fishery
  Ireland (Éire): KDK590+
  Scotland: KDC585+
Fishery law: KD2310+
Fishing industry
  Labor disputes: KD3091.F53+
Flats: KD850
Flax and hemp industry
  Wages: KD3126.F5
Fleta, seu Commentarius juris Anglicani
  (ca. 1290): KD600.F59
Flogging
  Military law: KD6332
Flood control: KD1071
F.O.B. clause: KD1673
Food: KD3450+
  Labeling: KD2209.F6
  Scotland: KDC700+

Food
  Weights and measures: KD2231.F6
Food additives: KD3456.P7
Food law: KD3453+
  Ireland (Éire): KDK940
Food processing industries: KD2405+
  Ireland (Éire): KDK645+
  Jersey: KDG310+
  Northern Ireland: KDE250.A+
  Scotland: KDC592+
Foot trails: KD1048
Footprints
  Criminal procedure: KD8385
Forcible entry: KD7994
Foreign corporations
  Government regulation and control:
    KD2084
Foreign exchange
  Conflict of laws: KD685.F65
Foreign exchange regulations: KD5288
  Ireland (Éire): KDK1434
Foreign investments
  Economic policy: KD2190
  Ireland (Éire): KDK545
Foreign investments, Income from
  Income tax: KD5479
Foreign investors
  Works for: KD665.B86
    Ireland (Éire): KDK175.B87
    Isle of Man: KDG31.B87
    Northern Ireland: KDE88.5.B86
Foreign judgments: KD7121
Foreign Office: KD4472
Foreign relations: KD4030+
Foreign Service: KD4474+
Forensic psychology: KD7487
Forest land
  Conservation
    Ireland (Éire): KDK572
Forestry: KD2280
  Income tax: KD5526.F65
  Ireland (Éire): KDK570+
  Scotland: KDC580+
Forfeitures
  Criminal procedure: KD8460
    Ireland (Éire): KDK1833
    Scotland: KDC935.7

Forgery: KD8090
Form books: KD318, KDK85
  Scotland: KDC156
Formalities
  Contracts: KD1568
Formularies: KD546
Fortescu, J., De laudibus legum Angliae
  (1468-1471): KD600.F6713
Foundations
  Income tax: KD5500
Foundries
  Labor hygiene and safety: KD3172.F6
Franchises
  Retail trade: KD2490
Franchises, Grants of
  Anglo-Norman period: KD590
Fraternal insurance: KD1913
Fraternities, Law student: KD448.A+
Fraud
  Contracts: KD1583
    Ireland (Éire): KDK375
  Criminal law: KD8000
    Ireland (Éire): KDK1774.F73
  Torts: KD1963
Frauds, Statute of: KD1568
Fraudulent conveyances: KD2162
Free tenure
  Feudal tenure: KD835+
Freedom of assembly and association:
  KD4117
Freedom of expression: KD4110+
  Ireland (Éire): KDK1262
Freedom of information: KD3756
  Ireland (Éire): KDK1101
Freedom of petition: KD4119
Freedom of religion and conscience:
  KD4100+
Freedom of the press: KD4112
  Ireland (Éire): KDK1262
Freehold estates: KD845+, KDC400
Friendly societies: KD1913
  Wales: KD9448
Frustration of contracts: KD1596
Fur industry
  Wages: KD3126.F87
Fur trade: KD2385

Furniture industry
  Wages: KD3126.F875
Future estates
  Personal property: KD863+
  Real property: KD863+
    Scotland: KDC403+
Future interests
  Personal property: KD863+
  Real property: KD863+
    Scotland: KDC403+

G

Galleries: KD3736
Gambling
  Contracts: KD1920+
  Criminal law: KD8072
  Ireland (Éire): KDK978
  Regulation: KD3527, KDE382
  Taxation: KD5597.W3
Gambling gains
  Income tax: KD5483.G3
Game laws: KD2290
  Ireland (Éire): KDK582
  Scotland: KDC584.5
Game protection: KD2290+
Games of chance
  Ireland (Éire): KDK978
  Northern Ireland: KDE382
  Regulation: KD3527
Garages: KD2517.G3
Gardens
  Legal aspects: KD667.G37
Garnishment: KD7592
Gas industry
  Public utilities: KD2550
Gavelkind: KD836.G3
General Eyre, Court of: KD6913
General trusts: KD1483
Gift tax: KD5560+
  Northern Ireland: KDE487
  Scotland: KDC821
Glanvill: Tractatus de legibus
  consuetudinibus et regni Angliae
  (1187-1189): KD600.G5513
Gold
  Weights and measures: KD2231.G6

Good faith: KD703.G6
Goodwill
  Intellectual property: KD1450
Government
  Church of England: KD8650+
  London: KD8910+
Government contracts: KD1610+
Government departments: KD4467+
Government expenditures: KD5292
Government lawyers: KD472.G6
Government officials and employees
  Civil service: KD4510+
  Inventions: KD1391
  Patents: KD1391
  Tort liability: KD1994
Government personal property:
  KD1465
Government tort liability: KD2004
Government torts
  Ireland (Éire): KDK470.7
Governmental investigations: KD4895
Grade crossings: KD2620
Grain
  Marketing regulations
    Scotland: KDC582.2.G7
  Price supports: KD2248.G7
  Shipping: KD2770.G7
Grain trade
  Export: KD2466.G7
  Import: KD2475.G7
Grand jury: KD8350
Grand Jury
  Ireland (Éire): KDK1806
Grants-in-aid
  Local finance: KD5752
Grants of franchises: KD590
Gravel and sand industry: KD2370.S3
Gray's Inn: KD504.G7
Great Sessions, Courts of: KD9482
Greater London Boroughs: KD9142.A+
Greater London Council: KD8913+
Grievances
  Labor law: KD3150
Groceries
  Retail trade: KD2510.G76
    Ireland (Éire): KDK685.G74
Ground effect machines: KD2840

Group medical practice: KD2960.P3
Guaranty insurance: KD1904+
Guardian and ward: KD785
  Scotland: KDC378
Guernsey: KDG421+
Gynecologists: KD2965.G95
Gypsies, Works for: KD665.G95

H

Habeas corpus: KD7612
Habitual criminals: KD7883
  Scotland: KDC918
Hale, M.: The History of the Common
  Law of England (1713): KD600.H3
Hallmarks: KD2231.G6
Halsbury's Statutes of England:
  KD135.H3
Handbooks for legal services to the
  poor: KD667.P68
Harbors and ports: KD2792+
  Ireland (Éire): KDK768+
Hard labor: KD7885.H3
Hartlepool, Port of: KD2796.H3
Hat industry
  Scotland: KDC647.H3
  Wages: KD3126.H3
Hazardous articles and processes
  Public safety: KD3494+
Hazardous occupations: KD3168+
Hazardous waste disposal
  Public safety: KD3495
Health insurance
  Private insurance: KD1871
  Social insurance: KD3205+
    Ireland (Éire): KDK873
    Isle of Man: KDG50.3
    Jersey: KDG329.3
    Northern Ireland: KDE342
    Scotland: KDC664+
  Wales: KD9448
Health services, Schools: KD3405.S3
Hearsay evidence: KD7525
Heirless property: KD1534
  Scotland: KDC470
Hemp industry
  Wages: KD3126.F5

Herbicides
  Public safety: KD3505.P46
Heresy
  Criminal trials: KD371.H47
  Ecclesiastical law: KD8763
Heritable jurisdictions
  Scotland: KDC865+
Herring fishery: KD2315.H4
Hidage: KD5327.H5
High Court
  Ireland (Éire): KDK1630+
High Court of Admiralty: KD1832+
  Ireland (Éire): KDK437
High Court of Justice: KD7154+
  Costs: KD7568.S82
High Court of Justiciary
  Scotland: KDC936+
Higher education: KD3680+
  Scotland: KDC728
Highest courts of appeals: KD7132+
Highway finance: KD1043
Highway law: KD1040
  Scotland: KDC441
Highway safety: KD2620
Highway transport workers: KD3177.H5
Hire-purchase: KD1759
  Scotland: KDC523
Historic buildings and monuments:
  KD3740
  Ireland (Éire): KDK1092
Historical documents: KD3753+
  Ireland (Éire): KDK1100
Holding companies: KD2112
Holidays
  Labor law: KD3142
Hollow ware industry: KD2398.H6
Home Guard: KD6115
Home labor: KD3163
Homicide: KD7963+
Horizontal property: KD850
Horn, A.: The Mirrour of Justices (1285-
  1290): KD600.H67
Horse racing: KD3525
  Taxation: KD5597.W3
Horses
  Legal aspects: KD667.H6
  Sales contracts: KD1657.H6

Hospitals: KD3400
  Armed Forces: KD6078
  Army: KD6118
  Ireland (Éire): KDK928
  Royal Air Force: KD6228
  Royal Navy: KD6158
  Scotland: KDC692
Hotels: KD2517.H6
  Ireland (Éire): KDK691.H6
Hours of labor: KD3136+
  Children: KD3159
    Northern Ireland: KDE335
    Scotland: KDC655
  Ireland (Éire): KDK850
  Women: KD3161
    Scotland: KDC656
Hours of Labor
  Scotland: KDC650+
House of Commons: KD4310+
  Northern Ireland: KDE450+
House of Lords: KD7132+
  Civil procedure: KD7632
    Scotland: KDC902.6
  Constitutional law: KD4260+
  Criminal procedure: KD8429+
    Original jurisdiction: KD8282.2+
  Law reports: KD187+
    Scotland: KDC110
House of Representatives Ireland (Éire):
  KDK1330+
Housebreaking: KD7993
Housing: KD1171+
  Armed Forces: KD6063
  Army: KD6103
  Finance: KD1183
    Ireland (Éire): KDK286
    Scotland: KDC452
  Ireland (Éire): KDK283+
  Jersey: KDG279
  London: KD8952.H6
  Northern Ireland: KDE138
  Royal Air Force: KD6213
  Royal Navy: KD6143
  Scotland: KDC452
Housing condominium: KD850
Housing cooperatives
  Scotland: KDC405.5.H6

Housing courts: KD911
Hovercraft: KD2840
Human body
  Legal aspects: KD667.H85
Human experimentation in medicine
  Medical legislation: KD3407+
Hundred courts: KD6976+
Husband abuse: KD7973
Husband and wife: KD753+
  Ireland (Éire): KDK203+
  Jersey: KDG265.M3
  Scotland: KDC367+
Husband's coercion
  Criminal liability: KD7898
Hygiene and safety
  Labor law: KDK857

I

Identification, Means of
  Criminal procedure: KD8385
Identification of individuals: KD4122
Illegal disclosure of official secrets:
  KD8024
Illegitimate children: KD775
  Ireland (Éire): KDK209
  Northern Ireland: KDE98.I4
  Scotland: KDC376
Immigration: KD4134+
  Ireland (Éire): KDK1270
Immigration inspection: KD3369
Immunity, Parliamentary: KD4246
Immunization
  Public health laws: KD3370
Impeachment
  Law officers of the Crown: KD7105.5
Impeachment power and procedure:
  KD4373
Imperial Yeomanry: KD6115
Implied warranties: KD1654.C6
Import bounties: KD5694.B6
Import trade: KD2470+
Impossibility of performance: KD1596
Impossibility, Supervening: KD1596
Impounding distress
  Ireland (Éire): KDK469

Impressment
  Armed Forces: KD6053
  Army: KD6093
  Royal Air Force: KD6203
  Royal Navy: KD6133
Imprisonment
  Criminal law: KD7885.I6
  Criminal procedure: KD8450+
    Ireland (Éire): KDK1831
    Northern Ireland: KDE557
  Juvenile criminal procedure:
    KD8492+
    Ireland (Éire): KDK1840+
Imprisonment for debt: KD7596
In vitro fertilization
  Medical legislation: KD3415
Incentive wages: KD3124.P7
Inchoate offenses: KD7953+
  Scotland: KDC920.I55
Incidental questions: KD681.P74
Income tax: KD5421+
  Channel islands: KDG164.I5
  Ireland (Éire): KDK1452+
  Isle of Man: KDG70.4.I5
Incorporated Law Society of Ireland:
  KDK134
Incorporated Society of Law Agents in
  Scotland: KDC247
Incorporation: KD2085
Incorporeal hereditaments: KD935+
Indemnity insurance
  Armed Forces: KD6062
  Army: KD6102
  Merchant mariners: KD6248
  Royal Air Force: KD6212
  Royal Navy: KD6142
Independent contractors: KD1638+
  Scotland: KDC500+
Indexes
  Law reports
    Common law courts: KD197.A+,
      KD200.4
    Common law reports: KD203.4
    Digests: KD300
    Equity courts: KD232.4
    In all the courts since 1865: KD285
    Ireland (Éire): KDK61+

Indexes
  Law reports
    Northern Ireland: KDE59
    Scotland: KDC110+
  Statutes
    Channel Islands
      Jersey: KDG226
    General: KD142+
    Ireland (Éire): KDK44+
    London: KD8876
    Northern Ireland: KDE47
    Scotland: KDC90
  Statutory instruments
    Ireland (Éire): KDK51
  Statutory rules and orders: KD170
    Ireland (Éire): KDK49
    Northern Ireland: KDE50
Indictment: KD8348+
  Ireland (Éire): KDK1806
  Scotland: KDC933
Indirect taxes: KD5580+
Individual and state: KD4050+
  Ireland (Éire): KDK1250+
Industrial bonds
  Corporations: KD2108
Industrial courts and tribunals: KD3073
  Scotland: KDC643.I53
Industrial espionage: KD2226.T7
Industrial insurance: KD1868.I6
Industrial lawyers: KD472.I5
Industrial property
  Antitrust aspects: KD1371
  Guernsey: KDG440.I5
  Income tax: KD5483.I53
  Ireland (Éire): KDK315+
Industrial rating relief: KD5739
Industrial societies: KD2122
Infant formulas: KD3456.I54
Infant welfare: KD3304
Infanticide: KD7967
Inflammable materials
  Public safety: KD3500
Influence of foreign law: KD540
  Scotland: KDC315
Influence of religion: KD540.5.R4
Influence of Roman law: KD540

Information
  Criminal procedure: KD8348+
    Ireland (Éire): KDK1806
    Scotland: KDC933
Information retrieval
  Legal research: KD394+
Informed consent
  Medical legislation: KD3410.I54
Infringement, Patent: KD1411
Inheritance and succession
  London: KD9090.I5
Inheritance tax: KD5560+
  Ireland (Éire): KDK1480
  Northern Ireland: KDE487
  Scotland: KDC821
Injunctions: KD7578
  Scotland: KDC896
Injunctions of Edward VI and Elizabeth I:
  KD8632
Inner Temple: KD504.I5
Innkeeper and guest: KD1685
Inns
  Ireland (Éire): KDK691.H6
Inns of Chancery: KD504.2+
Inns of Court: KD503.2+
Inns of Court and the Bar, Senate of:
  KD500
Inquisitiones post mortem: KD839
Insane persons
  Capacity and disability
    Ireland (Éire): KDK191
  Criminal liability: KD7897
Insanity
  Criminal liability
    Ireland (Éire): KDK1764
Insider trading in corporate securities:
  KD1777.I58
Insolvency and bankruptcy: KD2139+
  Conflict of laws: KD685.I5
  Directories: KD340.B34
  Ireland (Éire): KDK530+
  Jersey: KDG296
  Northern Ireland: KDE230
  Scotland: KDC560+, KDC561+
  Taxation: KD5405
Inspection
  Food: KD3455

Inspection, Factory: KD3170
Installment sale: KD1759
  Scotland: KDC523
Institute, The: KD456.I6
Institutions for criminal lunatics:
  KD8452+
Insurance: KD1851+
  Ireland (Éire): KDK440
  Real property taxes: KD5534
  Scotland: KDC534
Insurance brokers: KD1862
Insurance business
  Ireland (Éire): KDK440
Insurance companies
  Income tax: KD5526.I56
  Regulation: KD1862
Insurance fraud: KD8001
Intangible property: KD1238+
  Ireland (Éire): KDK315+
Intellectual property: KD1261+
  Antitrust aspects: KD1371
  Conflict of laws: KD685.I54
  Guernsey: KDG440.I5
  Ireland (Éire): KDK315+
Intent, Criminal: KD7892
Interdict
  Civil procedure
    Scotland: KDC896
Interest
  Income tax: KD5477
  Loans: KD1740
    Ireland (Éire): KDK412+
Interests arising from marriage:
  KD1523.D6
Intermediate appeals
  Civil procedure
    Ireland (Éire): KDK1711
Internal security: KD4160
  Northern Ireland: KDE423
International and municipal law:
  KD4015, KDK1227.5
International trade: KD2460+
Interpleader: KD7465
Interpretation and construction,
  Statutory: KD691
Interrogatories: KD7470
  Ireland (Éire): KDK1680

Intertemporal law: KD687
Intestate succession: KD1522+
  Scotland: KDC467
Inventions: KD1384+
Inventions, Employees': KD1390+
Inventors' awards: KD1394
Investigation, Criminal: KD8335
  Criminal procedure
    Scotland: KDC930.5
Investigations, Governmental: KD4895
Investment companies: KD1782
Investment trusts: KD1782
Investments: KD1774+
  Ireland (Éire): KDK420
Investments, Foreign, Income from
  Income tax: KD5479
Irish House of Lords
  Law reports: KDK61
Iron
  Tariff: KD5662.I7
Iron and steel industry: KD2395.I7
  Wages: KD3126.I7
Iron mining industry: KD2365.I7
Isle of Man: KDG21+, KDG21+
Itinerant justices, Court of: KD6913

J

Jersey: KDG220+
Jews
  Capacity and disability: KD744.J4
  Citizenship: KD4058.J48
  Discrimination: KD4102.J4
Job security: KD3110+
  Ireland (Éire): KDK820
Joint boards
  London: KD9120+
Joint obligations: KD1571
Joint-stock companies: KD2071+
Joint tenancy: KD880
Joint ventures
  Income tax: KD5502
Journalists: KD3177.J65
Journalists, Works for: KD665.J6
  Scotland: KDC335.J68
Judges: KD7285+
  Ireland (Éire): KDK1652

Judges
  Northern Ireland: KDE524.5
Judgment
  Civil procedure: KD7562+
    Ireland (Éire): KDK1694+
  Criminal procedure: KD8406
    Scotland: KDC935
Judgments
  Norman period: KD560
  Scottish legal history: KDC277
Judgments, Foreign: KD7121
Judicial assistance: KD7121.5
  Criminal procedure: KD8469
  Scotland: KDC843
Judicial Committee of the Privy Council:
  KD7134+, KD8693
  Appellate procedure: KD7634
  Costs: KD7568.P7
Judicial corruption: KD7286.J8
Judicial discretion: KD7558
Judicial education: KD435
Judicial error, Compensation for:
  KD8464
Judicial ethics: KD7286.J8
Judicial investigations: KD370+
  Ireland (Éire): KDK102+
  Jersey: KDG240+
  Northern Ireland: KDE72+
  Scotland: KDC184+
Judicial officers: KD7283+
  Ireland (Éire): KDK1650+
  Northern Ireland: KDE524+
  Scotland: KDC868+
Judicial power: KD4645
  Scotland: KDC783
Judicial review of administrative acts:
  KD4902
  Ireland (Éire): KDK1382
  Scotland: KDC802
Judicial statistics: KD327+
  Ireland (Éire): KDK89
  London: KD8886+
  Scotland: KDC161+
Judiciary
  Scotland: KDC783
Juridical Society of Edinburgh:
  KDC220.J8

Jurisdiction
  Civil procedure: KD7443
    Scotland: KDC879
  Constitutional law: KD4025
  Criminal law: KD7888
Jurisprudence and philosophy of English
  law: KD640+
Juristic persons: KD2057+
  Income tax: KD5504+
  Ireland (Éire): KDK496+
  Scotland: KDC556+
Juristic persons, Criminal liability of:
  KD7892.5
Jury and jurors
  Civil procedure: KD7540+
    Ireland (Éire): KDK1691+
    Northern Ireland: KDE530.J8
    Scotland: KDC891
  Criminal procedure: KD8400
Jus relictae
  Scotland: KDC465.R5
Justice, Military: KD6290+
Justice Society: KD456.J87
Justices of the peace: KD7301+
  Criminal procedure: KD8301+
    Ireland (Éire): KDK1820
  Ireland (Éire): KDK1610+
  Scotland: KDC860+
Justiciary, High Court of
  Scotland: KDC936+
Jute industry
  Wages: KD3126.J8
Juvenile courts: KD8473
  Ireland (Éire): KDK1837
  Scotland: KDC952
Juvenile crime
  Statistics: KD331
    London: KD8890
Juvenile criminal law: KD8471+
  Ireland (Éire): KDK1836+
  Northern Ireland: KDE561+
  Scotland: KDC951+
Juvenile detention homes: KD8492
  Ireland (Éire): KDK1840
Juvenile reformatories: KD8492
  Ireland (Éire): KDK1840

K

Keg and drum industry
  Wages: KD3126.K4
Kennels: KD3429.K45
King
  Religion: KD4456.R44
  Title: KD4456.T5
King's Bench: KD6895+
  Crown side: KD8260
  Law reports: KD190+
    Ireland (Éire): KDK70
King's Bench Division: KD7169+
  Costs: KD7568.S83
  Crown side: KD8285
  Law reports: KD277, KD277.7
King's Bench masters: KD7556
King's Inns, Dublin: KDK132
Knight's service
  Feudal tenure: KD836.K5

L

Labeling
  Trade regulations: KD2208+
Labor conditions: KD3095
  Ireland (Éire): KDK815
  Scotland: KDC644
Labor Court
  Ireland (Éire): KDK804
Labor discipline: KD3146+
Labor disputes: KD3070+
  Arbitration: KD3071
    Maritime laborers: KD1839
  Conciliation: KD3071
  Wartime disputes: KD3086+
Labor exchanges: KD3273
Labor hygiene and safety: KD3168+
  Merchant mariners: KD1842
  Northern Ireland: KDE333+
  Scotland: KDC653+
Labor law: KD3001+
  Conflict of laws: KD685.L3
  Ireland (Éire): KDK802+
  Isle of Man: KDG50.2
  Jersey: KDG329.2
  London: KD8996+

Labor law
  Northern Ireland: KDE322+
  Scotland: KDC640+
Labor protection
  Labor law: KD3168+
  Merchant mariners: KD1842
  Northern Ireland: KDE333+
  Scotland: KDC653+
Labor standards: KD3095+
  Ireland (Éire): KDK815+
  Northern Ireland: KDE326+
  Scotland: KDC644+
Labor unions
  Civil service: KD4524
  Ireland (Éire): KDK807
  Management-labor relations:
    KD3050+
    Northern Ireland: KDE324
  Tort liability: KD1996
Labor unions, Maritime: KD1839
Laboratories: KD3715.L3
Lace and lacemaking
  Wages: KD3126.L3
Lack of genuine consent
  Void and voidable contracts:
    KD1582+
    Ireland (Éire): KDK375
Land books: KD550
Land burning
  Ireland (Éire): KDK572
Land, Carriage by: KD1802
Land charges: KD1016
  Local: KD1128
Land Commission: KD1128
Land development: KD1125
Land drainage: KD1095+
Land law: KD821+
  Ireland (Éire): KDK217+
  Isle of Man: KDG33.2
  Scotland: KDC393+
Land ownership
  Income tax: KD5471
Land purchase acts
  Northern Ireland: KDE120
Land reclamation: KD1095+
Land surveying: KD988
Land tax: KD5535

Land tenure: KD833+
  Ireland (Éire): KDK219+
  Northern Ireland: KDE113+
  Scotland: KDC395+
Land titles
  Data processing: KD394.5.L3
Land transfer: KD966+
  Northern Ireland: KDE121+,
    KDK245+
  Scotland: KDC430+
Land valuation
  Real property taxes: KD5534
    Scotland: KDC817
Land value tax: KD5538
Land values duties: KD5536
Landed Estates Court
  Ireland (Éire)): KDK251
Landlord and tenant: KD891+
  Ireland (Éire): KDK222+
  Scotland: KDC412+
Lands of ecclesiastical corporations:
  KD8740
Lands Tribunal
  Eminent domain: KD1187
Landscape architects: KD2990.L37
Larceny: KD7992+
  Criminal law
    Ireland (Éire): KDK1774.L37
  Indictment: KD8348.5.L3
Laundry industry
  Labor hygiene and safety: KD3172.L3
  Wages: KD3126.L38
    Northern Ireland: KDE330.L3
Law agents
  Scotland: KDC229
Law as a career: KD460
  Ireland (Éire): KDK120
  Scotland: KDC225
Law books
  Anglo-Norman period: KD600
  Norman period: KD544, KD562
Law dictionaries: KD313
  Ireland (Éire): KDK84
  Scotland: KDC152
  Wales: KD9420
Law office management: KD492+
  Scotland: KDC238+

Law officers of the Crown: KD7105+
Law reporters and reporting: KD411
Law reports
  Channel Islands: KDG120
    Jersey: KDG232+
  Checklists: KD54
  Collections: KD186.2+
  Court of Common Pleas
    Digests: KD203.3
  Digests: KD200.3
  Ecclesiastical law: KD8638+
    Ireland (Éire): KDK1860+
  Indexes
    Common law courts: KD200.4,
      KD203.4
    Digests: KD300
    Equity courts: KD232.4
    In all the courts since 1865: KD285
    Ireland (Éire): KDK61+
    Northern Ireland: KDE59
    Privy Council Cases (Judicial
      Committee): KD247.4
    Scotland: KDC110+
  Ireland (Éire): KDK61+
  Isle of Man: KDG27+
  Northern Ireland: KDE55+
  Reports in all the courts: KD270+
  Scotland: KDC110+
  Wales: KD9410+
Law Reports: KD275+
Law Reports (Ireland), 1878-1893:
  KDK63
Law school, Admission to: KD444
Law school catalogs: KD428.A+
Law schools: KD452.A+
  Scotland: KDC215.A+
Law societies: KD456.A+
  Scotland: KDC220.A+
Law society journals: KD345
  Ireland (Éire): KDK93
  Scotland: KDC170
Law Society of Scotland: KDC247
Law Society (United Kingdom): KD509
Law students: KD446+
Lawyers: KD460
  Ireland (Éire): KDK120
  Scotland: KDC225

Lawyers' clubs: KD510.A+
Lay days
  Maritime law: KD1834.D4
Lay time
  Maritime law: KD1834.D4
Lead industry
  Labor hygiene and safety: KD3172.L4
Leaseholds: KD891+
  Ireland (Éire): KDK222+
  Northern Ireland: KDE120
  Scotland: KDC412+
Leases
  Income tax: KD5483.L4
Leases, Ecclesiastical
  Ireland (Éire): KDK227
Leave regulations
  Civil service: KD4531
Leaves of absence
  Labor law: KD3142
Legacies: KD1515.L4
Legacy and succession duty
  Ireland (Éire): KDK1480
Legal abbreviations: KD400
Legal advertising: KD703.N6
Legal aid: KD512+
  Ireland (Éire): KDK137
  Scotland: KDC260
Legal aid societies: KD509+
Legal assistance to the poor: KD512+
  Scotland: KDC260
Legal bibliography: KD392+
  Ireland (Éire): KDK110
  Scotland: KDC200
Legal composition: KD404
  Scotland: KDC202
Legal draftsmanship: KD404
  Scotland: KDC202
Legal education
  Ireland: KDK113+
Legal Education Association: KD430.L4
Legal ethics: KD479+, KDC234
Legal etiquette: KD479+, KDC234
Legal fees
  Law practice: KD489, KDK126.3
    Northern Ireland: KDE77
Legal investments: KD1787
  Government bonds: KD5300

Legal investments
  Mortgages: KD1013
  Stocks: KD2096
Legal maxims: KD315
  Scotland: KDC154
Legal profession: KD460+
  Ireland (Éire): KDK120+
  Jersey: KDG243
  Northern Ireland: KDE75+
  Scotland: KDC225+
Legal protection of the poor:
  KD667.P68
Legal quotations: KD315
  Scotland: KDC154
Legal reform: KD654
  Ireland (Éire): KDK166
  Northern Ireland: KDE87
  Scotland: KDC320
Legal research: KD392+
  Ireland (Éire): KDK110
  Scotland: KDC200
Legal status of students: KD3688
Legislation: KD124+
  Ireland (Éire): KDK38+
  Isle of Man: KDG25.2+
  Northern Ireland: KDE42+
  Scotland: KDC69+
  Wales: KD124+
Legislation of the Church of England
  (1559-): KD8624+
Legislative documents: KD4354.A3
Legislative process: KD4230+
  House of Commons: KD4354+
  Northern Ireland: KDE440+
  Scotland: KDC766
Legislators: KD4246+
  Ireland (Éire): KDK1310+
Legislature
  Ireland (Éire): KDK1305+
Legitim
  Scotland: KDC465.R5
Legitimacy: KD774
Legitimation of children: KD774
  Northern Ireland: KDE98.I4
Lender liability
  Torts: KD1990.5.B35
Lesser historical courts: KD6965+

Lesser historical courts
  Ireland (Éire): KDK1610+
Letters of credit: KD1735
Letters of patent: KD178
Liability
  Attorney and client: KD486.M35
  Carriage by sea: KD1825+
  Ireland (Éire)
    Carriers: KDK430
    Minors: KDK189
    Railways: KD2696+
    Strict liability: KD1983+
     Ireland (Éire): KDK467+
    Trustees: KD1493
Liability, Criminal: KD7890+
Liability for condition and use of land:
  KD1977
  Ireland (Éire): KDK461
Liability for marine accidents: KD1825+
Liability for torts of others: KD1999+
Liability insurance: KD1890+
Libel and slander
  Criminal law: KD7980
  Scotland: KDC543
  Torts: KD1960
    Ireland (Éire): KDK454
  Trials: KD371.L5
Liberties
  Scotland: KDC758
Libraries: KD3746
  Jersey: KDG344
Library catalogs: KD56
  Ireland (Éire): KDK22
  Scotland: KDC53
License fees: KD5750
Licensed premises
  Local taxation: KD5732.L5
Licenses, Drivers': KD2607
Licenses, Excise: KD5600
Licenses, Local taxation: KD5750
Licenses, Patent: KD1400
Licensing
  Corporations: KD2083+
  London: KD8980
  Motor carriers: KD2627
  Pilots: KD2726
  Radio stations: KD2905

Licensing
  Service trades: KD2515
    Ireland (Éire): KDK690
    Scotland: KDC597
Lien, Attorney's: KD490
Liens: KD1762+
  Real property: KD1010+
    Scotland: KDC438
Liens, Contractors': KD1640
Liens, Maritime: KD1834.B6
Liens, Mechanics': KD1640
Liens, Workers': KD1640
Life insurance: KD1864+
Life insurance companies: KD1866
Life insurance proceeds
  Income tax: KD5483.L5
Life interests
  Land tenure: KD857+
Lifesaving apparatus
  Ship safety regulations: KD2764
Light and air easements: KD940
Light railways: KD2710
Limitation of actions: KD703.L5
  Civil procedure: KD7455
  Conflict of laws: KD685.L55
  Negotiable instruments: KD1697.L5
Limited partnership: KD2054
Lincoln's Inn: KD504.L5
Linen industry
  Regulation: KDK635.L55
  Wages: KD3126.L5
    Ireland (Éire): KDK840.L5
    Northern Ireland: KDE330.T4
Linguistic rights
  Ireland (Éire): KDK1261
Liquidation
  Corporations: KD2125
    Ireland (Éire): KDK520
    Scotland: KDC558
Liquidators in bankruptcy: KD2155.R4
Liquor laws: KD3466+
  Ireland (Éire): KDK952
  Jersey: KDG337
  London: KD9028
  Northern Ireland: KDE378
Liquor production
  Scotland: KDC704

Liquor taxes: KD5590+
  Ireland (Éire): KDK1492.A5
  Jersey: KDG366+
Liquor traffic
  Scotland: KDC704
Literary copyright: KD1300+
Litigants in person: KD7463.5
Liverpool Court of Passage: KD7246
Liverpool, Port of: KD2796.L5
Livestock
  Standards and grading: KD2259+
Livestock industry and trade: KD2267+
Living wills: KD3410.E88
Loan of money: KD1740
  Ireland (Éire): KDK412+
  Scotland: KDC517
Local civil service: KD4805+
Local councils: KD4779.L6
Local courts
  Before 1873: KD6965+
  Ireland (Éire): KDK1610+
  Northern Ireland: KDE523
  Scotland
    Law reports: KDC121+
  Since 1873: KD7228+
Local Defense Volunteers: KD6115
Local elections: KD4347
  Ireland (Éire): KDK1295
  Scotland: KDC774
Local finance: KD5710+
  Ireland (Éire): KDK1520+
  Scotland: KDC825
Local government: KD4746+
  Ireland (Éire): KDK1365+
  Isle of Man: KDG64
  Scotland: KDC788+
  Wales: KD9468
Local government and central
  government: KD4765
Local laws
  England: KD8849.2+
  Ireland (Éire): KDK1909.2+
  Northern Ireland: KDE570+
  Scotland: KDC979.2+
  Wales: KD9500.2+
Local offenses
  London: KD9085+

Local option
  Liquor laws: KD3480.L6
Local revenue: KD5718+
Local taxation: KD5718+
  London: KD9073+
Local taxation licenses: KD5750
Local transit: KD2710
  Ireland (Éire): KDK748
  London: KD8970
Locus standi reports: KD4372
London
  Local laws: KD8860+
London Authority, Port of: KD9120
London County Council: KD8920+
London Gazette: KD62
London, Port of: KD2796.L6
London Stock Exchange: KD1778.L6
Longshoremen: KD3177.L6
Lord Chancellor's Departments:
  KD7107
Lord High Chancellor: KD6945
Lord High Steward: KD8283
Lords spiritual: KD4263
Lord's Supper: KD8751.5+
Lords temporal: KD4265+
Lotteries
  Criminal law: KD8072
  Ireland (Éire): KDK978
  Regulation: KD3527
    Northern Ireland: KDE382
Lower courts
  General
    Before the Judicature Act of 1873:
      KD6965+
    Since the Judicature Act of 1873:
      KD7228+
  Ireland (Éire): KDK1610+
  Northern Ireland: KDE523
  Scotland
    Law reports: KDC121+
Lowtonian Society: KD456.L6
Lunacy proceedings: KD740+
  Ireland (Éire): KDK191

M

Machinery
  Local taxation: KD5732.F3
Magistrates: KD7301+
Magistrates' courts: KD7249.2+,
  KD7301+
  Criminal procedure: KD8301+
    Ireland (Éire): KDK1820
    Scotland: KDC941
Mail-order business
  Trade regulation: KD2501
Maintenance and champerty: KD8057
Maintenance relief
  Income tax deductions: KD5462.M3
Malicious prosecution: KD1962
Malpractice: KD1978
  Attorney and client: KD486.M35
  Economic and financial advisors:
    KD2974+
  Medical: KD2960.M55
  Torts: KD1978
    Ireland (Éire): KDK462
Malt trade
  Export controls: KD2466.M3
Management
  Business corporations: KD2088+
    Ireland (Éire): KDK504
Management-labor relations: KD3040+
  Ireland (Éire): KDK804+
  Northern Ireland: KDE324
  Scotland: KDC642+
Management of courts: KD7122+
Mandamus: KD7613
Manorial courts: KD6968+
  Ireland (Éire): KDK1613+
  Law reports: KD225
Manorial laws
  General collections: KD594
  Particular manors
    England: KD9310.A+
    Wales: KD9350.A+
Manors
  Feudal tenure: KD838.M3
Manual training
  Educational law: KD3662
Manufacturing industries: KD2375+

Manufacturing industries
  Ireland (Éire): KDK629+
Manx law reports: KDG27.A5+
Marine accidents
  Liability: KD1825
Marine insurance: KD1845+
Marital law: KD4442
Marital property: KD760+
  Conflict of laws: KD685.M3
    Ireland (Éire): KDK180.M37
    Scotland: KDC342.M3
  Scotland: KDC370
Maritime commercial law: KD1811+
  Ireland (Éire): KDK435+
  Scotland: KDC530+
Maritime labor law: KD1836+
Maritime labor unions: KD1839
Maritime liens: KD1834.B6
Maritime torts: KD1825
Marketing agreements, Agricultural:
  KD2250
Marketing controls, Agricultural:
  KD2250
Marketing of legal services: KD491
Marketing of securities: KD1774+
  Ireland (Éire): KDK420
Marketing regulations, Agricultural
  Scotland: KDC582+
Markets
  Retail trade: KD2500
Marks of origin: KD1444+
  Ireland (Éire): KDK345
Marriage
  Conflict of laws: KD685.M3
    Ireland (Éire): KDK180.M37
    Scotland: KDC342.M3
  Domestic relations: KD753+
    Ireland (Éire): KDK203+
    Jersey: KDG265.M3
    Scotland: KDC367+
Marriage contracts: KD762
Marriage settlements: KD762
  Ireland (Éire): KDK204
Marriage, Void and voidable: KD756
Married women: KD758
Marshalsea, Court of: KD6980
Mass media: KD2870+

Master and servant
  Contract for service
    Scotland: KDC498+
  Contract of service: KD1634+
    Ireland (Éire): KDK380
  Tort liability: KD1999
Master of Chancery: KD6940
Master of Rolls Court: KD6947
  Law reports: KD238+
Masters (Civil procedure): KD7554+
Matches, White phosphorus
  Public safety: KD3505.W4
Maternal and infant welfare: KD3304
Maternity leave
  Labor law: KD3144
Mayor's Court
  London
    Modern: KD7248+
    Old: KD6974
Measures and weights: KD2230+
Meat
  Inspection
    Jersey: KDG310
    Standards and grading: KD2259+
Meat industry: KD2417+
  Inspection: KD2417+
    Scotland: KDC593.M4
  Jersey: KDG310
  Scotland: KDC593.M4
Mechanical reproduction
  Copyright
    Literary copyright: KD1305.2
Mechanics' liens: KD1640
Medical associations: KD2950+
Medical Department, Army
  Military law: KD6116.M4
Medical economics: KD2960.F4
Medical education: KD2960.E4
Medical evidence
  Civil procedure: KD7523
Medical examiners: KD7296
  Northern Ireland: KDE524.7.C65
Medical fees: KD2960.F4
Medical genetics: KD3410.G45
Medical instruments and apparatus
  Products liability: KD1988.M42
Medical legislation: KD3395+

Medical legislation
  Ireland (Éire): KDK926+
  London: KD9018+
  Scotland: KDC690+
Medical partnership: KD2960.P3
Medical personnel: KD2945+
  Labor law: KD3177.M42
Medical practice, Group: KD2960.P3
Medical records
  Medical legislation: KD3410.R43
Medical technology: KD3407+
Medical witnesses: KD7523
Meetings
  Legal aspects: KD667.M4
Meetings, Stockholders': KD2104
Men's furnishings industry
  Wages: KD3126.M4
Mens rea: KD7892
Mentally disabled
  Capacity and disability
    Ireland (Éire): KDK191
Mentally ill
  Capacity and disability: KD737+
    Scotland: KDC358
  Medical care: KD3412
    Ireland (Éire): KDK931
    Scotland: KDC694
Mercantile customs
  Anglo-Norman period: KD597
Mercantile Marine Fund: KD2794
Mercantile transactions
  Ireland (Éire): KDK378
  Scotland: KDC495
Merchant marine
  Organization: KD6240+
  Shipping laws: KD2810+, KD2830+
Merchant mariners
  Labor law: KD1836+
  Safety regulations: KD2762
Mergers
  Corporations: KD2127
  Taxation: KD5528.M4
Messengers-at-arms
  Scotland: KDC869.M3
Metalworkers
  Wages: KD3126.M47
Methodist Church in Ireland: KDK1895

Metropolitan Police: KD9140
Mews, J., Digest of English Case Law:
  KD296.M4
Middle Temple: KD504.M5
Midwives: KD2968.M5
Military awards: KD4657
Military criminal law: KD6270+
  Ireland (Éire): KDK1560+
  Northern Ireland: KDE507
Military discipline: KD6250
Military establishment
  Northern Ireland: KDE506+
Military establishment (Ireland (Éire)):
  KDK1545+
Military justice: KD6290+
Military law: KD6000+
  Ireland (Éire): KDK1540+
  Northern Ireland: KDE505+
  Scotland: KDC835
Military prisons: KD6330
Military procurement: KD1613
Military training: KD6055+
  Army: KD6095+
  Royal Air Force: KD6205+
  Royal Navy: KD6135+
Militia: KD6114+
Milk production and distribution
  Regulation: KD2423
  Wages
    Ireland (Éire): KDK840.D3
Mineral rights duties: KD5536
Mines
  Property tax: KD5732.M5
Minimum wage: KD3118+
  Ireland (Éire): KDK830+
  London: KD8998.W3
  Northern Ireland: KDE328+
  Scotland: KDC646+
Mining
  Regulation: KD2331+
  Scotland: KDC588
Mining industry
  Hygiene: KD3172.M5+
  Income tax: KD5526.M5
  Regulation
    Ireland (Éire): KDK610+
  Safety regulations: KD3172.M5+

Ministry of Defense: KD6032
Ministry of Labor: KD3015
Ministry of Transport: KD2582
Minority lawyers: KD472.M55
Mint regulations: KD5286
Misbranding
  Trade regulations: KD2208+
Miscarriage, Induced: KD7969
Misrepresentation
  Contracts: KD1583
Mistake
  Void and voidable contracts: KD1583
    Ireland (Éire): KDK375
Mobile homes (Legal aspects):
  KD667.M63
Model building bylaws: KD1152
Molasses (Trade agreements):
  KD5662.M6
Money: KD5284+
  Ireland (Éire): KDK1432
Money laundering: KD1737.R43
Monopolies: KD2218+
Moot courts: KD440.A+
Mortgages: KD1010+, KD1013
  Real property
    Scotland: KDC438
Mortgages, Chattel: KD1757
Mortgages, Ship: KD1834.B6
Mortmain: KD873
Motion picture theaters (Local taxation):
  KD5732.M6
Motion pictures
  Censorship: KD3730+
  London: KD9054.M6
  Regulation (Scotland): KDC735
Motor carriers: KD2625+
Motor Insurers' Bureau: KD1894
Motor vehicles
  Insurance: KD1892, KD5593
  Regulation: KD2591+
Motorbus lines (Collective labor
  disputes): KD3091.S8+
Motortrucks (Road traffic): KD2611.T76
Multinational enterprises
  Government regulation and control:
    KD2084

Municipal and international law:
  KD4015, KDK1227.5
Municipal and mercantile customs
  Anglo-Norman period: KD597
Municipal bonds: KD5715
Municipal charters: KD4772
  Scotland: KDC792
Municipal civil service: KD4807+
Municipal contracts: KD1611
Municipal corporations: KD4770+
  Ireland (Éire): KDK1367
  Scotland: KDC790
  Tort liability: KD1991
Municipal government: KD4770+
  Ireland (Éire): KDK1367
  Scotland: KDC790+
Municipal services: KD4770+
  London: KD8960+
  Scotland: KDC790+
Munitions
  Public safety: KD3492
  Shipping: KD2770.E9
Munitions of war acts: KD3086+
Munitions tribunals: KD3086+
Murder: KD7964
  Trials: KD371.M8
    Ireland (Éire): KDK103.M8
    Scotland: KDC185.M8
Museums: KD3736
Musical copyright: KD1310
Muslims
  Civil rights: KD4102.M86
Mutiny
  Military criminal law: KD6278.M8

N

Name: KD727
Narcotic addiction
  Medical legislation: KD3413.N3
Narcotics
  Drug laws: KD3462
Nasciturus: KD744.U53
National Assembly
  Ecclesiastical law: KD8652.A+
National banks: KD1718
National defense: KD6000+

INDEX

National defense
  Ireland (Éire): KDK1540+
  Northern Ireland: KDE505+
  Scotland: KDC835
National defense contribution
  Income tax: KD5506
National emblem: KD4650
National Health Service: KD3210+
  Scotland: KDC666
National parks
  Public land law: KD1105+
National preserves: KD1102+
National revenue: KD5320+
  Ireland (Éire): KDK1440+
  Isle of Man: KDG70.2+
  Northern Ireland: KDE482+
National solicitors' associations:
  KD509+
  Ireland (Éire): KDK134+
Nationality and citizenship: KD4050+
  Ireland (Éire): KDK1250
Nationalization
  Eminent domain: KD1189
Nationalization of coal industry:
  KD2360
Nationalization of transportation:
  KD2584
Natural persons: KD725+
  Ireland (Éire): KDK186+
  Northern Ireland: KDE90+
  Scotland: KDC354+
Naturalization: KD4056
Navigation and pilotage: KD2780+
  Ireland (Éire): KDK764
Navigation and shipping: KD2750+
  Ireland (Éire): KDK750+
Ne exeat regno: KD7580
Negligence
  Torts: KD1975+
    Ireland (Éire): KDK460+
Negligence, Contributory: KD1976
Negligence, Criminal: KD7892
Negotiable instruments: KD1695+
  Scotland: KDC510
Negotiated settlement: KD7644
Netmaking and repair industry
  Wages: KD3126.N4

Newgate (Prison): KD8454.N4
Night work: KD3136+
  Children: KD3159
  Ireland (Éire): KDK850
  Women: KD3161
Nisi prius: KD7530.N5
Nisi prius courts
  Assize courts: KD6913
  Civil procedure: KD7440
    Ireland (Éire): KDK1668
  Law courts
    Circuit courts: KD210+
  Law reports
    Ireland (Éire): KDK74
Noise control
  Public health: KD3380
  Ships: KD2772.N64
Nolo contendere: KD8360
Non-support
  Domestic relations: KD780
Nonconformists
  Civil rights: KD4102.D5
Nonprofit corporations: KD2061+
  Income tax: KD5501+
  Ireland (Éire): KDK498+
Nonresidents
  Income tax: KD5494.N6
Nonwage payments: KD3130+
Norman compilations
  Anglo-Saxon period legal sources:
    KD544
Norman period
  Legal history: KD558+
Notaries: KD470
  Ireland (Éire): KDK121.7
  Scotland: KDC230
Notice: KD703.N6
Nuisance: KD1968
  Abatement of public nuisances:
    KD3372+
  London: KD9090.N84
  Scotland: KDC545
Nullity: KD703.N84
  Divorce: KD764+
  Marriage: KD756
    Ireland (Éire): KDK203.6

Nursery schools
  Ireland (Éire): KDK691.D39
Nurses: KD2968.N8
  Works for: KD665.N87
Nursing homes: KD2517.O43

O

Oath
  Legal aspects: KD667.O28
Oath and affirmation
  Witnesses: KD7516
Obligations
  Conflict of laws: KD685.C6
  Scotland: KDC482+
Obscenity: KD8075
  Ireland (Éire): KDK1787.O3
Obstetricians: KD2965.G95,
  KD2965.P75
Occupational diseases
  Workers' compensation: KD3221+,
    KD3235
Occupational law: KD2200+
  Ireland (Éire): KDK550+
  Jersey: KDG300+
  London: KD8980+
  Northern Ireland: KDE235+
  Scotland: KDC570+
Occupational therapists: KD2968.T47
Occupations, Hazardous: KD3168+
Ocean bills of lading: KD1827
Offenses against government and public
  order
  Ireland (Éire): KDK1775+
Offenses against property: KD7990+
  Ireland (Éire): KDK1773+
Offenses against public convenience
  and morality: KD8070+
  Ireland (Éire): KDK1786+
Offenses against public property, public
  finance, and currency: KD8090+
Offenses against religion: KD8760+
Offenses against reputation: KD7980+
Offenses against the administration of
  justice: KD8054+
  Ireland (Éire): KDK1780+
Offenses against the person: KD7960+

Offenses against the person
  Ireland (Éire): KDK1770+
  Scotland: KDC920.O44
Offenses against the public
  administration: KD8044+
Offenses, Local
  London: KD9085+
Officers
  Armed Forces: KD6068
  Army: KD6108
  Royal Air Force: KD6218
  Royal Navy: KD6148
Official gazettes: KD62+
  Ireland (Éire): KDK25+
  Northern Ireland: KDE24+
  Scotland: KDC56+
Official secrets, Illegal disclosure of:
  KD8024
Offshore oil and gas: KD2368
  Labor hygiene and safety:
    KD3172.O33
Offshore oil industry workers:
  KD3177.O35
Oil and gas
  Regulation: KD2366+
Oil pollution damages
  Liability: KD1989.5
Oireachtas
  Ireland (Éire): KDK1305+
Old age homes: KD2517.O43
Old age pensions: KD3241+
  Ireland (Éire): KDK885
  Northern Ireland: KDE346
Old Bailey: KD8289
Older courts
  Criminal procedure: KD8235+
  Scotland: KDC863+
Older people
  Employment: KD3103.O43
  Public welfare: KD3306
  Works for: KD665.A43
    Ireland (Éire): KDK175.A43
Ombudsman: KD4900
Open and closed shop: KD3053
Open spaces
  Local laws
    London: KD8952.P3

Open spaces
  Public land law: KD1105+
Ophthalmic services
  National Health Service: KD3213.O6
Order of the Coif: KD456.C7
Orders-in-Council: KD176
Organized crime: KD8006
Ornaments
  Ecclesiastical law: KD8714
Orphans
  Social legislation: KD9005.O7
Orphans' pensions
  Northern Ireland: KDE346
Outlawry in civil proceedings:
  KD7451.5.O9
Overseas sales: KD1673
Ownership
  Personal property: KD1213.2+
  Property: KD810
    Ireland (Éire): KDK215
  Real property
    Ireland (Éire): KDK219+
    Scotland: KDC399+
Ownership, Concurrent: KD878+
Ownership, Equitable: KD858
Oyer and Terminer and General Gaol
  Delivery, Courts of: KD8240

P

Package tours
  Contracts: KD1642.T73, KDK382.T72
Pakistanis
  Aliens: KD4145
Palatine courts, practice, and procedure
  Before the Judicature Act of 1873:
    KD6916+
  Since the Judicature Act of 1873:
    KD7220+
Paper bag and box industry
  Wages: KD3126.P3
    Ireland (Éire): KDK840.P3
    Northern Ireland: KDE330.P3
Parcel post: KD2854.P3
Pardon
  Criminal procedure: KD8440
Parent and child: KD772+

Parent and child
  Ireland (Éire): KDK207+
  Scotland: KDC374+
Parent companies: KD2112
Parental kidnapping: KD779+
Parental leave
  Labor law: KD3144
Parental rights and duties: KD779+
Parish priests: KD8660.P3
Parishes
  County government: KD4791
  Ecclesiastical law: KD8700
    Scotland: KDC968
  Local laws
    Ireland (Éire): KDK1930.A+
    Northern Ireland: KDE580.A+
    Scotland: KDC985.A+
Parking rules
  Traffic regulations: KD2622
Parks
  Local laws
    London: KD8952.P3
Parks, National
  Public land law: KD1105+
Parliament
  England and Wales: KD4190+
  Ireland (Éire): KDK1305+
  Northern Ireland: KDE440+
  Scotland: KDC762+
Parliamentary immunity and privileges:
  KD4246
Parliamentary reporting: KD4220
Parochial clergy
  Scotland: KDC968
Parochial councils
  Ecclesiastical law: KD8700
Parochial officers
  Ecclesiastical law: KD8705+
    Scotland: KDC968
Parole: KD8462
Parties
  Civil procedure: KD7463+
Parties to crimes: KD7910
Partition
  Real property: KD883
Partnership: KD2049+, KD2051+
  Income tax: KD5502

Partnership
   Isle of Man: KDG42
   Jersey: KDG290
   Scotland: KDC554
Partnership, Limited: KD2054
Partnership, Medical: KD2960.P3
Party walls
   Real property: KD942
Passenger carriers
   Contracts
      Ireland (Éire): KDK430+
   Regulation: KD2632
      Scotland: KDC610
Passports: KD4124
Patent assignments: KD1401
Patent attorneys: KD1413
Patent conveyancing: KD1401
Patent infringement: KD1411
Patent law: KD1360+, KD1361+
   Antitrust aspects: KD1371
   Guernsey: KDG440.I5
   Ireland (Éire): KDK330
Patent licenses: KD1400
Patent Office: KD1374
Patent practice: KD1413
Patent procedures: KD1374
Patents
   Income tax: KD5483.I53
Paternity: KD774
Patriotic observances in schools:
   KD3632
Patronage
   Ecclesiastical law: KD8725
      Scotland: KDC971
Pawnbroking: KD1742
   Ireland (Éire): KDK414
Pay
   Armed Forces: KD6059+
   Army: KD6099+
   Merchant marine: KD6246+
   Royal Air Force: KD6209+
   Royal Navy: KD6139+
Pay, Dismissal: KD3111
Payment in kind
   Wages: KD3124.P3
Payroll deductions
   Income tax: KD5490

Payroll deductions
   Income tax
      Ireland (Éire): KDK1458
Peat industry (Ireland (Éire)):
   KDK615.P4
Pedophilia: KD7976.P4
Peerage
   House of Lords: KD4265+
   Parliament (Scotland): KDC764+
Penal institutions: KD8452+
   Ireland (Éire): KDK1831.2+
Penalties
   Criminal law: KD7882+
      Scotland: KDC917+
   Military law: KD6330+
Penitentiaries: KD8452+
Pension funds
   Income tax: KD5500
Pension plans: KD3131+
Pension trusts: KD3132
Pensions
   Civil service: KD4529
   Local
      County: KD4818
   Local government
      Municipal civil service: KD4809+
      Scotland: KDC797
   Northern Ireland: KDE460
   Clergy: KD8658+
   House of Commons: KD4375
   Income tax: KD5473
   Judges: KD7286.S3
   Legislators
      Ireland (Éire): KDK1312
   Orphans
      Northern Ireland: KDE346
   Postal service: KD2849
   Survivors
      Armed Forces: KD6061
      Army: KD6101
      Royal Air Force: KD6211
      Royal Navy: KD6141
   Teachers: KD3640
      Scotland: KDC720
   War veterans: KD6355
   Widows
      Northern Ireland: KDE346

People, The
  Constitutional law
    Ireland (Éire): KDK1285+
People with disabilities
  Public welfare: KD3313+
People with mental disabilities
  Capacity and disability: KD737+
    Scotland: KDC358
People with physical disabilities
  Capacity and disability: KD737+
    Scotland: KDC358
Performance
  Contracts: KD1590
  Sales contracts: KD1671+
Performance, Specific: KDK1603
Performing arts: KD3720+
  London: KD9052+
Performing rights
  Copyright
    Literary copyright: KD1305.3
Perjury: KD8059
Personal injuries
  Ireland (Éire): KDK452
  Northern Ireland: KDE195
  Railway liability: KD2698
  Reparation: KD2007
    Northern Ireland: KDE210
    Scotland: KDC542
  Torts: KD1954
Personal insurance: KD1864+
Personal property: KD1205+
  Ireland (Éire): KDK300+
  Scotland: KDC455
  Valuation of: KD5534
Personation at elections
  Northern Ireland: KDE430
Personnel
  Armed Forces: KD6051+
  Army: KD6091+
  Merchant marine: KD6244+
  Royal Air Force: KD6201+
  Royal Navy: KD6131+
Personnel records: KD3097
Persons: KD723+
  Conflict of laws: KD685.P47
    Ireland (Éire): KDK180.P47
  Ireland (Éire): KDK185+

Persons
  Jersey: KDG260+
  Northern Ireland: KDE90+
  Scotland: KDC350+
  Torts: KD1954+
  Wales: KD9432
Persons of unsound mind
  Capacity and disability
    Ireland: KDK191
Pesticides
  Public safety: KD3505.P46
Pet shops: KD3429.P48
Petition, Freedom of: KD4119
Petroleum
  Mining: KD2366+
  Shipping: KD2770.P4
Petroleum industry
  Income tax: KD5526.M5
Petty Sessions
  Lower courts
    Ireland (Éire): KDK1610+
  Magistrates' Courts: KD8312
Pews and pew rights
  Ecclesiastical law: KD8716
Pharmacists: KD2968.P4
Photographers: KD2517.P5
Photography
  Copyright: KD1320+
Physical therapists: KD2968.T47
Physician and patient
  Privileged communications:
    KD7519.P48
Physicians
  Regulation: KD2945+
  Tort liability: KD1978
Picketing: KD3077
Piepowder courts: KD6985
Pilot licensing: KD2726
Pipe fitting
  Building laws: KD1162
Pipe rolls
  Anglo-Norman legal sources: KD584
Pipelines: KD2714
Plants
  Armed Forces: KD6077
  Army: KD6117
  Local taxation: KD5732.F3

Plants
    Royal Air Force: KD6227
    Royal Navy: KD6157
Plastics industry
    Labor hygiene and safety:
        KD3172.P55
Plea bargaining: KD8360
Pleading and motions: KD7453+
    Ireland (Éire): KDK1676
    Scotland: KDC883
Pleas of guilty
    Criminal procedure: KD8360
Pleasure craft
    Safety regulations: KD2768.P5
Pledges
    Real property
        Scotland: KDC438
Plumbing
    Building laws: KD1162
        Ireland (Éire): KDK280
Poisons
    Drug laws: KD3462
    Public safety: KD3503+
Police: KD4831+
    Ireland (Éire): KDK1375
    London: KD8931
    Municipal civil service: KD4812.P6
    Northern Ireland: KDE462
    Scotland: KDC798
    Works for: KD665.P6
        Ireland (Éire): KDK175.P64
Political activity
    Civil service: KD4517
Political disabilities: KD8460
    Criminal procedure
        Scotland: KDC935.7
Political offenses
    Ireland (Éire): KDK1775
    Trials: KD371.P6
Political rights: KD4080+
    Ireland (Éire): KDK1255+
    Northern Ireland: KDE420
    Scotland: KDC758
Pollution liability insurance:
    KD1896.P64
Poor
    Public welfare: KD3310+

Poor laws: KD3291+
    Ireland (Éire): KDK895
    London: KD9004+
    Scotland: KDC670+
Poor rate
    Local taxation: KD5721+
Population control: KD3340
Port of Bristol: KD2796.B7
Port of Liverpool: KD2796.L5
Port of London Authority: KD9120
Possessory estates
    Land tenure: KD857+
Post-mortem inquisitions: KD839
Postage: KD2860
Postal notes: KD2858.P6
Postal service: KD2845+
Poultry industry: KD2272
Poverty
    Legal works on: KD667.P68
Power, Judicial: KD4645
Power of appointment: KD865
Power of attorney: KD2022
Power supply
    Public utilities: KD2540+
Powers, Separation and delegation of:
    KD4000
Practice Court: KD7605
Practice of law: KD474+, KDE75+
    Ireland (Éire): KDK122+
    Scotland: KDC232+
Practicks
    Scottish legal history: KDC284.A+
Preferential employment: KD3098+
    Veterans: KD3098+
        Civil service: KD4520
Preferred stock: KD2108
Prelaw-school education: KD444
Preliminary crimes: KD7953+
Preliminary questions: KD681.P74
Prenuptial contracts: KD762
Prerogative Court of Canterbury:
    KD8690.5
Prerogative instruments
    Ecclesiastical law: KD8631.92+
Prerogative legislation: KD175+
Prerogative writs and orders: KD7610+

Prescription
  Property: KD960.P7
    Scotland: KDC426.P7
Presentation, Right of
  Ecclesiastical law: KD8725
Preservation of cultural property
  Ireland (Éire): KDK1092
Preserves, National: KD1102+
President, The
  Ireland (Éire): KDK1342
Press censorship: KD4114
Press, Freedom of the: KD4112
Press law
  Regulation: KD2875
    Ireland (Éire): KDK774
    Scotland: KDC628
Presumptions: KD7508.P7
Pretrial procedure: KD7470+
  Ireland (Éire): KDK1680+
Prevention of cruelty to animals:
  KD3424+
Preventive detention: KD7883
Price maintenance
  Retail trade: KD2492+
Price regulations: KD2215
Price supports
  Agriculture: KD2247+
Priests, Parish: KD8660.P3
Primary production: KD2241+
  Ireland (Éire): KDK570+
  Scotland: KDC580+
Prime Minister and the Cabinet:
  KD4462
  Ireland (Éire): KDK1344
Primogeniture: KD1523.P7
Printing industry
  Labor disputes: KD3091.P7+
  Purchase tax: KD5585.P7
Priority of claims
  Bankruptcy: KD2160
Prison administration: KD8450
  Ireland (Éire): KDK1831
  Northern Ireland: KDE557
Prison discipline: KD8450
  Ireland (Éire): KDK1831
Prisons: KD8452+
Prisons, Military: KD6330

Privacy, Violation of: KD1956+
Private bill legislation
  Scotland: KDC768
Private companies: KD2115
Private education: KD3670
Private law: KD720+
Private property, Public restraints on:
  KD1034+
  Ireland (Éire): KDK270+
  Jersey: KDG276+
  Northern Ireland: KDE125+
  Scotland: KDC440+
Private schools: KD3670
Private trusts: KD1483
Privileged communications: KD7518+
Privileges, Parliamentary: KD4246
Privy Council: KD4460
  Law reports: KDC136
Privy Council Cases (Judicial
  Committee)
  Law reports: KD247+
Privy Council records
  Scottish legal sources: KDC287
Prizefighting: KD3525
Probate Division (The Law Reports):
  KD1518
Probate, Divorce, and Admiralty Division
  (High Court of Justice): KD7210+
  The Law Reports: KD279.3
Probate, Divorce, and Admiralty Series
  (The Law Reports): KD279+
Probate law and practice: KD1518+
  Ireland (Éire): KDK365
  Northern Ireland: KDE149
  Scotland: KDC463+
Probation: KD8462
  Scotland: KDC948
Proclamations and instructions, Royal:
  KD175
Proclamations, Statutory: KD176
Procurement, Military: KD1613
Procuring
  Criminal law: KD8077
Procuring miscarriage: KD7969
Product counterfeiting
  Unfair competition: KD2226.P76

Products liability
  Torts: KD1987+
    Scotland: KDC547
Products liability insurance: KD1896.P7
Professional corporations: KD2941
Professional discipline
  Legal profession: KD479+
Professional discipline (Legal
  profession): KDC234
Professional tenancies: KD905
Professions: KD2940+
Professions, The
  Jersey: KDG328.A+
Profit sharing
  Labor law: KD3124.P7
Profit-sharing trusts: KD1782
Profit tax: KD5506
  Ireland (Éire): KDK1462
Profitmaking organizations
  Income tax: KD5501+
Profits
  Incorporated hereditaments: KD936+
Profits à prendre: KD950
Promotions
  Armed Forces
    Officers: KD6068
  Army
    Officers: KD6108
  Royal Air Force
    Officers: KD6218
  Royal Navy
    Officers: KD6148
Proof of foreign law: KD7508.P74
Property: KD810+
  Guernsey: KDG440.P7
  Ireland (Éire): KDK215+
  Isle of Man: KDG33+
  Jersey: KDG268+
  Northern Ireland: KDE110+
  Scotland: KDC390+
Property, Alien: KD813
Property damage
  Liability
    Railways: KD2696
Property, Horizontal: KD850
Property insurance: KD1881+
Property of minors: KD779+

Property, Separate: KD761.S4
Property taxes: KD5532+
  Ireland (Éire): KDK1467+
  Scotland: KDC816+
Property transfer
  Conflict of laws: KD685.T7
Prostitution
  Criminal law: KD8077
Protection, Court of: KD740+
Protection of labor: KDK857
Protest
  Bills of exchange: KD1697.P7
Provident societies: KD2122
Provincial Courts of the Archbishops:
  KD8690+
Provocation
  Criminal defenses: KD7900
Psychiatric evidence: KD7524
Psychiatrists: KD2965.P75
Psychological evidence: KD7524
Psychologists: KD2965.P75
Psychotherapists: KD2965.P75
Public accounting: KD5295
Public acts: KD124+
Public assistance
  Ireland (Éire): KDK895
Public auditing: KD5295
Public authorities
  London: KD9120+
Public contracts: KD1610+
Public control of land: KD831
Public corporations: KD4481+
Public debts: KD5300
  Ireland (Éire): KDK1438
  Local finance: KD5715
Public defenders: KD8358
Public domain
  National revenue: KD5323+
Public education: KD3600+
  Scotland: KDC715+
Public finance: KD5280+
  Channel islands: KDG160+
    Jersey: KDG356+
  Ireland (Éire): KDK1430+
  Isle of Man: KDG70+
  London: KD9070+
  Northern Ireland: KDE480+

INDEX

Public finance
  Scotland: KDC807+
Public general acts: KD124+
  Northern Ireland: KDE42+
  Scotland: KDC69+
Public health: KD3351+
  Ireland (Éire): KDK910+
  Jersey: KDG331
  London: KD9012+
  Northern Ireland: KDE355+
  Scotland: KDC680
Public housing
  Government contracts: KD1616
Public institutions: KD3291+
Public interest law: KD667.P83
  Ireland (Éire): KDK177.P82
Public interest lawyers: KD472.P82
Public land law: KD1090+
Public lending rights: KD1305.5
Public officers
  Tort liability: KD1994
Public policy: KD703.P9
  Land law: KD831
Public property: KD815
  London: KD8950+
  Real property: KD1034+
    Scotland: KDC440+
Public prosecutor: KD8348+
  Ireland (Éire): KDK1806
  Scotland: KDC933
Public Record Office: KD3755
Public safety: KD3490+
  London: KD9032+
Public sanitation: KD3351+
  Ireland (Éire): KDK910+
  Jersey: KDG331
  London: KD9012+
  Scotland: KDC680
Public trustees: KD1530.S6
Public utilities: KD2535+
  Ireland (Éire): KDK695+
  London: KD8960+
Public welfare: KD3291+
  Ireland (Éire): KDK895
  London: KD9004+
  Scotland: KDC670+
Public works: KD1195

Publicly chartered corporations:
  KD2117
Publishing contract: KD1340
Punishment
  Criminal law: KD7882+
    Scotland: KDC917+
  Military law: KD6330+
Purchase tax: KD5584+
Purchasing and procurement: KD1610+
Purveyance: KD5324.P8

Q

Quakers
  Civil rights: KD4102.Q3
Quarantine
  Immigrants: KD3369
Quarrying: KD2331+
  Ireland (Éire): KDK610+
  Scotland: KDC588
Quasi contracts: KD1924
  Scotland: KDC538
Quasi delicts
  Scotland: KDC541+
Queen Anne's Bounty: KD8745
Queen's Bench: KD6895+
  Law reports: KD190+
    Ireland (Éire): KDK70
Queen's Bench Division: KD7169+
  Costs: KD7568.S83
  Crown side: KD8285
  Law reports: KD277, KD277.7
Queen's Bench masters: KD7556
Quo warranto: KD7615

R

Racial discrimination
  Labor law: KD3102
  Scotland: KDC644.4
Racial minorities
  Civil rights: KD4095
Radiation
  Public safety: KD3497
Radio: KD2880+
Radio broadcasting
  Ireland (Éire): KDK780

Radio communication: KD2900+
Radio stations: KD2905
Radiologists: KD2965.R33
Ragpickers
  Wages: KD3126.R3
Railroad crossings: KD2620
Railroads
  Income tax: KD5526.R3
  Labor disputes: KD3089+
  Regulation: KD2651+
    Ireland (Éire): KDK730+
    Scotland: KDC620
Railway and Canal Commission:
  KD2684
Railway Commission: KD2684
Railway lands: KD2665
Railway Rates Tribunal: KD2684
Railways, Light: KD2710
Rape: KD7976.R3
Ratemaking
  Electricity: KD2545.5
  Railways: KD2680+
  Transportation (Northern Ireland):
    KDE282
Rates
  Canals: KD2787
  Church: KD8718
  Postal services: KD2852+
  Railways: KD2680+
Reading County Gaol: KD8454.R4
Real covenants: KD954
Real estate agents: KD2517.E7
Real estate management: KD1020+
Real estate transactions
  Ireland (Éire): KDK245
  Property taxes: KD5545
Real property: KD821+
  Guernsey: KDG440.P7
  Ireland (Éire): KDK217+, KDK270+
  Isle of Man: KDG33.2
  Jersey: KDG269+
  Northern Ireland: KDE112+,
    KDE125+
  Scotland: KDC393+
  Valuation of: KD5534
Real property taxes
  Local finance: KD5721+

Real property taxes
  Local finance
    Scotland: KDC816+
  National revenue: KD5534+
Receivers for mentally disordered
  persons: KD741
Receivers in bankruptcy: KD2155.R4
Receivers in equity: KD7584
  Ireland (Éire): KDK1700
Receivership to avoid bankruptcy:
  KD2170
  Ireland (Éire): KDK540
Receiving stolen goods: KD7995
Reclamation of land: KD1095+
Record keeping: KD2043
  Banking: KD1737.R43
Record retention: KD2043
Recording and registration: KD703.R4
  Individual: KD746
    Ireland (Éire): KDK195
    Jersey: KDG261.R4
    Scotland: KDC362
  Real property: KD984
Records management
  Courts: KD7123
  Research: KD3755
    Ireland (Éire): KDK1100
Recoveries
  Land transfer: KD992
Recreation grounds
  Local laws
    London: KD8952.P3
  Public land law: KD1105+
Recruiting
  Armed Forces: KD6053
  Army: KD6093
  Royal Air Force: KD6203
  Royal Marine: KD6182.E5
  Royal Navy: KD6133
Referees, Court of: KD4370
Referees, Official
  Judicial officers: KD7286.R43
Refugees
  Aliens: KD4142
Refuse disposal
  Public health: KD3382.R44
    Ireland (Éire): KDK924.R44

Regalia
  Public finance: KD5332+
Regality courts
  Scotland: KDC865+
Regency
  Constitutional law: KD4456.R4
Regiam Majestatem and Quoniam
  Attachmenta: KDC275
Regional and city planning: KD1125+
  Ireland (Éire): KDK275+
  London: KD8952.C5
  Northern Ireland: KDE135+
  Scotland: KDC446+
Registers of births, marriages, and
  deaths: KD746
  Ireland (Éire): KDK195
  Jersey: KDG261.R4
  Scotland: KDC362
Registers of brieves
  Scottish legal history: KDC280
Registration
  Business names: KD1450
  Copyright: KD1295
  Land titles: KD984
    Ireland (Éire): KDK247+
    Northern Ireland: KDE122
    Scotland: KDC436
  Motor vehicles: KD2605
  Trademarks: KD1442
  Voters
    House of Commons: KD4340
    Ireland (Éire): KDK1287
    Scotland: KDC772
Registration of individuals: KD4122
Registries, District
  High Court of Justice: KD7167
Registry of ships: KD2757
Regulation of corporations: KD2083+
Regulation of industry, trade, and
  commerce: KD2200+
  Ireland (Éire): KDK550+
  Jersey: KDG300+
  London: KD8980+
  Northern Ireland: KDE235+
  Scotland: KDC570+
Regulatory agencies: KD4882+
Rehabilitation of criminals: KD8463

Rehabilitation, Vocational: KD3313+
Reinsurance: KD1906+
Relief from rates
  Real property tax: KD5737+
Religion and conscience, Freedom of:
  KD4100+
Religion, Influence of: KD540.5.R4
Religion of the monarch: KD4456.R44
Religious instruction in public schools:
  KD3632
Religious minorities
  Civil and political rights: KD4100+
  Criminal laws against: KD4100+
Religious observances in schools:
  KD3632
Remainders
  Future estates and interests: KD867
Remedies: KD681.R34
  Civil procedure: KD7576+
    Ireland (Éire): KDK1698+
    Scotland: KDC895+
Remuneration
  Civil service: KD4527+
  County: KD4818
Rent: KD902
  Ireland (Éire): KDK223
  Scotland: KDC412+
Rent charges: KD956
Rent control: KD902
  Ireland (Éire): KDK223
  Scotland: KDC413
Renvoi: KD681.R4
Repairs
  Income tax deductions: KD5462.R4
Reparation: KD2007
  Ireland (Éire): KDK471
  Northern Ireland: KDE210
  Scotland: KDC541
Replevin: KD1225
Reprinting
  Copyright
    Literary copyright: KD1305.2
Reputation, Torts in respect to:
  KD1960+
Res judicata: KD7564
Rescission contracts: KD1605

Reservation of the Sacrament: KD8751.5

Reserves
  Armed Forces: KD6071
  Army: KD6111
  Royal Air Force: KD6221
  Royal Navy: KD6151
Resignation of employees: KD3110+
  Ireland (Éire): KDK820
Resources, Water: KD1070+
Respondeat superior doctrine: KD1952
Respondentia: KD1834.B6
Restaurants: KD2517.H6
  Ireland (Éire): KDK691.H6
Restitution
  Breach of contract: KD1605
  Unjust enrichment: KD1924
Restraint of alienation: KD928
Restraint of trade: KD2212
Restrictive covenants: KD954
Restrictive Practices Court: KD2218
Resulting trusts: KD1485
Retail and service establishments
  Hours of labor: KD3140.R4
Retail trade: KD2485+
  Ireland (Éire): KDK680+
  Northern Ireland: KDE260
Retired persons
  Works for: KD665.A43
    Ireland (Éire): KDK175.A43
Retirement contributions
  Income tax deductions: KD5462.R45
Retirement pensions
  Armed Forces: KD6060
    Officers: KD6068
  Army: KD6100
    Officers: KD6108
    Volunteers: KD6114+
  Civil service: KD4529
    Northern Ireland: KDE460
  Ireland (Éire): KDK885
  Local government
    Municipal civil service: KD4809+
  Northern Ireland: KDE346
  Royal Air Force: KD6210
    Officers: KD6218
  Royal Navy: KD6140

Retirement pensions
  Royal Navy
    Officers: KD6148
  Scotland: KDC797
  Volunteers: KD6115
Retirement plans: KD3131+
Retroactive law: KD687
Revenue, Local: KD5718+
Reversions: KD866
Right of presentation
  Ecclesiastical law: KD8725
Right of unpaid seller: KD1673.2+
Right to die: KD3410.E88
Right to work laws: KD3053
Rights of shareholders: KD2100+
Rights of spouses and children
  Scotland: KDC465.R5
Rights of suspects: KD8335
  Criminal procedure
    Scotland: KDC930.5
Rights of war
  Roads: KD1045
Rights of way
  Easements: KD938
Riots: KD8037
  Trials: KD371.R5
Riparian rights: KD923
  Ireland (Éire): KDK240.W3
  Scotland: KDC421
Rites
  Ecclesiastical law: KD8751+
River and harbor improvement: KD1072
Rivers
  Navigation and pilotage: KD2789+
  Public property: KD1070+
Road traffic: KD2591+
  Ireland (Éire): KDK710+
  Scotland: KDC604+
Road transport workers: KD3177.H5
Roads: KD1040+
  Scotland: KDC441+
Roadside protection: KD1045
Robbery: KD7992+
Rolls of letters patent and letters close
  Anglo-Norman legal sources: KD587
Roman Catholic Church: KD8785
Romanies, Works for: KD665.G95

Romney Marsh: KD9312.R6
Ropemakers
  Wages: KD3126.R6
    Northern Ireland: KDE330.R6
Rotuli Pipea
  Anglo-Norman legal sources: KD584
Rotuli scaccarii: KD586
Royal Air Force: KD6198+
  Courts-martial: KD6326
Royal College of Physicians of London:
  KD2952.R5
Royal Commissions: KD4479+
Royal Court
  Channel Islands
    Jersey: KDG232.A5+
Royal documents
  Anglo-Saxon legal sources: KD548
Royal Marine: KD6180+
Royal Military Academy, Woolwich:
  KD6097.W6
Royal Military College, Sandhurst:
  KD6097.S3
Royal Navy: KD6128+
  Courts-martial: KD6320+
Royal prerogative
  Constitutional law: KD4435+
  Public finance: KD5332+
Royal proclamations and instructions:
  KD175
Royal supremacy
  Church of England: KD8603
Rubber industry
  Wages: KD3126.R8
Rule against perpetuities
  Real property: KD871
    Scotland: KDC403
Rule in Shelley's case: KD869
Rule of law
  Constitutional law: KD3995
Rural districts
  County government: KD4789
Rural estate management: KD1020.4

S

Sack and bag industry
  Wages: KD3126.S3

Sacraments
  Ecclesiastical law: KD8751+
Safety, Air: KD2723
Safety equipment
  Motor vehicles: KD2603
Safety regulations
  Aviation: KD2723
  Labor law: KD3168+
    Northern Ireland: KDE333+
  Shipping: KD2760+
Sailors
  Civil status: KD6335
Salaries
  Civil service: KD4528
    County: KD4818
    Foreign Service: KD4477
    Municipal
      Police: KD4812.P6
    Northern Ireland: KDE460
  Clergy: KD8658+
  House of Commons: KD4375
  Income tax: KD5481
  Judges: KD7286.S3
  Legislators
    Ireland (Éire): KDK1312
  Local government employees
    Scotland: KDC797
  Postal service: KD2849
  Teachers: KD3640
    Scotland: KDC720
Sale of business enterprises
  Taxation: KD5528.S25
Sale of goods: KD1650+
  Scotland: KDC505
Sales, Overseas: KD1673
Sales tax: KD5580+, KD5588+
Salmon fishery: KD2315.S3
  Ireland (Éire): KDK591.S3
  Scotland: KDC586.S2
Salt
  Tariff: KD5662.S3
Salvage
  Maritime law: KD1834.S4
Sand and gravel industry: KD2370.S3
Sanitation
  Northern Ireland: KDE355+
Sark: KDG532+

Savings banks: KD1720
Sawmill workers
  Wages: KD3126.S33
Scholarships
  Higher education: KD3687
  Northern Ireland: KDE395.S7
School attendance: KD3628
School boards: KD3611
School buildings
  Building laws: KD1154.S3
    Scotland: KDC449.S3
    Wales: KD9444
School districts: KD3609
School government and finance:
  KD3607+
School health services: KD3405.S3
Schools
  Armed Forces: KD6056+
  Army: KD6096+
  Royal Air Force: KD6206+
  Royal Navy: KD6136+
  Wales: KD9460
Schools, Denominational: KD3605
Schools, Private: KD3670
Science and arts: KD3710+
  Ireland (Éire): KDK1090+
  Jersey: KDG342+
  London: KD9050+
  Scotland: KDC732+
Scientific exchanges: KD3758
Scire facias: KD7586
Scotland: KDC51+
Scottish Bar: KDC245+
Scottish government departments:
  KDC781
Scottish Office, The: KDC781
Scrap metal industry: KD2513.S3
Scriveners: KD472.S35
Sea, Collisions at: KD1825
Seal of government: KD4650
Seanad Éireann: KDK1320+
Searches and seizures
  Criminal procedure: KD8338
Secondhand trade: KD2512+
Secret commissions
  Unfair competition: KD2226.S4
Secrets, Trade: KD2226.T7

Secured transactions: KD1755+
  Ireland (Éire): KDK417
  Scotland: KDC522+
Securities
  Corporate finance: KD2096
  Income tax: KD5475
  Marketing: KD1774+
  Stock exchanges: KD1774+
Securities fraud: KD8002
Security classification: KD6350.S4
Sederunt, Acts of
  Scotland: KDC875.A+
Sedition: KD8026
  Trials: KD371.P6
Seeds
  Standards and grading: KD2257.S4
Selden Society: KD456.S4
Seldon, J., Ad Fletam dissertatio (1647):
  KD600.S4413
Select Committee on Statutory Rules
  and Orders: KD4361.S8
Selective Employment Tax: KD5605
Self-incrimination: KD8386
Senate
  Ireland (Éire): KDK1320+
  Northern Ireland: KDE445
Sentence
  Criminal procedure: KD8406
    Scotland: KDC935
Separate property: KD761.S4
Separation
  Marriage law: KD764+
    Ireland (Éire): KDK205
    Scotland: KDC372
Separation of power: KD4000
Separation of powers
  Ireland (Éire): KDK1227
Sequestration
  Bankruptcy
    Scotland: KDC563
Serjeants-at-law: KD464
Serjeants Inn: KD504.S4
Serjeanty
  Feudal tenure: KD836.S4
Service establishments
  Hours of labor: KD3140.R4

Service insurance
  Armed Forces: KD6062
  Army: KD6102
  Merchant mariners: KD6248
  Royal Air Force: KD6212
  Royal Navy: KD6142
Service marks: KD1443
Service stations
  Local taxation: KD5732.A9
Service trades: KD2515+
  Ireland (Éire): KDK690+
  Scotland: KDC597+
Service voters: KD4334
Services
  Armed Forces: KD6051+
  Army: KD6091+
  Merchant marine: KD6244+
  Royal Air Force: KD6201+
  Royal Navy: KD6131+
Servitudes
  Ireland (Éire): KDK240.E27
Session Court of Chester: KD6918
Session laws
  Anglo-Norman period: KD125
  Ireland (Éire): KDK38+
Settled land: KD861
Settlements
  Income tax: KD5483.D35
Settlements and trusts for sale
  Land tenure: KD861
Settlements, Marriage: KD762
Sewers
  Building laws: KD1162
Sex crimes: KD7975+
  Scotland: KDC920.S4
  Trials: KD371.S48
Sex discrimination
  Constitutional law: KD4103
    Ireland (Éire): KDK1259
Sex-oriented businesses
  Zoning law: KD1132
Sexual offenses
  Ireland (Éire): KDK1771.S49
Shareholders' rights: KD2100+
Shares, Corporate: KD2100+
Shelley's case, Rule in: KD869
Sheriff Court (Scotland): KDC852+

Sheriff Court (Scotland)
  Law reports: KDC121+
Sheriffs
  Ireland (Éire): KDK1656.S4
Sheriff's Court (London): KD7248+
Ship brokers: KD2024.S4
Ship money: KD5327.S5
Ship mortgages: KD1834.B6
Shipbuilding contracts: KD1642.S55
Shipbuilding industry
  Regulation: KD2395.S5
Shipping
  Income tax: KD5526.S5
Shipping industry: KD2815+
Shipping laws: KD2810+
Ships: KD2755+
Ships' papers: KD2757
Shire courts: KD6972+
Shire government
  Scotland: KDC794
Shires
  Local laws
    England: KD8850.A+
    Scotland: KDC980.A+
    Wales: KD9320.A+
Shirtmaking industry
  Wages
    Ireland (Éire): KDK840.C5
Shoe polish industry
  Wages: KD3126.S5
Shop committees: KD3148
Shop stewards: KD3148
Shore protection: KD1098
Sick leave: KD3143
Signboard restrictions: KD1045
Silver
  Weights and measures: KD2231.G6
Simony
  Ecclesiastical law: KD8765
Slaughtering of animals: KD3427
Slave trade
  Criminal law: KD7852.S5
Slum clearance: KD1171+
Small boats
  Safety regulations: KD2768.P5
Small business: KD2227

Small estates administration
  Decedents' estates: KD1530.S6
Small holdings: KD907+
Smoke control
  Public health: KD3378
    Scotland: KDC685
Smuggling: KD5692
Social insurance: KD3191+
  Ireland (Éire): KDK870+
  Isle of Man: KDG50.3
  Jersey: KDG329.3
  Northern Ireland: KDE340+
  Scotland: KDC662+
Social legislation: KD3000+
  Ireland (Éire): KDK800+
  Isle of Man: KDG50+
  Jersey: KDG329+
  London: KD8996+
  Northern Ireland: KDE320+
  Scotland: KDC635+
Social security: KD3241+
  Ireland (Éire): KDK885
  Isle of Man: KDG50.3
  Jersey: KDG329.3
  Northern Ireland: KDE346
Social security taxes: KD3252
Social services: KD3302
Social work: KD3302
Social workers: KD3302
  Works for: KD665.S6
Societies, Cooperative credit
  Scotland: KDC515
Societies, Industrial: KD2122
Society journals: KD345
  Ireland (Éire): KDK93
  Scotland: KDC170
Society of Advocates in Aberdeen:
  KDC220.S6
Society of Clerks to His Majesty's
  Signet: KDC220.S65
Society of Friends
  Civil rights: KD4102.Q3
Society of Writers to Her Majesty's
  Signet: KDC220.S65
Sodomy: KD7976.S6
Soft drink industry: KD2430.C3

Soil conservation
  Ireland (Éire): KDK572
Soldiers
  Civil status: KD6335
Solicitor General: KD7105+
Solicitors: KD466+
  Scotland: KDC229
Solicitors' associations: KD498+
  Ireland (Éire): KDK130+, KDK134+
  Northern Ireland: KDE80
  Scotland: KDC245+
Solidarity
  Contracts: KD1571
Special districts
  London: KD9120+
Special jurisdiction, Courts of: KD7260+
Specific performance: KD1603
Speedy trial
  Criminal law: KD7878
Sports: KD3525
Sports medicine: KD2965.S66
Spouses' rights
  Scotland: KDC465.R5
Squatting: KD1966
Stair Society: KDC220.S7
Stalking: KD7974.5
Stamp duties: KD5612
  Ireland (Éire): KDK1494
Standard time
  Regulation: KD2233
Standards and grading
  Agriculture: KD2256+
  Containers: KD2230+
  Forestry: KD2256+
  Weights and measures: KD2230+
Stannaries, Courts of (Devonshire and
  Cornwall): KD6990
Staple Inn: KD505.S7
Stare decisis: KD695
  Ireland (Éire): KDK181
  Scotland: KDC345
Statute of frauds: KD1568
Statute of uses
  Land tenure: KD859
Statutes
  Channel Islands
    Guernsey: KDG421+

Statutes
  Channel Islands
    Jersey: KDG220+
  General
    By period
      Anglo-Norman period: KD571
      Anglo-Saxon period: KD543
    Checklists: KD53
    Citators: KD141
    Compilations: KD129+
    Construction: KD691
    Digests: KD140
    Indexes
      General: KD142+
      Ireland (Éire): KDK44+
      Isle of Man: KDG26+
      London: KD8876
      Northern Ireland: KDE47
      Scotland: KDC90
    Interpretation: KD691
    Isle of Man: KDG25.2+
    Revision: KD132
      Acts and committees: KD150
    Sessional volumes: KD125
  Ireland (Éire): KDK38+
  Northern Ireland: KDE42+
  Scotland: KDC69+
    Citators: KDC87
  Wales: KD9407+
Statutes and customs
  Scottish legal history: KDC272
Statutes at large: KD129+
  Ireland (Éire): KDK38+
Statutory construction: KD691
Statutory instruments
  Administrative process: KD4885
  Ireland (Éire): KDK50
  Subordinate legislation: KD166+
Statutory interpretation: KD691
Statutory law: KD4018
Statutory proclamations: KD176
Statutory rules and orders: KD166+
  Channel Islands
    Guernsey: KDG425
    Jersey: KDG225
  Ireland (Éire): KDK48
  Northern Ireland: KDE49

Steam boilers
  Public safety: KD3510
Steerage passengers
  Shipping laws: KD2818
Sterilization: KD3417
Stipendiary curates: KD8660.S7
Stock-exchange transactions: KD1774+
  Ireland (Éire): KDK420
Stock transfers: KD2100+
  Taxation: KD5528.S25
Stockholders' meetings: KD2104
Stoppage in transitu: KD1675
Street railroads
  Labor disputes: KD3091.S8+
  Regulation
    Ireland (Éire): KDK748
Streetcar lines
  Ireland (Éire): KDK748
Streetcars
  London: KD8972.S7
Strict liability: KD1983+
  Ireland (Éire): KDK467+
  Scotland: KDC546+
Strikes: KD3076+
  By industry: KD3089+
Student aid
  Higher education: KD3687
  Northern Ireland: KDE395.S7
Student discipline: KD3688
Student government: KD3688
Student workers
  Immigration law: KD4139.S7
Students: KD3624+
  Northern Ireland: KDE394+
Students, Law: KD448.A+
Students with mental disabilities:
  KD3666
Students with physical disabilities:
  KD3664
Submerged lands: KD2368
Subordinate legislation: KD166+
  Ireland (Éire): KDK48+
Subornation of perjury: KD8059
Subrogation: KD1574
Subsidiary companies: KD2112
Succession and legacy duty
  Ireland (Éire): KDK1480

Succession to the throne: KD4456.S8
  Scotland: KDC779
Succession upon death: KD1500+
  Conflict of laws: KD685.S9
  Ireland (Éire): KDK360+
  Jersey: KDG284
  Northern Ireland: KDE145+
  Scotland: KDC462+
Suffrage: KD4332+
  Ireland (Éire): KDK1287
Sugar refining: KD2411
Summary judgment: KD7572
Sunday legislation: KD2488
Superior courts
  Before the Judicature Act of 1873:
    KD6870+
  Ireland (Éire): KDK1595+, KDK1630+
    Law reports: KDK65+
  Since the Judicature Act of 1873:
    KD7139+
Supervening impossibility: KD1596
Support
  Domestic relations: KD769
    Ireland (Éire): KDK207
  Income tax: KD5483.A4
Support of land
  Real property: KD942
Supremacy of law: KD3995
Supreme Court appeals
  Civil procedure
    Ireland (Éire): KDK1713
Supreme Court of Judicature: KD7139+
  Costs: KD7568.S8
  Ireland (Éire): KDK1605+
  Northern Ireland: KDE521
Suretyship and guaranty
  Contracts: KD1752
    Scotland: KDC520
  Insurance: KD1900+
Suretyship insurance: KD1900+
Surtaxes
  Income tax: KD5467
    Corporations: KD5521+
Surveying
  Land transfer: KD988
Surveys
  Anglo-Norman legal sources: KD582

Surveys of local administration of justice
  London: KD8886+
Surveys on legal education: KD421
Survivors' benefits
  Armed Forces: KD6061
  Army: KD6101
  Ireland (Éire): KDK885
  Northern Ireland: KDE346
  Royal Air Force: KD6211
  Royal Navy: KD6141
Suspects, Rights of: KD8335
  Criminal procedure
    Scotland: KDC930.5
Swans
  Game, bird, and fish protection:
    KD2295.S9
Systems of citation: KD400

T

Tangible personal property: KD1220
Tanning
  Labor law: KD3172.T3
Tariff: KD5641+
  Ireland (Éire): KDK1510+
  Isle of Man: KDG70.6
  Scotland: KDC823
Tax accounting: KD5387
Tax administration: KD5375+
  Ireland (Éire): KDK1445+
  Scotland: KDC812
Tax boards: KD5401
Tax collection: KD5385+
  Income tax: KD5490
Tax consultants: KD5395
Tax courts: KD5401
Tax evasion: KD5410
Tax havens: KD5372
Tax on servants: KD5597.S4
Tax planning: KD5370+
Tax procedure: KD5375+
  Ireland (Éire): KDK1445+
  Scotland: KDC812
Tax saving: KD5370+
Taxation: KD5326+, KD5351+
  Channel Islands: KDG162+
  Jersey: KDG358+

Taxation
   Guernsey: KDG440.T38
   Ireland (Éire): KDK1443+
   Isle of Man: KDG70.2+
   Local finance: KD5718+
      London: KD9073+
   Northern Ireland: KDE484+
   Scotland: KDC810+
Taxation of capital: KD5532+
   Ireland (Éire): KDK1467+
   Scotland: KDC816+
Taxes, Historical: KD5326+
Taxicabs: KD2634
   London: KD8972.T3
Tea
   Trade agreements: KD5662.T4
Teachers: KD3636+
   Ireland (Éire): KDK1070
   Scotland: KDC718+
   Wales: KD9460
Technical education: KD3662
Technologists, Works for: KD665.T4
Teind Court (Scotland): KDC850
Teinds
   Scotland: KDC972
Telecommunication: KD2880+
   Ireland (Éire): KDK775+
Telegraph: KD2885
Telephone: KD2890
Television: KD2915
Television broadcasting
   Ireland (Éire): KDK780
Tenancy: KD891+
   Ireland (Éire): KDK222+
   Northern Ireland: KDE120
   Scotland: KDC412+
Tenancy, Joint: KD880
Tenure
   Civil service: KD4527+
   Local
      County: KD4818
      Municipal
         Police: KD4812.P6
Territorial and Army Volunteer Reserve:
   KD6115
Territorial Army: KD6115
Terrorism: KD8039

Testate succession: KD1501+
   Scotland: KDC463+
Textile industry
   Regulation: KD2380+
      Ireland (Éire): KDK630+
   Wages: KD3126.T4
      Northern Ireland: KDE330.T4
Thames River (England)
   Navigation and shipping laws:
      KD2790.T4
Theater: KD3725+
Theater buildings: KD1154.T4
Theft: KD7992+
Therapists, Occupational: KD2968.T47
Therapists, Physical: KD2968.T47
Threats: KD8005+
Time
   Computation: KD703.T5
Tin mining industry: KD2365.T5
Tithes: KD8747
   Ireland (Éire): KDK1875+
   Scotland: KDC972
Title, Documents of
   Sales contracts: KD1660+
Title investigation: KD982
   Ireland (Éire): KDK247+
   Scotland: KDC435
Title of the monarch: KD4456.T5
Title transfer
   Motor vehicles: KD2605
   Sales contracts: KD1660+
Tobacco
   Import trade: KD2475.T6
   Taxation: KD5595
      Jersey: KDG368.T6
Tobacco industry: KD2415.T6
   Wages: KD3126.T63
      Ireland (Éire): KDK840.T3
Toothprints
   Criminal procedure: KD8385
Tort liability: KD1990+
Tort liability, Government: KD2004
Tort liability of children: KD735
Tort liability of corporations: KD1990+
Tort liability of government employees:
   KD1994
Tort liability of labor unions: KD1996

Tort liability of minors: KD735
Tort liability of municipal corporations:
  KD1991
Tort liability of physicians: KD1978
Tort liability of public officers: KD1994
Torts: KD1941+
  Conflict of laws: KD685.T67
  Ireland (Éire): KDK450+
  Northern Ireland: KDE194+
  Scotland: KDC541+
Torture
  Criminal procedure: KD8225.T6
Tourism: KD2517.T67
Towage
  Maritime law: KD1834.T67
Town tenancy
  Ireland (Éire): KDK229
Towns
  Local laws
    England: KD8860+
    Ireland (Éire): KDK1930.A+
    Northern Ireland: KDE580.A+
    Scotland: KDC985.A+
    Wales: KD9325.A+
Toxic substances
  Public safety: KD3503+
Toy industry
  Wages: KD3126.T68
Traction engines
  Motor vehicle laws: KD2611.T7
Trade agreements
  Ireland (Éire): KDK1512+
  Isle of Man: KDG70.6
Trade and commerce: KD2455+
  Ireland (Éire): KDK670+
  Northern Ireland: KDE260+
  Scotland: KDC597+
Trade associations: KD2228
Trade, International: KD2460+
Trade regulations: KD2204+
  Ireland (Éire): KDK552+
  London: KD8985+
Trade, Restraint of: KD2212
Trade secrets: KD2226.T7
Trade unions
  Ireland (Éire): KDK807
Trademarks: KD1360+, KD1431+

Trademarks
  Guernsey: KDG440.I5
  Income tax: KD5483.I53
  Ireland (Éire): KDK345
Trading stamps
  Retail trade regulation: KD2494
Trading with the enemy: KD1607
Traffic accidents
  Ireland (Éire): KDK463.T7
Traffic regulations: KD2617+
  Ireland (Éire): KDK712+
  Scotland: KDC607
Traffic signs and signals: KD2620
Traffic violations: KD2618
  Ireland (Éire): KDK713
Trailbaston, Courts of: KD8242
Trailer camps: KD2517.T7
  Sites development: KD1107.T7
Training, Manual
  Educational law: KD3662
Training, Military: KD6055+
  Army: KD6095+
  Royal Air Force: KD6205+
  Royal Navy: KD6135+
Transfer inter vivos
  Land transfer: KD966+
    Ireland (Éire): KDK245+
    Scotland: KDC430+
Transfer of personal property: KD1220+
Transfer of property
  Conflict of laws: KD685.T7
Translators
  Court employees: KD7314
Transplantation, Medical: KD3409
Transport Tribunal: KD2684
Transportation: KD2571+
  Ireland (Éire): KDK705+
  Jersey: KDG320+
  London: KD8970+
  Northern Ireland: KDE280+
  Scotland: KDC601+
Transportation contracts: KD1642.T73,
  KDK382.T72
Transportation workers
  Wages: KD3126.T7
Travel contracts: KD1642.T73,
  KDK382.T72

INDEX

Treason: KD8022
  Scotland: KDC920.T7
  Trials: KD371.P6
    Ireland (Éire): KDK103.T7
    Scotland: KDC185.T7
Treasure troves: KD5333.T7
Treatymaking power: KD4452
Trespass to goods: KD1970
Trespass to land: KD1966
Trial
  Civil procedure: KD7480+
    Ireland (Éire): KDK1685+
    Scotland: KDC885+
  Criminal procedure: KD8362+
    Ireland (Éire): KDK1810+
    Scotland: KDC934+
Trial by battle
  Criminal procedure: KD8225.W3
Trial by jury
  Civil procedure: KD7540+
Trial by newspaper: KD7879
Trial of peers: KD8283
Trial practice
  Civil procedure: KD7483+
    Scotland: KDC885+
  Criminal procedure: KD8364
Trial tactics: KD7483+
Trials
  Civil: KD370+
    Ireland (Éire): KDK105+
    Scotland: KDC187+
  Courts-martial
    Army: KD6315+
    Navy: KD6322+
  Criminal
    Ireland (Éire): KDK102+
    Scotland: KDC184+
  Ecclesiastical
    Scotland: KDC963+
  General: KD370+
Tribal law
  Wales: KD9405+
Tribunals, Administrative: KD4890
Tribunals, Munitions: KD3086+
Tribunals of inquiry: KD4895
Trover: KD1970
Truancy: KD3628

Truck system
  Wages: KD3124.P3
Trucklines: KD2636
Trust companies: KD1491
Trust investments: KD1787
Trustees in bankruptcy: KD2155.R4
Trustees, Public: KD1530.S6
Trusts
  Income tax: KD5494.T7
Trusts and trustees: KD1480+
  Ireland (Éire): KDK350+
  Jersey: KDG281
  Northern Ireland: KDE140+
  Scotland: KDC460
Trusts for sale: KD861
Trusts, General: KD1483
Trusts, Investment: KD1782
Trusts, Private: KD1483
Trusts, Resulting: KD1485
Tuberculosis
  Public health laws
    Ireland (Éire): KDK919.T8
Tugboats
  Safety regulations: KD2768.T8
Turnover taxes: KD5580+

U

Ultra vires
  Corporations: KD2059.U5
Unborn children: KD744.U53
Unclaimed estates: KD1534
  Scotland: KDC470
Undertakers: KD2517.U5
Undue influence
  Void and voidable contracts: KD1582
    Ireland (Éire): KDK375
Unemployment insurance: KD3261+
  Northern Ireland: KDE348
Unfair competition: KD2225+
Unfair labor practices: KD3095
Unfair trade practices: KD2204
  Ireland (Éire): KDK552+
Unfree tenure: KD837+
Uniform regulations
  Armed Forces: KD6065
  Army: KD6105

Uniform regulations
  Royal Air Force: KD6215
  Royal Navy: KD6145
Unincorporated associations: KD2046+
  Scotland: KDC552+
Union security: KD3051+
Union shop: KD3051+
Unions, Maritime Labor: KD1839
United Reformed Church: KD8790
Unjust enrichment: KD1924
Unlawful contracts: KD1578+
Unmarried couples: KD771
Unpaid seller, Right of: KD1673.2+
Unsatisfied judgment funds: KD1894
Urban districts
  County government: KD4787
Urban estate management: KD1020.6
Usage and custom: KD693
Uses and trusts
  Land tenure: KD859
Usury
  Contracts: KD1580.U7
  Ireland (Éire): KDK412+
  Loans: KD1740

V

Vacations
  Labor law: KD3142
Vaccination
  Public health laws: KD3370
Vagrancy: KD8079
Valuation of buildings
  Real property taxes: KD5534
Valuation of tenant right
  Farm tenancy: KD908.V3
Value-added tax: KD5586
  Ireland (Éire): KDK1491
Vending machines: KD2503
Vendor and purchaser: KD966
  Ireland (Éire): KDK245
  Scotland: KDC430
Venue
  Civil procedure: KD7443
    Scotland: KDC879
Veterans: KD6335
  Preferential employment: KD3098

Veterans
  Preferential employment
    Civil service: KD4520
Veterinarians: KD2990.V4
Veterinary Corps
  Army: KD6116.V4
Veterinary hygiene: KD3420+
  London: KD9024
Veterinary laws
  London: KD9024
Veterinary medicine: KD3420+
Veterinary public health: KD3420+
Vicarious liability: KD1999+
Vice-Chancellors' Courts
  Law reports: KD234+
Vice Warden of the Stannaries, Court of
  the: KD6990
Victims of crimes: KD8470
Villeinage
  Feudal tenure: KD838.V5
Violation of ordinances
  London: KD9085+
Violation of privacy
  Ireland: KDK453
  Torts: KD1956+
Visas: KD4140
Vital statistics
  Ireland (Éire): KDK195
Vivisection: KD3426
Vocational education: KD3660+
Vocational rehabilitation: KD3313+
Void and voidable contracts: KD1576+
  Ireland (Éire): KDK374+
  Scotland: KDC487
Void and voidable marriage: KD756
Volunteers, Army: KD6114+
Voting, Absentee: KD4342

W

Wage and Hour laws: KD3118+
Wage control: KD3120+
Wage discrimination: KD3102+
Wager of battle
  Criminal procedure: KD8225.W3
Wages
  Income tax: KD5481

INDEX

Wages
  Labor law: KD3118+
    Ireland (Éire): KDK830+
    Northern Ireland: KDE328+
    Scotland: KDC646+
  Postal service: KD2849
Waiver: KD703.W34
Wales: KD9400+
War and contracts: KD1607
War and emergency powers: KD4440
War contracts: KD1613
War risks
  Accident insurance: KD1875.W3
  Marine insurance: KD1847
  Reinsurance: KD1907+
Wards and liveries, Courts of: KD6992
Warehouse receipts: KD1667
Warehouses
  Contracts: KD1681
  Regulation: KD2525+
Warehouses, Bonded: KD2530
Warrant of arrest: KD8335
  Criminal procedure
    Scotland: KDC930.5
Warranties: KD1654.C6
Warranties, Implied: KD1654.C6
Wartime and emergency legislation:
  KD5110+, KD6004+
  Ireland (Éire): KDK1400+
  Local government: KD4751+
  Scotland: KDC804
Wartime debtors' relief: KD2168
Wartime deferment of executions:
  KD7598
Wartime finance: KD5336+
Wartime labor disputes: KD3086+
Wartime regulation of wages: KD3120+
  By industry: KD3126.A+
Waste products industry
  Wages: KD3126.W3
    Ireland (Éire): KDK840.W3
    Northern Ireland: KDE330.W3
Water pollution and drainage: KD3375
  Ireland (Éire): KDK910+
  Scotland: KDC684
Water resources: KD1070+
Water rights: KD923

Water rights
  Ireland (Éire): KDK240.W3
  Scotland: KDC421
Water supply
  Public utilities law: KD2555
    London: KD8962.W3
Water transportation: KD2750+
  Ireland (Éire): KDK750+
Wealth tax: KD5533
  Ireland (Éire): KDK1468
Weapons
  Armed Forces: KD6077
  Army: KD6117
  Public safety: KD3492
  Royal Air Force: KD6227
  Royal Navy: KD6157
Weight restrictions
  Motor vehicles: KD2603
Weights and measures: KD2230+
Welsh Church, The: KD9498+
Wheat
  Price supports: KD2248.W4
White phosphorus matches
  Public safety: KD3505.W4
Whitecross Street Prison: KD8454.W45
Whitley councils: KD3148
Wholesale trade: KD2480
Widows
  Public welfare
    Scotland: KDC674
Widow's pensions
  Northern Ireland: KDE346
Wife abuse: KD7973
Wilderness preservation
  Public land law: KD1105+
Wildlife conservation
  Ireland (Éire): KDK580+
  Scotland: KDC584+
Wills: KD1501+
  Scotland: KDC463+
Wine
  Taxation: KD5591.W5
Wiretapping: KD8388
Witchcraft
  Criminal law: KD7852.W5
    Scotland: KDC911.W5
  Trials: KD371.W56

Witchcraft
 Trials
  Scotland: KDC185.W67
Withholding tax: KD5490
 Ireland (Éire): KDK1458
Witnesses
 Civil procedure: KD7514+
  Scotland: KDC889
 Criminal procedure: KD8391
Witnesses, Medical: KD7523
Woman labor: KD3161
 Scotland: KDC656
Women
 Capacity and disability: KD734
  Scotland: KDC356
 Citizenship: KD4058.W6
 Employment: KD3103.W6
  Scotland: KDC644.5.W65
 Jury duty
  Ireland (Éire): KDK1692
 Suffrage: KD4336
Women lawyers: KD472.W65
Women, Married: KD758
Women's services
 Armed Forces: KD6073
 Army: KD6113
 Royal Air Force: KD6223
 Royal Navy: KD6153
Wood-using industries
 Labor hygiene: KD3172.W62
Wool industry
 Labor disputes: KD3091.W6+
Wool trade
 Export: KD2466.W6
Worcester & Birmingham Canal
 English law: KD2785.W6
Words and phrases
 Ireland (Éire): KDK84
 Scotland: KDC152
 Wales: KD9420
Words of limitation
 Future estates and interests: KD869
Work councils: KD3148
Work rules: KD3146+
Workers' compensation: KD3221+
 Ireland (Éire): KDK878
 Isle of Man: KDG50.3

Workers' compensation
 Jersy: KDG329.3
 Northern Ireland: KDE344
Workers' liens: KD1640
Workers, Student
 Immigration law: KD4139.S7
Works councils: KD3045
Wreck
 Maritime law: KD1834.S4
Writ of extent: KD7594
Writers
 Scotland: KDC229
Writers to Her Majesty's Signet, Society
 of: KDC220.S65
Writs
 Anglo-Norman legal sources: KD576
Writs and orders, Prerogative:
 KD7610+
Written contracts: KD1568

X

Xenografts: KD3409

Y

Yachts
 Safety regulations: KD2768.P5
Year Books, The (ca. 1280-1535):
 KD193+
Yearbooks
 General: KD325
 Legal education: KD421
 London: KD8886+
York, Chancery Court of: KD8693
Youth employment service: KD3273
Youth welfare: KD3305
 Scotland: KDC672

Z

Zoning: KD1125+
 Ireland (Éire): KDK275+
 Northern Ireland: KDE135+
 Scotland: KDC446+

INDEX

GPO U.S. GOVERNMENT PRINTING OFFICE: 2008-340-014/60015